COLLABORATIVE
REFORM
AND OTHER
IMPROBABLE DREAMS

SUNY series, Teacher Preparation and Development
Alan R. Tom, editor

COLLABORATIVE REFORM AND OTHER IMPROBABLE DREAMS

The Challenges of Professional Development Schools

edited by

MARILYN JOHNSTON
PATTI BROSNAN
DON CRAMER
and
TIM DOVE

State University
of New York
Press

Published by
State University of New York Press, Albany

© 2000 State University of New York

Production by Susan Geraghty
Marketing by Mike Campochiaro

Printed in the United States of America

For information, address State University of New York
Press, State University Plaza, Albany, N.Y., 12246

Library of Congress Cataloging-in-Publication Data

Collaborative reform and other improbable dreams : the challenges of
    professional development schools / edited by Marilyn Johnston . . .
    [et al.].
        p.   cm. — (SUNY series, teacher preparation and development)
    Includes bibliographical references and index.
    ISBN 0-7914-4465-1 (hard : alk. paper). — ISBN 0-7914-4466-X
(pbk. : alk. paper)
    1. Laboratory schools—United States. 2. Educational change-
-United States. I. Johnston, Marilyn, 1942–   . II. Series: SUNY
series in teacher preparation and development.
LB2154.A3C65 2000
370'.71'1—dc21   99-28354
                                                                      CIP

10 9 8 7 6 5 4 3 2 1

Dedicated to the memory of
Cindy Dickens,
who lived life with a collaborative spirit,
and
to all our PDS colleagues

CONTENTS

FOREWORD

In 1986, The Ohio State University and its College of Education joined the Holmes Group, a national reform-minded consortium of research-oriented universities committed to excellence in the preparation of teachers. While Ohio State had never lost its commitment to teacher education, it had, along with its peers, never paid the kind of quality attention to teacher preparation called for in the reform initiatives of the early 1980s. A small group of deans saw the possibilities and formed the Holmes Group around a renewed sense of excellence required in their preparation programs, if teaching was ever to attain its rightful stature as a profession.

The decision to join the Holmes Group was roundly debated in our college, including the then sitting president, who both encouraged us to join and promised resources. Ultimately, our Faculty Senate voted to join, not unanimously, but nonetheless committing us to the redesign of our teacher preparation programs over the next decade. Taking our lead from *Tomorrow's Teachers*, we began with a reexamination of our initial preparation program, and after much debate, ultimately forged a model for a free-standing masters of education degree, which is now fully implemented. We no longer offer a baccalaureate option to licensure; rather, licensure candidates complete a bachelor's degree in the teaching discipline prior to admission to our five quarter, yearlong master's program

In 1990, the college took another page out of the Holmes text, following the publication of *Tomorrow's Schools*. Drawing on the design principles articulated in this second volume, we set about to create professional development schools—the "Ohio State way." With the dean making a clear commitment to the task, working committees were established around which program, governance, resource, personnel, and evaluative guidelines were framed. Since these committees were composed of both college and local school district personnel, the groundwork for collaboration was laid. For twenty years, the college had worked closely with local school districts; the PDSs movement would intensify those existing relationships.

As I look back, and you the reader look forward to this text, I want to signal what you will find. First, and most importantly, a word about the authors. I recognize them! They are the wonderful heroes and heroines that for nine years now have worked on the frontiers of this new concept. In this story are the very professors who risked the initial design work, clinical faculty and field professors who signed up for the task, knowing fully that the role had not yet been adequately defined. You'll see doctoral students who experienced firsthand the stresses of their professors and the challenges dealt their role, once very traditionally defined and now changing almost daily. And you'll see students, both our initial preparation candidates and real-life pupils in our PDS sites. You will hear administrators invoked, both positively and with disappointment. And all I can say to you is, this is real. This is a story I know. This really happened.

Second, I believe this is a text about "getting it." The stories told in this text proclaim the new profession of teaching. They concede the need for reform at the outset. They embrace new ways of teaching and learning. They simultaneously affirm experiences and condemn exasperations. The programs move forward to this day. And yet, you will see the authors readily acknowledging that in their midst were many who didn't get it, and still don't. Therein lies the shift in thinking about how one learns to teach, which is really at the heart of these stories.

Third, you will see diversity. We let a thousand flowers bloom. We said a PDS could be a single site, a school within a school, a district, a discipline-based network, and/or an entity whose purpose was to serve the others. In many ways, that is our greatest strength, and yet our greatest challenge.

I must observe that Ohio State was one of those institutions years ago that created an on-campus laboratory school, called University School. It opened in the fall of 1932, and closed in 1967. Many graduates still actively recall the wonder of this place, as do faculty who recall vividly the vision of education enabled at this school. Today, when others hear us talk about the Professional Development School (PDS) initiative, they ask longingly, "Are you going to reopen the lab school?" Our response is unequivocal. We are committed to everything that was right about University School, save for its locale. I believe that we must have a "teaching school," and in many respects a mirror image of former lab schools. But we also believe that teaching schools (read: PDSs) should be a part of the lived experience of schooling—in the neighborhoods, in the districts—in the real settings where children, youth, and families live. That's a fourth distinction you will see in the stories that unfold.

Finally, you will see us raising many questions throughout this text that I hear raised at national conferences. You will see us struggle with issues of culture and climate, personnel and resources, integrity and results. And you will hear unresolved attributes of partnerships, so pivotal now to the issues being addressed in the new Holmes Partnership. Hopefully, this text will guide our thinking, not only here at home, but in the national dialogue, about how to form lasting partnerships to support teacher education and school renewal. These will be the kinds of partnerships that will undergird professional development for decades to come. Only by looking back carefully can we look forward creatively.

NANCY ZIMPHER

INTRODUCTION

Context, Challenges, and Consequences: PDSs in the Making

Marilyn Johnston

The stories in this book tell of a continuing attempt to reform teacher education at a major university and the challenges that followed. Faculty at The Ohio State University and local school administrators and teachers have been working together since 1986 to change how we prepare new teachers and promote professional development. This has meant changing our institutions while working in them and studying both the process and outcomes as we go. The context, challenges, and consequences of this large-scale reform are complex and uneven but some of the outcomes are clear: teacher education is done differently now, professors and teachers teach differently, and the schools and university have changed in significant ways.

But many questions remain. Is collaboration a viable means to reform in teacher education? Can the initial enthusiasm of collaborative reform survive changes in personnel, administration, and policies? Will those involved continue to be willing to meet the strenuous time-commitments required? Will the distinctive character of our diverse PDS projects be smothered by further institutionalization? Can one college support diverse kinds of PDSs and goals? Can sufficient resources be garnered to support these kinds of collaborative efforts? In short, is cross-institutional collaboration a viable model for long-term reform?

The chapters in this book address these questions through a case study of what we have done in central Ohio. Donmoyer (1990) argues that the value of a case study is the insight it may offer for another situation. The results of case studies cannot be transferred directly from one context to another (Lincoln & Guba, 1985) nor generalized across many contexts, but insights into the assumptions and practices of one's own context may best occur when they are compared with another. We hope our case study provokes such insights.

We have developed PDSs in ways that do not conform with the standard Holmes Group recommendation for school-based sites. Our several PDSs grew out of the needs of those who created them and work in them, and there are significant differences between them. The ways collaboration has been defined within our PDS projects have also varied considerably. Within this diversity, however, there are shared goals and assumptions that have had a significant impact on schools in the area and on the College of Education.

As at many universities, our reform initiatives grew out of the national critiques of teacher education (Carnegie Forum on Education and the Economy, 1986; National Commission on Excellence in Education, 1983). Ten years after the first Holmes Group publication (1986), there is hardly an educational conference or teacher education institution that has not been touched or taken over by these and other critiques and recommendations, especially the recommendations for professional development schools (PDSs).

The Ohio State University was an early institutional member of the Holmes Group. Our deans (Don Anderson, then Nancy Zimpher) tried to create a climate that encouraged, even mandated, the development of PDSs. Gradually our PDSs have become tightly associated with the emerging MEd programs. As most certification programs have moved from the baccalaureate to the masters level, they have developed a PDS or allied themselves with an existing one. While PDS issues and developments have to be seen in the context of these larger college reform initiatives, this book will focus specifically on the evolution and evaluation of our PDSs.

Neither our membership in the Holmes Group nor our move toward PDSs was undisputed. Many of our faculty are still vehemently opposed to the time and resources required to initiate and sustain the PDSs. Others are supportive but feel their own contributions to the college, which do not fit into PDS agendas, have been underappreciated and underfunded. And those working in PDSs feel overworked and often exploited. For the latter, neither the resources, the compensation for time spent, nor the tenure and promotion criteria, adequately support the challenges of establishing and maintaining PDSs (although there have been attempts in the college to address all three).

But there is an equally bright side of the story. Our PDSs have made a difference. Teacher education programs are stronger and more focused now, collaborative work with schools makes it possible to connect theory and practice, inquiry pervades everything we do, and students come out of these programs with more professional attitudes and abilities than were apparent in earlier, more traditional programs. It is rare to find a PDS participant who does not wax eloquent about the benefits of PDSs for teacher education, and also for professional development and school change. In our experience, PDSs do produce many of the things that advocates initially claimed they would.

Of course there are qualifications to be made. Poor leadership, lack of commitment and time, inconsistent membership, political issues, and/or lack of support from principals, school districts, or college administrators easily interfere with PDS outcomes.

Collaboration is a fragile process on which to base a reform agenda. It is easily subverted and depends on relationships that must be nurtured and attended to in ways that more hierarchical arrangements do not. Collaboration is more easily undermined than sustained. It requires changes in attitudes, working relationships, and pedagogies, as well as in organizational structures. There are few proven models and most participants have had little personal experience with this kind of organizational structure.

The narratives in this book reflect both the dark and the bright sides of PDSs. Of course, the bright side is easier to write about, and some of the problems are too political to have been put into print. Nevertheless, the book is a realistic portrayal of our reform efforts.

CONTEXT

There are several important characteristics of the development of our PDSs. Overarching all is their diversity. We have variation in organization, goals, levels of collaboration, and patterns of working with students. We have PDSs that are situated primarily in one school, networks that bring specialist teachers from many schools together (in physical education, art education, special education, foreign language), and consortiums of groups of teachers and their administrator from several schools. Some PDSs have a particular subject matter focus (literacy based education, art education), some have planned diversity in teaching approaches (ECC, one of the elementary PDSs), and others have a subject matter focus (English, social studies, and math, science, and technology). Even for a large university, this is a lot of variation.

The college administration's orientation to reform has encouraged this diversity. As associate dean in charge of these reforms and then dean, Nancy Zimpher favored a "Ready, Fire, Aim" approach. She felt that the time was ripe for reform and the appeal of new ideas in the national arena was enough to get things going. Her faith in individuals to create meaningful reform has nurtured vibrant projects and individual commitment. Her approach could be described as both top-down and bottom-up.

Top-down and Bottom-up

From the top, the deans (Dean Anderson, then Nancy Zimpher) since 1986 have been strong supporters of the Holmes Group reforms—MEd certification and PDSs in particular. Once the difficult collegewide decision about joining the Holmes Group was made, there were consistent pressures to move in the directions of the Holmes proposals. The deans established a series of committees and guided collaborative decision making with school colleagues. From this process, a procedure and criteria for inviting and screening PDS applications was established. A subgroup from these task groups screened applications and eleven PDSs were established in 1991.

From the bottom-up, the call for proposals in spring 1991 laid out only very general principles—PDSs needed to include both school and university participants and to adhere to the broad principles of the Holmes Group. This allowed consortiums of school- and university-based personnel to develop proposals that fit their context and interests. From a PDS in a single school, to networks of physical education specialists across many schools, to a large three district consortium, our initial PDSs were a diverse group. Within individual PDSs, there was almost total autonomy for participants to develop and experiment. In this book you will encounter a wide range of organizational structures, collaborative arrangements, purposes, and programs.

Cross-PDS Communication

Another characteristic of our PDS organization has been ongoing conversations between PDSs. Once the first group of PDSs was identified, monthly meetings of PDS co-coordinators were organized. Each PDS had a clinical educator who was a classroom teacher released half-time from teaching responsibilities (funded by the college) to help co-coordinate the PDS with a university faculty (some who were given release time from their departments and others not). Together the clinical educator and faculty person for each PDS were called co-coordinators and they met monthly to compare notes across diverse contexts and projects and construct recommendations to be taken to the Policy Board for discussion.

A PDS Policy Board, initially co-chaired by Nancy Zimpher and a school principal, Don Cramer, included superintendents, school board members, university faculty, teacher union representatives, teachers, and clinical educators. The board discussed policy and public relation issues. Attempts to evaluate PDSs in order to make funding decisions had the flavor of top-down decision making but otherwise there was little pressure to do things in particular ways.

The clinical educators began meeting as a group during the second year. These monthly meetings helped them deal with an emerging role that placed them half time in two very different institutions, a role that Lampert (1991) describes as "boundary blurring." While no two clinical educators operationalized their role in the same way, the meetings provided support and encouragement.

Another strategy that provided cross-PDS communication was setting up email. The college provided computers and modems for each PDS and technical assistance to get equipment installed and people trained to use it. Two years later, after much time and effort, PDSs were able to communicate between school and university participants and across PDSs. A separate enabling PDS, Technology in Education (TIE), with a university faculty member, Keith Hall, and clinical educator, Bill Gathergood (high school English teacher) was established expressly for this purpose (see chapter 12). Bill, in particular, wore out several sets of tires as he ran from school to school fixing things and training teachers to use email. This communication across PDSs has been critical to keeping people informed of meetings and sharing information. A few of the PDSs have taken this to the next step and used listserves and chat rooms to discuss issues (see chapters 7 and 8).

Funding

Funding the PDSs has been a major challenge. Initially there was the agreement that funding would come one third from the college, one third from the school districts, and one third from outside sources. This was an admirable goal but it has never been met. The college provided significant funding initially to support each clinical educator at $10,000, used primarily for substitutes or co-teachers for their half-time release. If the release time was supplied by substitute teachers, the district probably profited. If the district provided a regularly salaried half-time teacher, they had to support the position with additional district funds. Many school districts have provided additional support for substitutes for PDS teachers, travel to conferences, and space for meetings and classes, but this has not nearly added up to a third of the funding for PDSs. There has been very little external funding.

Faculty in the college were supported in different ways. Individual departments worked out their own arrangements. There was some funding from the dean's office to support credit offerings within PDSs, but this was essentially overload time and pay. Some program areas gave faculty course load credit for administration and work within the PDSs, others did not. Most faculty working in PDSs felt overextended and some untenured faculty resigned because they could not get their publishing completed.

In some programs, PDS work is shared among all faculty; more commonly, a few individuals shoulder the responsibility. Some programs did not establish PDSs, thinking that this wave of reform would be short-lived. In a couple of programs, faculty were not able to work collaboratively, and while their arrangements may have a PDS label, their students are still in traditional placements and supervision. Such programs are not represented in this book.

The funding within the college changed over time. Initially, the dean's office allocated funds to be used in specific ways. Each PDS was given support for the half-time, school-based clinical educator to be a co-coordinator of the PDS with a university-based faculty. Each PDS also got an annual $500 petty cash fund; there was financial support for faculty to teach courses in the PDSs on an overload basis, and teachers and faculty were reimbursed for some of the costs of making conference presentations. These were specific funds to be used for particular kinds of activities.

By 1997–98, funding was allocated directly to the school and the director of the school worked with PDS co-coordinators to set up their budget. Allocations were based on the number of MEd students in each PDS. This funding approach has supported even wider diversity in the structures and goals of the PDSs while at the same time inexorably linking MEd certification and PDS work.

Evaluation

The diversity of the PDSs made accountability challenging. Partly because money was being given to the PDSs, the Policy Board felt some obligation to evaluate the projects. After much discussion in the Policy Board and Co-coordinator's group, three areas of activity were established as defining characteristics of PDSs: (1) collaborative reform in teacher education, (2) professional development, and (3) inquiry. In order to qualify for further funding, each PDS had to write an annual report describing their efforts in the three areas. If there were perceived weaknesses in one area or another, suggestions were made for the coming year. As a result of this process, a couple of PDSs eventually dissolved because they could not initiate activities in all three areas. For most of the PDSs, however, the report was a rather straightforward matter. The process of writing the report, which was often done collaboratively by PDS members, provided a time to reflect on progress and challenges.

The college also supported a professor who specialized in evaluation, to study the PDSs. His graduate students took field notes of meetings, interviewed participants, and visited PDS schools. This same faculty person had a larger, longitudinal study of college graduates that then included graduates from PDS programs. While some internal reports from these data were produced, the enormity of the PDS endeavor made assessment difficult. In addition, the professor in charge of this evaluation moved on to other projects, and so the data wait for further analyses. More recently, evaluation efforts have been relocated in the Office of Career Services where renewed evaluation efforts are under way.

Most of us that work consistently in PDSs are convinced that this work makes a difference for students in our PDS schools. Professional development of teachers, careful mentoring of interns, and school reform initiatives ultimately provide a richer learning environment for students. These environments are rich because interns are in long-term school assignments where they can attend to students' needs, there is careful and collaborative planning for student learning, teachers and interns critically reflect on their teaching, and there is regular implementation of innovative teaching strategies. None of the PDS projects have adequately assessed student learning. Time and resources are two reasons, but in addition, many of our urban PDS schools have high student turnover that make longitudinal and comparative studies difficult if not impossible.

Good-Faith Agreements

For better or worse, there were no formal agreements signed between the college and the school districts. Rather than formal arrangements and prestructured plans, diversity and innovation were encouraged. This allowed for PDS-based decision making and promoted commitment on the part of participants. The down side, however, meant that it was difficult for individual PDSs to get bureaucracies to respond to their needs. Each PDS had to negotiate individually with district personnel to get substitutes or manage reform plans. Idiosyncratic decisions by administrators or the effectiveness of a particular principal or university faculty could make or break a PDS. Some people were just better at playing the system than others. This was advantageous in some situations and devastating in others. It supported variation but sometimes limited the larger initiatives. On the other hand, lots of things probably got done in small and experimental ways that would not have been allowed if more general agreements had been made.

CHALLENGES

Jeanne Oakes and colleagues (1986) describe collaboration as "a congenial paradigm in a cantankerous world." The norms of collaboration are often antithetical to the ways power and decision making occur within schools and universities. For this reason, working in PDSs often makes us feel schizophrenic. We move back and forth adjusting our psychologies to the differences in expectations, relationships, and reward systems.

When we come together in a PDS we bring our different contexts and histories with us. Within PDSs, most participants were initially wary of each other. We had to learn how to work collaboratively. This required overcoming previous stereotypes and perceptions. The process took time, trust, and a willingness to change. Establishing institutional structures, meeting the time demands, deciding whether to jump on the bandwagon, collaborating without imposing, and creating shared goals have continued to be equally prevalent challenges.

No-Person's Land

Much of the organizational work has occurred in the cracks of the institutional structures within which our PDSs have existed. We have struggled to carve out a space for the PDS initiative without knowing where it should fit. What do you do with a Policy Board that has representatives from both the schools and the college but is not clearly answerable to either institution? The Policy Board and Co-coordinators' group met regularly, made decisions about programs and budgets, and yet neither group ever showed up on their respective institution's organizational flowchart. To whom were these groups accountable? Who gave them authority to make these decisions? Departments within the college were often left out of decisions, and funds to faculty for PDS work sometimes bypassed department chairs. School districts seldom had decision procedures in place or categories for clinical educator issues. Initially some clinical educator funds and positions were approved at the district office before the principal in their building had been consulted.

After several years of district support for clinical educators, some superintendents began to wonder if this arrangement was pulling their best teachers away from the classroom. Even though clinical educators were developing professionally and returning to their classrooms refreshed and with new ideas to implement in their schools and classrooms, the superintendents were not convinced. They pointed to the few who completed graduate work and moved to university positions. As a result of these concerns, and the fact that most teachers wanted to continue their full-time work in the district, a few subsequent PDSs opted for clinical educator roles to be shared by "field professors" that did not take teachers out of the classroom.

During the 1996–97 academic year, the PDS initiative was moved to the associate dean's office and we were on our way to a more institutionalized place for the PDSs. The Policy Board was renamed the Partnership Board. Chaired by Susan Sears, the associate dean, it meets once or twice a quarter and has wide representation. Issues are discussed and coordinating activities planned, but there is less consistent membership and less sense that this group has any direct decision-making responsibilities. Fewer meetings are a welcome reality for many, on the other hand, there is less communication across PDSs. During the same period, PDSs have become more tightly associated with MEd programs in particular areas, and this means decision making for each PDS is now more the shared responsibility of the faculty in that program. What started as rather autonomous and sometimes maverick PDS projects are now fully institutionalized into certification programs with wider participation of university faculty. Almost all certification students in the college, with the notable exception of educational administration, now do their internships in PDS settings.

Institutionalization of PDSs has had both advantages and disadvantages. There is more stability and predictability. There are more equitable policies so that PDSs have similar support and faculty get similar credit for working in them. There is, however, less autonomy as PDSs are now closely associated with program areas and more people have input into their purposes and programs. This increases faculty involvement, but sometimes hampers reform initiatives. This is not always the case, of course. Some PDSs continue to be hotbeds of reform, others seem to be dragging under the weight of more recalcitrant faculty.

Time

The time required for collaboration and PDS work is one of the most consistent topics in this book. If we could calculate the number of additional hours PDS work has added to the involvement of both school and university participants, it would be staggering. While the time commitment to get things started is often more than anticipated, the time required to sustain PDSs seems not to decrease to any significant degree. We wonder, even when there is strong commitment to these reforms, whether these arrangements can be sustained? Is there personal as well as institutional will to continue this kind of work long term? If we cut the time involvement, will we sacrifice the innovation? Are the rewards, although readily apparent, enough to sustain what's required to continue? Will institutions be willing to maintain sufficient, which means probably increased, levels of support and personnel to create manageable modes of participation? If we cut back on the time, will we lose the relationships that have nurtured and sustained these PDSs? Can we sustain their relationships with new members joining and others retiring or leaving for other reasons? Can we even maintain the outcomes we have achieved without the same levels of time and involvement?

Inquiry

The obligation to include inquiry in all the PDSs has presented a challenge. This expectation added another layer to an already full reform initiative. As clinical settings, we were supposed to study what we did in order to inform further development and also to add to the scholarly literature. Many faculty working in PDSs were untenured and were well aware of the need to make their work turn into publications. School-based participants, however, were typically leery of inquiry. They did not feel like researchers, nor did they initially want to turn into, or be turned into, miniprofessors. There are no tangible rewards in schools for doing this kind of inquiry and writing, and even less time for actually getting the work done.

Some have argued that the requirement for inquiry is an imposition of university norms on school contexts (Labaree, 1995). Others contend that helping teachers do research, especially with approaches like action research, supports reflective teaching and professional development (Miller & Pine, 1990; Oja, 1987). Others emphasize the potential of action research to produce a knowledge base that reflects teachers' expertise gained from experience (Cochran-Smith & Lytle, 1993). Further, some suggest that action research will help teachers to be critical change agents in their classrooms and give them tools to change undemocratic and controlling school contexts (Noffke & Stevenson, 1995; Zeichner, 1993).

Should We? Should We Not?

Another issue for those in schools and at the university has been the political question of whether to "jump on the PDS wagon." Encouragement, sometimes even strong pressure, came from college administrators to move to graduate-level MEd programs and PDSs. Some faculty and program areas were reticent because they were opposed to these kinds of changes. Others waited to see if these initiatives would be sustained. Other programs jumped on the wagon and moved speedily into programmatic changes and PDS development. The consequences of each of these approaches have been varied, both in terms of resources and institutional rewards.

In the schools, some district administrators and school principals were anxious to be part of the PDS movement. Part of this interest was motivated by the fee waiver system that has existed between OSU and local school districts for the past 30 years. The development of PDSs meant more focused work in fewer schools. Districts were therefore anxious about losing their access to fee waivers if they did not participate in PDSs.

Eight years later, the trend is clear and consistent, especially at the university. In the college, all program areas now have had proposals accepted to tie their MEd programs and a PDS together. While the future is always uncertain, it is clear that our college now has graduate level certification programs and associated PDS projects. In the school districts, there are generally good feelings about PDS efforts, and superintendents and school boards are increasingly more willing to support PDSs in their districts.

Whose Interests are Served?

It is difficult, in some cases, to distinguish between a PDS and a collaborative effort that is based on a faculty member's individual research agenda. It has been advantageous for individual university faculty to fold their research interests into their PDS work. The greater the overlap the more productive they could be to serve both PDS work and the need to do research and publish. But what if the PDS is primarily a springboard for the faculty member's research or it solely reflects the ideology or interests of the university faculty? Are there questions to be raised about mutual influence from both school and university participants? If this is a collaborative endeavor, should one point of view prevail throughout?

A more general, but parallel distinction, has to do with PDS philosophy. To what extent should a PDS reflect the orientation of the college program in which it is situated? If the program area, for example, art education or elementary education, has a particular theoretical orientation to instruction, should the PDS only work with teachers who share this philosophy? Or should the PDS develop a philosophy that reflects the theory/practice connections collaboratively constructed by those involved in the PDS?

In many cases, a PDS was initiated by a group who had a history of working together prior to the PDS, for example, the LEADS/PDS that grew out of a 25-year program in literacy education. (For other examples, see art education, chapter 13; foreign and second language, chapter 15; special education, chapter 16; middle school, chapter 6.) In some cases, PDSs formed out of consortia that represented diverse teaching styles and philosophies (see ECC, chapter 5).

Changing Personnel

What happens to a PDS when key members of the group leave? New participants and new leadership make it hard to sustain the collaborative goals established by previous members. Continuity within projects has been challenging because both school- and university-based participants come and go. If there is genuine collaboration, the PDS ought to reflect the interests of the present group, and yet, if the present group is continually changing there is the ongoing and time-consuming need to continually reconstruct goals and procedures. In some of the longer term projects, participants who have been in the PDS for some time, get tired of continually orienting and negotiating with new participants instead of continuing their own professional development. It feels to them like walking backwards to bring new participants along.

Initially, Dean Nancy Zimpher advocated changing PDS affiliation with particular schools every three years. The goal was to influence more schools and school-based educators. Some PDSs have naturally fallen into this kind of cycle, especially as university participants leave a PDS and new faculty came in. Others have continued with at least some consistent schools and school and university participants. At this point, neither of these options seem best in all situations. Many variables influence the ability of a PDS to continue, including the longevity of participants, administrators' continuity and support, changing district politics or agendas, and funding sources. Each of these can affect whether a PDS continues in any given shape or form.

Has It Made a Difference?

It has been a major challenge to demonstrate the value of all of this work. The tendency has been to investigate local questions, classroom-based questions, PDS successes, and projectwide issues rather than to look systematically across the PDSs. While a wide range of publications and studies have been published, it's hard to get a handle on the overall impact.

The dean did support an evaluation effort led by a faculty person with expertise in this area. A large amount of data was collected but little helpful reporting was produced. The college either lacked the expertise and/or available personnel for this kind of evaluation, or was expending resources in the work of PDSs rather than evaluation. With college restructuring nearly completed, there is a renewed effort to do more systematic studies, but this is only at a beginning stage.

The impact of PDSs, nevertheless, is readily apparent in the publications produced by PDS participants (see appendix for a list of PDS publications). This book and other writings and presentations describe ways in which interns are better prepared, professional development is accomplished, and school and college programs are changing. This is a reform initiative that has actually promoted reform. Few people who have had substantive involvement with PDSs feel their time has been wasted; typically they are tired but exuberant about what they have learned and how they have changed.

CONSEQUENCES

The chapters that follow describe the consequences of our work. Our PDSs are diverse in shape, purposes, and outcomes, and so are these chapters. They vary in their content, focus, authorship, and format. Across this diversity, however, you will see consistent themes and continuous attempts to address the challenges just discussed. Overall, we are convinced that our PDSs are better preparing future professionals, supporting our own professional growth, and contributing significantly to reform in the schools and at the university.

One indication of the consequences of our PDSs is the change in how we talk about and to each other. What follows is a comparison of typical comments made before PDS and quotations from after PDS. They serve to foreground the changes you will see in this book and the description of the chapters that follows.

TYPICAL BEFORE PDS COMMENTS

Schools folks said to university folks:

I tried that once and it didn't work.

What's in it for us?

Why can't you be here, you only teach two classes?

I have to teach to the tests. That's how I'm evaluated.

Teachers said to student teachers:

If you need me, I'll be in the lounge reading.

If you teach like I do, you'll get a good recommendation.

The theories you learn at the university are well and good, but I will show you how things really work.

Interns said:

That theory just doesn't work in the classroom.

My professors tell me to vary my instruction, but they usually lecture.

My cooperating teacher shows me how she/he wants me to teach, but I'm not allowed to do anything else.

University folks said:

We need quality teachers with whom to place our student teachers.

Teachers are quick to criticize new ideas we present to students and won't support them trying new things in the classroom.

AFTER PDS COMMENTS

After seven years of collaborative work, many things have changed. We think differently about each other and understand better how our separate institutions shape our perspectives and reward us differentially. The following "after PDS" comments are quoted from the book chapters as well as from recent interviews with PDS participants.

- "As anyone who had tackled a difficult task and lived to relate it will tell you, there are both rewards and challenges inherent in any new endeavor." (Clinical educator, chapter 2)
- "My own learning about teacher preparation, teaching, schools and students has been deeply enhanced by the collective process, sometimes in obvious ways, at other times more subtly." (Professor, chapter 8)
- "If the student teacher is not from a PDS, I am not interested in having them teach in my classroom." (PDS cooperating teacher interview, 1995)
- "I feel like I am a part of the staff, not a visitor." (PDS intern interview, 1995)
- "Because of the great successes of our middle school students, graduate students from the university were intrigued and wanted to study the student-centered curriculum phenomenon." (Professors and cooperating teachers, chapter 6)
- "It was challenging for university faculty. Some had a difficult time giving up control of the content and delivery of a program that they felt had been successful." (Professor, chapter 14)
- "Using inquiry as a basis for our PDS, we have woven together multiple perspectives and furthered our goals to improve student learning, teacher education, and educators' professional development." (Team of professors, chapter 4)

- "I have been a classroom teacher for over 28 years and involved with student teachers for a long time. There is no question in my mind that our PDS Network has vastly improved the preparation of preservice teachers." (Cooperating teacher, chapter 7)
- "No, I do not do playground duty on my clinical educator days, but it is important to me that my colleagues see me working for them in other ways during this time." (Clinical educator, chapter 2)
- "As I try to make sense of who I am as a teacher and what I want to bring to a classroom, I have changed the way I mentor our year-long interns. Through their struggles, I see my weaknesses. Just as each child teaches me about myself as a person, the interns have had this same effect on my practice." (Cooperating teacher, chapter 5)

CHAPTER PREVIEWS

The introduction to the book provides some background for reading the book. It was written by one of the editors and has attempted to lay out the context, challenges, and consequences of the book. Chapter 1 is a critical review of the literature on collaboration. It draws from literature in teacher education, school administration, college teaching, and feminist theories. In chapter 2, Rhonda Dailey Dickinson describes her role as a clinical educator. The clinical educator role has been a unique part of the development of PDSs at Ohio State and this chapter describes the character of this role as it was first developed. Chapter 3 describes the role of an administrator who works in both school and university cultures.

In the second part, the elementary and middle school PDSs describe their diverse and varied approaches to reform, professional development, and inquiry. The LEADS PDS in chapter 4 is grounded in a 30-year collaborative program focusing on literacy and urban education. Chapter 5 is written by teachers and university participants in the ECC PDS that is distinguished by particular attention to establishing collaborative relations and reform through professional development. The middle school PDS described in chapter 6 uses a metaphor of the artist to describe their approach to developing a PDS for middle school–level education.

Part III includes chapters at the secondary level. Chapters 7 and 8 are two PDSs associated with social studies education, chapters 9 and 10 are a single site PDS where their school reform initiatives with the Coalition for Essential Schools incorporated PDS activities, and chapter 11, LEARN PDS is a broad network of educators interested in learning styles.

Part IV includes a chapter on an "enabling" PDS, Technology in Education (TIE) that supports the development of technology in all our

PDSs (chapter 12), and our network PDSs associated with particular subject matters (art, physical education, and foreign and second language, chapters 13 through 15) and special education (chapter 16).

In the conclusion the editors each give a pre- and post-PDS account of their own experience and then we draw together some themes, issues, and hopes for the future.

READING ROUTES

There are several ways to read this book. The chapters are not arranged in a linear order, but rather are clustered by types of PDSs. There are, however, numerous ways to read this book. Below we lay out several interests that might direct your reading.

- If you are interested in reading about starting a PDS, see chapters 6, 9, 13, 15 and 16.
- If you are interested in PDSs that have a longer history, see chapters 4, 5, 7 and 11.
- If you are interested in the perspective of school-based participants see chapters 2, 3, and 5 through 12.
- If you are interested in the role of clinical educators see chapters 2, 5, 7, and 9 through 12.
- If you are interested in PDSs developed for elementary and middle school programs, see chapters 4 through 6.
- If you are interested in PDSs developed around subject matter orientations at the high school level, see chapters 7 through 10.
- If you are interested in research done in PDSs, see chapters 4, 5, 7, 9 and 15
- If you are interested in how a PDS might support technology interests in PDSs generally, see chapter 12.
- If you are interested in PDSs that are built around a particular philosophical orientation, see chapters 4, 6, 7, 8, 9, 11, and 13 through 16.
- If you are interested in the consequences of PDSs for professional development, see chapters 4 through 9 and 11.

REFERENCES

Carnegie Forum on Education and the Economy. (1986). *A nation prepared: Teachers for the 21st century.* New York: Author.

Cochran-Smith, M., & Lytle, S. (1993). *Inside/Outside: Teacher research and knowledge*. New York: Teachers College Press.

Donmoyer, Robert. (1990). Generalizability and the single-case study. In E. Eisner and A. Peshkin (Eds.), *Qualitative inquiry in education: The continuing debate* (pp. 175–200). New York: Teachers College Press.

Holmes Group. (1986). *Tomorrow's teachers: A report of the Homes Group*. East Lansing, MI: Author.

Holmes Group. (1990). *Tomorrow's schools: Principles for the design of professional development schools*. East Lansing, MI: author.

Labaree, D. F. (Ed.). (1995). *Why do schools cooperate with university-based reforms: The case of professional development schools*. Albany: State University of New York Press.

Lampert, M. (1991). Looking at restructuring from within a restructured role. *Phi Delta Kappan, 72*(9), 670–674.

Miller, D. M., & Pine, G. J. (1990). Advancing professional inquiry for educational improvement through action research. *Journal of Staff Development, 11*(3), 56–61.

National Commission on Excellence in Education. (1983). *A nation at risk: The imperative for educational reform*. Washington, DC: Government Printing Office.

Noffke, S. E., & Stevenson, R. B. (1995). *Educational action research: Becoming practically critical*. New York: Teachers College Press.

Oja, S. N., & Pine, G. J. (1987). Collaborative action research: Teachers' stages of development and school contexts. *Peabody Journal of Education, 64*(3), 96–115.

Zeichner, K. M. (1993). Action research: Personal renewal and social reconstruction. *Educational Action Research, 1*(2), 199–219.

PART I

Contextualizing PDS Work and Roles

CHAPTER 1

Too *Valuable to Be Rejected,*
Too *Different to Be Embraced:*
A *Critical Review of*
School/University *Collaboration*

Cindy Dickens

In this chapter, Cindy Dickens surveys the literature on school/university collaboration using writings in teacher education, school administration, college teaching, and feminist theories to examine critically the definitions, assumptions, and silences in this literature. The author raises questions as well as suggests areas where research and writing are needed.

Collaboration is increasingly *en vogue* in the United States. Heralded as a response to complex global problems, resource limitations, and an eroding faith in Western social and economic institutions, proponents of collaboration offer it as a practical solution to a multitude of complex problems. The American public school system, a perennial scapegoat during periods of intense international competition, has not been exempt from scathing criticism. Critics have placed responsibility for the decline of American economic competitiveness and scientific preeminence heavily on the shoulders of the nation's educators. Declining SAT scores with large numbers of high school graduates ill prepared for college-level work, sky-rocketing dropout rates, and a host of other numeric indicators attest to the apparent inability of the public schools to prepare the technologically sophisticated work force needed for the twenty-first century. Perhaps it is not surprising that a series of blue-ribbon commissions, borrowing heavily from Japanese group-centered practices, have urged greater cooperation between government and business, business and universities, and universities and schools.

Collaboration in Western culture, although seemingly in conflict with the American ethic of rugged individualism is not a foreign concept. Schools of artists flourished in Europe during the Renaissance, and since World War II, teamwork has become the normative pattern for scientific research in medicine, physics, biology, and engineering. Formal and informal relationships between university-based teacher education programs and local school personnel are as old as the nineteenth-century normal schools from which many of our schools of education evolved. Within our own century, events of such political magnitude as the Soviet Union's launching of Sputnik and the U.S. Supreme Court's ending of racial segregation in public schools have drawn university faculty as researchers, evaluators, and consultants into active, although sometimes unwelcomed, partnership with their public school colleagues.

Within the context of recent national recommendations for reform (Carnegie Forum on Education and the Economy, 1986; National Commission on Excellence in Education, 1983), school/university collaboration has taken on a different meaning. Some reformers are encouraging and even demanding that people from diverse sectors of our society become actively involved in education. At the same time, other educators are raising serious questions regarding the role that university faculty and other "outsiders" can and should play in the restructuring of K–12 schools and teacher education (Ladwig, 1991; Maeroff, 1988; Darling-Hammond, 1992; Lieberman, 1992). In the center of this controversy, school and university leaders around the country are coming together in recognition of their common problems and responsibilities. What is different about the school/university collaborations that are appearing in the 1980s and 1990s?

This essay looks critically at the educational literature that has appeared during the last two decades in order to see what has been learned about school/university collaborations. What theories are emerging from twenty years of practice to guide future collaborations between such different organizations? Is there more here than "feel good" rhetoric? Even more fundamentally, are the values that are basic to collaboration changing the way we think and write about schools, teachers, and knowledge?

TOWARD A CLEARER DEFINITION OF COLLABORATION

Part of the difficulty in reviewing this literature is determining just what researchers and practitioners mean by collaboration. Our vocabulary is filled with words that attempt to express the range of formal and informal, ad hoc and permanent, organized and dynamic relationships that exist between individuals or groups pursuing common goals. Teams, partnerships, coalitions, collectives, cooperatives, consortia, collaborations, and networks are the most commonly used. Some writers use similar terms interchangeably, implying no differences in their meaning. Clark (1988) concludes that frequently used terms—network, partnership, consortium, cooperative, and collaborative—are imprecise and overlapping. The use of imprecise terms reinforces the notion that there are no clear distinctions of their constitutive processes and values.

If It Looks Like Collaboration . . .

Parallel to the imprecise and interchangeable use of terms, definitions of school/university collaboration are often broad and all inclusive—collaboration is shared intellectual labor or working together. Qualifying this broad definition only slightly, Hawthorne and Zusman (1992) define school/university collaborations "as formal projects or activities in which representatives from the public schools and postsecondary education (public and private, two- and four-year) work together toward resolving common problems" (pp. 322–323). This definition includes all formal activity in which schools and colleges engaged jointly. Differences in values and processes that arise in these endeavors are concealed by this broad definition.

Falling frequently into hyperbole, some enthusiastic proponents describe school university collaboration as a change-enhancing, morale-boosting process. They also tout it as a panacea not just for restructuring troubled schools but for combating the alienating, hierarchical, and competitive aspects of contemporary social life. In contrast to this romantic view, we also find writers who are working toward a more precise definition in an attempt to understand its advantages, limitations, requirements, and unique applications.

Appley and Winder (1977) approach collaboration as a value system that eschews the older, dominating system based on the Darwinian and free market principles of scarcity, competition, and maximizing self-interest. They argue that the old value system was relatively functional in simple societies, however, our increasingly turbulent environment requires a value system based not on competition for limited resources but on collaboration, trust, and sharing. This definition emphasizes human caring, commitment, and justice, values that can be learned and incorporated successfully into work settings.

Hord (1986) differentiates between collaborating and cooperating organizations. She asserts that collaboration and cooperation are different operational processes and that each process evokes different expectations from its members. Cooperation is a limited process in which one organization seeks the assistance or permission of another for the attainment of a goal. Collaboration, in contrast, involves exchanges on the part of both organizations. Hord includes six dimensions: beginning processes, communication, resources and ownership, requirements and characteristics, leadership and control, and rewards. Conceptualizing collaboration as the more demanding relationship, she cautions:

> When participants are willing to relinquish personal control and assume more risk, they create a more flexible environment and can move closer to collaboration. Control must be shared, and a tolerance for plasticity must be fostered. For people or organizations needing stability and specificity, collaboration is a difficult process—the cooperative model is more suitable. (Hord, 1986, p. 26)

Goodlad (1988) turns to the concept of symbiosis to describe the type of school/university collaboration that offers the greatest promise for educational reform. "Symbiosis," he asserts, "refers to unlike organisms (or institutions) joined intimately in mutually beneficial relationships" (p. 14). Schlechty and Whitford (1988) call for school/university collaborations conceptualized as organic rather than symbiotic. They explain:

> In organic relationships, the parts fulfill unique functions, sometimes in a semi-autonomous fashion, but the purpose of these functions is to serve the body of the whole. Indeed, each part has a major investment in the survival of the whole. . . . Thus, unlike symbiotic relationships, which emphasize mutual self-interest, organic relationships stress the common good above all else. (p. 192)

Effective school/university collaborations are still relatively uncommon and not without problems. However, even experienced school/university collaborators such as Goodlad and colleagues (also see Clift, Veal, Holland, Johnson, & McCarthy, 1995; Johnston, 1997; Darling-Hammond, 1994; Petrie, 1995), boast that these partnerships can promote significant and long-lasting change and renewal. Increasingly, their stories are appearing in the published educational literature (Hoffman, Reed, & Rosenbluth, 1997; Hoz & Silberstein, 1995; Slater, 1996). From these stories, we can begin to learn what successful school/university collaborations look like, what changes they have fostered, and what those changes mean to the educators and organizations who experience them. If we listen to these stories carefully, we will, in addition, detect the silences that also tell us about the challenges of collaboration.

Defining Collaboration in School/University Research

Most researchers would agree that collaboration involves more than merely working together harmoniously. However, even when committed teachers, administrators, and faculty are able to agree upon the desired goals and outcomes, collaboration is not an inevitable process. Tikunoff and Ward (1983), whose early NIE (National Institute of Education) funded work became the model for later federally supported school/university research collaborations, identify four common characteristics of collaborative research projects:

1. Researchers and school practitioners work together on all phases of the effort.
2. The collaborative effort is focused on "real world" as well as theoretical problems.
3. Both groups gain in understanding and mutual respect.
4. The effort is concerned with both research and development/implementation issues throughout.

Oakes, Hare, and Sirotnik (1986), also writing on research relationships between university and school personnel, suggest "pushing the collaborative paradigm toward a democratic approach that is equitable and consensual rather than merely participatory" (pp. 546–547). Calling this mode "collaborative inquiry," they argue for a process in which collaborators work toward the same end rather than helping one another achieve goals unique to each:

> So defined, collaboration includes the conditions of equality, of responsibility, and equality of status. Decision making at all stages of the work becomes an appropriate collaborative task. . . . Diverse opinions are not simply respected, they have equal influence in decision making. (p. 547)

COLLABORATIVE VALUES IN REAL WORLD PARTNERSHIPS

Articles in the early to mid-1980s, frequently co-authored by researcher/practitioner teams, appear in retrospect to lack some of the key features of the democratic collaboratives described above. One of the earliest reports of school/university collaborations is a study by Huling, Trang, and Correll (1981), three university-based researchers. They report on a project in which a team of classroom practitioners, trained in research methods and working with a university researcher, selected disruptive student behavior for study, carried out the research, and implemented a peer-tutoring program based on their research findings. The project was reported to be extremely successful based on measurable improvement in the targeted students' behavior as well as teachers' attitudes toward integrating research with practice. The authors concluded that other teacher educators (for whom the article was written) can benefit from the underlying principle of IR&D (Institute for Research and Development), "that all programs intended ultimately to involve practitioners should be developed collaboratively so that the persons who are to be most affected by change can participate in every phrase of the change" (p. 14). In retrospect, however, we might argue that this collaborative arrangement was somewhat limited. The change was only to be experienced by the practitioner and the role of the university researcher remained essentially that of expert consultant. By participating as researchers in a school-based study, the practitioners indicated a greater willingness to engage in research and to act on it, a finding that appears to advantage university faculty and academic knowledge and to perpetuate hierarchical relationship between universities and schools.

More recently, university partners have begun to examine their own involvement and learning. Lampert (1991), associated with the Michigan State University Institute for Research on Teaching (IRT), did her research in collaboration with teachers. She writes from the perspective "of one who occupies the sort of restructured role that many reform proposals advocate" (p. 672). As she relives a typical day in the elementary school where she teaches math to fifth-graders, she reflects in a stream-of-consciousness style on her multiple selves and her feelings of conflict as a person in a boundary-blurring situation: "My fundamental strain is that it takes a different sort of 'me' to be good at each of these jobs, and the 'me' in one job is often in conflict with the 'me' in another" (Lampert, 1991, p. 674). Her personal experience raises new questions about the demands that school/university collaborations place on the individuals involved. Furthermore it provides insight into one teacher's values and how those values shape and are shaped by the way she interacts with students, parents, and colleagues in the construction of her own identity.

Susan Florio-Ruane (1986), reflecting on her experiences in collaborative inquiry groups composed of teachers and faculty members, learned to value teacher conversation and narrative, forms of discourse often dismissed by university researchers as unscientific and lacking in academic value. She reports on her own growth as an educational ethnographer interested in writing instruction:

> Incorporating the teachers' voices and stories into texts for diverse audiences taught us that not all knowledge can be represented by struc-

tural models. Because our initial formal accounts were biased toward the typical, they were unable to capture conflict, compromise, and change. In story and conversation we had access to a great many more of the tensions and contradictions in teachers' work. Whereas a year before we would have waited patiently for teachers to vent their complaints about the district or the principal before getting down to talking about how they teach writing, we now realized that those concerns were intimately tied to teaching writing. (p. 23)

Trubowitz (1986, p. 19) describes an ongoing school/university collaboration (six years at the time of the article) between Queens College in New York City and the Armstrong Middle School. Focusing on collaboration in the process of school renewal, Trubowitz identified eight stages of development—ranging from hostility and skepticism to renewal and continuing progress—through which the project and its participants passed. Many of the values that have come to be associated with current definitions of collaboration emerged in the Queens/Armstrong experience: active listening, empathy, merging of roles, building trust, open communication, supportive leaders, shared goals, and a long-term commitment to the project. Still missing from this success story, however, is a careful look at the other side of the equation (the university) in order to understand how collaborations can also challenge universities as sites of power and authority.

IS THERE THEORY IN THIS PRACTICE?

Not surprisingly, concern with the practical and methodological problems (for example, Kyle & McCutcheon, 1984; Metzner, 1970) associated with school/university collaborations—the how to's and what about's—have superseded the theoretical ones. As the traditional boundaries that have separated researchers and practitioners begin to fade, we cannot help but theorize why this collaborative way of doing things might or might not be working, if it might not be based on something more profound and epistemologically valid. By conjoining theory with practice and refusing to see them as separate and opposite, we express the belief that our understanding of collaboration might be informed not only by practice but by an emerging body of theory.

Underlying Assumptions

Theory is not a word that appears frequently in much of the literature describing school/university collaboration. When it appears, it is often isolated in theoretical positions that are rarely used in research or more descriptive writings. There are, however, shared assumptions about social reality and human relationships that have begun to emerge in this diverse literature. The values inherent in the available theoretical papers often reflect a constructivist view of social reality that differs radically from the more common view of knowledge as individual, internal, and preexisting the self. Many of the arguments that explain and justify collaborative learning and teaching turn to philosophy for theoretical force. Greene (1991), for example, draws on philosophers as diverse as Dewey, Sartre, Mead, Camus, Merleau-Ponty, and Arendt to argue for an image of teachers as reflective and purposeful people who can "create themselves as the teachers they want to be" (p. 13). The teacher's personal reality, however, cannot be separated from "cooperative action within a community. It is when teachers are together as persons, according to norms and principles they have freely chosen, that interest becomes intensified and commitments are made" (p. 13).

Also reflecting a constructivist view of organizations and schooling, Maloy (1985) frames school/university collaboration as an "example of social interactions based on multiple, rather than mutual, realities" (p. 342) and uses that frame for explaining why collaborations often do not succeed. Maloy contends that schools and universities face a mandate to collaborate but approach one another without mutually examining their perspectives and assumptions. He explains: "Reality is not a single, fixed set of ideas or assumptions shared by social actors. Constructing what is real, people may create alternative or multiple views of the same events, and act according to those differing interpretations."

Similarly, Hostetler (1992), in a philosophical argument that both critiques and defends Rorty's writings on collaboration, challenges the "privileged status" currently given to collaborative forms of work and argues that conversations between school and university personnel may be fruitless until "a richer, more complex vocabulary of education and life" is developed.

Bruffee (1983, 1984) embraces a collaborative theory of knowledge and learning whose theoretical roots he also traces to Rorty's social justification of belief, to Vygotsky's work in language development, to Kuhn's description of paradigmatic revolutions in the development of scientific knowledge, and to other contemporary constructivist thinkers such as Clifford Geertz and Stanley Fish. Writing from the perspective of a college-level composition teacher, Bruffee (1984) argues persuasively for a collaborative writing pedagogy that recognizes that all forms of communication—reading, writing, talking, even thinking—are inherently social acts that take place within and are sanctioned by peer communities.

A poststructural concern with language and metaphor frames McGowan and Powell's (1990) discussion of school/university collaboration. They observe that the image of school as machine (and teachers as interchangeable parts) that dominated school reform in the 1980s limited our thinking and failed to transform traditional school structures and climate. They argue that the brain metaphor is more suited to a transitional society such as ours where individuals must be able to question what they are doing and alter their behaviors in response to feedback. McGowan and Powell mount a persuasive argument that links poststructural thinking about language and reality with the contemporary school-based reform movement's emphasis on change which is "flexible, situation-specific, practitioner-formulated and monitored, interactive, relatively egalitarian, and directed at targets which all participants recognize." These are the same core values that we see emerging in the literature on successful school/university collaboration.

Johnston (1997) also uses poststructural feminists theories to consider issues of institutional norms and arrangements that influence collaboration as well as the silences around who speaks and about what topics—this include the unspoken and unsayable that reflect the power and politics inherent in this kind of work.

Theory in Action Research

A significant portion of work on collaboration is linked to action research, including the early work of James Collier, the U.S. Commissioner of Indian Affairs (1933–45), and Kurt Lewin, a German social psychologist working in the 1930s and 1940s, who are probably best known for their early work in action research. Lewin challenged the traditional experimental orientation of social scientists, believing that theory about social action could develop from observation of the effects of action in context. Lewin directly influenced Stephen Corey's work on schooling at Columbia University and Eric Trist's work in England.

Given the strong ideological ties between American business and public education, it is not surprising that the organizational change and development literature from the behavioral sciences most often provides theoretical underpinnings for research on school/university collaborations. Austin and Baldwin (1991, p. 47), reviewing the literature on collaboration in faculty research and teaching, conclude that negotiated order theory "is the single theory that is most useful for analyzing and understanding these team efforts among faculty." They too credit Lewin, Trist, and action research for making significant contributions to the theoretical perspectives that inform much of the current research on collaboration.

Theory Building

A growing body of rich literature, informed by anthropological and sociological theories and methods, links schools and universities through collaborative inquiry. Approaching schools as unique cultural settings, educational ethnographers no longer view teachers as objects of study but as cultural informants, knowledgeable participants, and partners in school-based research who must assume an active role in school renewal and their own development if change is to be meaningful and long lasting (McCutcheon, 1981). Studies in this tradition bring interpretive and critical perspectives to bear on school/university partnerships, often linking collaborative inquiry with curricular innovation and staff development (Florio & Walsh, 1981; Lieberman, 1986). Campbell (1988), for example, reports on a multiyear research and staff development project involving teachers, principals, and university researchers that was designed to "engage participants in reflection and dialogue grounded in respect for teachers' knowledge and modeled on the nonjudgmental and non-intervening features of ethnographic inquiry" (p. 99). His report reveals role conflicts, contradictions, power differences, and control issues that surfaced during the project, leading ultimately to reflective thinking and growth on the part of practitioners and researchers alike.

Adult developmental stage theories form the foundation for Oja and Ham's (1984) collaborative work with teachers. In their action research, they noted similarities between teacher behaviors and the stages of moral/ethical and ego development hypothesized by Kohlberg, Rest, Loevinger, and others. They suggest that university professors engaged in action research with classroom teachers can serve a dual function as researchers and staff developers.

Eschewing an impositional stance in a researcher/practitioner relationship, Hunsaker and Johnston (1992) and Johnston (1990) report on the complexities and risks that surround collaborative inquiry. Johnston (1990), responding to the "cry for collaboration in teacher education and research" (p. 172) concludes from her experience as a faculty collaborator that there are burdens as well as benefits from this mode of work and that collaborative procedures are not appropriate for all projects. She adds, however, "if the research goal is to understand teachers' meanings and beliefs, it seems reasonable, if not morally required, that teachers have some say in the telling of their stories" (p. 180).

TOWARD A FEMINIST THEORY OF
SCHOOL/UNIVERSITY COLLABORATION

Anyone familiar with feminist theory since Gilligan's 1982 assault on the androcentric bias in adult developmental theory will recognize the themes of caring, affiliation, and personal connections that appear repeatedly in the literature on collaboration. Although it may be possible to collaborate without caring for one's collaborators (and even this qualified contention is being questioned), it is difficult to understand how collaboration can be divorced from caring and personal concern in the context of schooling. Teaching is about helping others to learn and grow, a role that has been linked historically to women's capabilities to gestate and nurture children. And since this linkage was publicly recognized and reinforced in the early nineteenth century by the hiring of women to teach in common schools, teaching, especially at the elementary level, has been a profession dominated by women. It seems particularly odd that so much of the literature on school/university collaboration, teacher development, and school reform fails to mention this salient fact.

The curriculum, the work of teachers, as well as the isolated classroom environment in which it is situated, is increasingly controlled and regulated by administrators, bureaucrats, legislators, and other outsiders who are often males. Patriarchy, with its valuing of the masculine over the feminine, the public over the private, the instrumental over the expressive, is an ever present feature of teachers' professional lives.

Noddings (1986) points out that teaching is a constitutively ethical activity, implying that teachers and students are inherently connected as people in the work of learning. She explains, "It is a moral type of friendship in which teachers and students work together to construct and achieve common ends. Those who enter classrooms become part of this ethical activity" (p. 509). Theorizing from a feminist perspective, Noddings offers collaborative inquiry as a way to meet colleagues in genuine mutuality—as peers—rather than to make persons (teachers and students) the objects of research. In arguing for fidelity to persons as a guide to teacher education, research, and school reform, she is not limiting her comments to women, although she recognizes, just as Gilligan does, that the different voices expressing an ethic of caring is more typically female than male.

Feminist theory and feminist values inform a small but relatively diverse literature on school/university collaboration. Some researchers like Grumet (1989) and Connor and Sharp (1992) address the gendered context of schools directly. Others, like Lampert (1991), do not claim a feminist stance but express the feminist desire to empower women. They take their own and other women's experiences seriously and use them as the grounding for a more complete theory of education.

The feminist concern for voice is also a dominant theme is two papers co-authored by Hollingsworth and Gallego (1991) and Hollingsworth and Minarik (1991). In a paper that is both experimental and lyrical in its form, as well as explicitly feminist in its methodology, faculty member Hollingsworth and practitioner/former student

Minarik reflect upon the conflict between the public perception of schooling and teachers' private realities, and its consequences upon teachers' professional lives and career decisions. Minarik's journal, kept during the course of her collaboration with Hollingsworth's inquiry group, reveals a conspiracy of public silence where teachers conceal their concerns from the distant authority of state and district bureaucrats and university curriculum experts, sharing their private knowledge only among themselves.

As we hear so clearly from these studies, teacher talk, like "women talk" is commonly dismissed as complaining, idle chatter, or a time-wasting release of frustrations that prevents researchers from getting on with the real work. Hollingsworth and Minarik discover that school/university collaboration conducted in an atmosphere of mutual trust and respect with active listening and support can promote significant learning and risk taking for all participants.

In jarring contrast to Hollingsworth and Minarik's experience, a participant's comment included in another study suggests that some individuals may prefer a more masculine, product-oriented approach to collaboration. Oakes, Hare, and Sirotnik (1986) reporting on the problems they encountered in a collaborative research project, list one of the comments included on the final project evaluation, "Tendency of women to be groupish makes collaboration difficult" (p. 552). This criticism warns us that men and women may in general approach collaborative partnerships with different skills and expectations shaped by their experiences as gendered subjects. Furthermore women's behaviors may be stereotyped, undervalued, and differentially acted upon depending on whether they are perceived as enhancing or detracting from the goals of the collaborative.

From a feminist perspective, we might consider whether there are different masculine and feminine models of collaboration and how these different models might work. Do some men perceive caring and connected behavior as "groupish" and inhibiting collaboration? Will such conflicting views of collaborative behavior ultimately lead to conflicts or can collaboration be enhance by multiple perspectives? What role does gender play in the construction of those multiple realities? Feminist theorists would argue that the role is a significant but not insurmountable one. And as Nodding suggests, it is time to learn a feminine way of being in the world. Working collaboratively with others in genuine mutuality and concern may be one feminine way of being in the world.

LISTENING FOR THE SILENCES

The teeth of collaborative inquiry are the act of making it critical—that is, the act of people confronting descriptive information and the

knowledge they derive from it with the value base driving their programmatic efforts. It is for this reason that the assumptions, beliefs,
and agenda forming the foundation of partnership efforts must, at
every opportunity, be made as explicit as possible. This reservoir of
values forms the basis for critique; moreover, the values are themselves
subject to critique. (Sirotnik, 1988, p. 175)

Sirotnik admonishes us to deconstruct our assumptions, our positions,
and our political interests so that we may expose our views and knowledge as always partial and value-laden. Most American writers and
researchers, however, have approached school/university collaborations
uncritically (Johnston, 1994). Alert to the differences in power, prestige,
and resources that so often limit faculty/teacher partnerships, we too
often fail to confront the social categories that shape and limit the experiences of students, teachers, administrators, and researchers. Most
classroom teachers in the United States, for example, are White, middle-
class women. And except for principals in private schools, a majority of
school and university administrators are White, middle-class men
(National Center for Education Statistics, 1993). University education
faculty are highly educated men and women, the majority of whom also
are White. In contrast, the majority of students who attend urban
schools are members of ethnic and racial minority groups, many living
in poverty. In order to model the democratic, egalitarian, person-cen-
tered values that collaboration represents, we must confront these differences and incorporate multiple viewpoints in our thinking, in our
writing, and in our research.

Before we can hear silence and detect absence, we must distinguish
among the many voices that have contributed to this growing body of
literature. Research and writing are acts that not only privilege but
reflect material and intellectual resources. Not unexpectedly, the majority of literature reviewed for this essay has been written by college and
university faculty members, often associated with large research or comprehensive universities, many the recipients of large research grants.
Reflecting the demographics of the discipline of education (more than
university faculties as a whole where women comprise only a third of the
faculty), many if not most of these authors are women. Many of the articles, furthermore, are co-authored by women who are teachers, students, research associates, and occasionally, administrators.

Although it is almost impossible to identify the race or ethnicity of
the authors of academic articles, one can probably assume that an overwhelming majority of the articles in this review are contributed by White
men and women. Although it is becoming clear that the literature on
school/university collaboration is informed by a relatively small and
homogeneous group of academic faculty and their school colleagues, I

focus on three groups whose marginality is particularly harmful to our project. I will look at K–12 school administrators, African and Hispanic Americans and other low-income minority groups, and the women of all races who continue to teach the majority of the nation's children.

A Conspicuous Absence

With collaboration's antihierarchical stance and its promise of teacher empowerment, shared decision making, and school restructuring, it is not surprising that school-level administrators feel threatened, estranged, and vulnerable (see Cramer and Johnston, chapter 3). School administrators rarely have the time, training, or the motivation to conduct research, write for academic journals, and participate in long-term partnerships with external organizations. As faculty member turned elementary school principal, Linda DeMarco Miller (1991) discovered "exciting and needed concepts like participative leadership, teacher empowerment. parent partnership, and school reform are much easier to discuss in the abstract than to carry out in the real world" (p. 22).

Although it is easy to accept a principal, superintendent, or other central administrative officer lacking the time to participate in collaborative partnerships—and certainly lacking the incentive and motivation to write about them—still the administrator's silence cannot always be interpreted as benign. Central office administrators, viewed by teachers and principals alike as powerful figures, are in a position to mandate or prevent compliance by issuing orders from the top. Building principals, responsible for implementing unpopular central office policies, are frequently caught in the middle of a struggle between teachers and central office personnel. Often the last to be consulted and the first to feel accountable, principals can be difficult to persuade that an innovative school/university collaboration is in their interest. The building-level administrator who aspires to a central office position may appear to have little to gain by embracing collaborative values. The administrative and teaching skills that have distinguished the principal from other teachers and contributed to his advancement in the school's hierarchical system may prevent the principal from working comfortably and effectively in a collaborative inquiry group.

Although books and articles on school/university collaboration frequently mention the importance of acquiring administrative support and involvement, the administrator's role and perspective is rarely studied. Stump, Lovitt, and Perry (1993), two faculty members and a woman elementary school principal, analyze their experiences in the development of a yearlong collaborative focusing on high-risk students. There are two aspects of this collaboration that are particularly noteworthy. First, the principal's role in the partnership is made explicit:

> Involving the principal in the initial conception of the partnership was an essential component to the success of our endeavor. By keeping her informed of our activities and involvements with teachers, we kept lines of communication open that led to additional undertakings. (Stump, Lovitt, & Perry, 1993, p. 153.)

In this project, the faculty researchers occasionally played an active role in the management of classes so that teachers would have the time and flexibility to work collaboratively with others in the partnership. The inability of classroom teachers to escape the demands of their students is recognized in much of the literature as a serious impediment to professional development. Rarely is that problem adequately addressed in a researcher/practitioner partnership.

The November 1992 issue of *School Administrator* is devoted entirely to school/university collaborations. Reynolds (1992), writing from the perspective of the chancellor of the City University of New York, endorses egalitarian school/university partnerships and offers the New York City College Preparatory Initiative as a model for a large-scale curriculum initiative. An even more significant and innovative commitment to school/university collaboration is revealed in the same issue ("Profile," 1992, p. 39) in an article that reports on the creation of shared senior-level administrative positions at the University of Southern Colorado and School District 60 in Pueblo, Colorado. Both articles highlight the views and accomplishments of successful top level administrators and might be more appropriately categorized as public relations pieces targeted toward other administrators than as academic articles. Nevertheless, they provide insight into the ways in which some central administrative officers are promoting school-collaboration.

Collaboration and Diversity

Goodlad (1988) acknowledges that the challenges presented to community and school leaders by court-ordered school desegregation in the 1960s and the increasing racial and ethnic diversity of students in the 1990s have played an important role in highlighting the need for schools and universities to form partnerships. Still, rarely are minority perspectives adequately represented in the mainstream literature. Lacking the benefit of a diversity of views, we might assume that it is only the White, male heads of elite institutions who are capable of leading the school reform movement. Little is written about the skills and experiences that minority educators bring to these partnerships or about the efficacy of linkages between historically Black colleges and the nation's troubled schools. Furthermore, little is written by the men and women of color and diverse ethnic backgrounds who work as teachers, principals, curriculum specialists, and university faculty. The number of qualified and committed Black, Hispanic, and other ethnic minority educators in service in the nation's colleges and schools warrants a greater visibility in the mainstream educational journals and in school reform. It may be that we lack significant insights into collaboration without perspective as they are informed by various cultural influences. Saleem and Tyson (1997) suggest that a European American approach to collaboration may in fact be very different from African American practices of collaboration in the same way Lisa Delpit (1996) suggests that Eurocentric pedagogical approaches may not be culturally appropriate for African American children. We have much to learn from writings informed by different cultural perspectives.

Teaching the Nation's Children

The sound that is most difficult to explain is the low grumble of the teaching majority, the women who comprise the nation's corp of public and private school teachers. I have used examples of explicitly and implicitly feminist collaborations to shed light on the way in which women teachers develop a public voice and the courage to raise that voice in opposition to school policies. These have provided partial explanations.

The values that are promoted by participative, democratic school/university collaborations should empower isolated classroom practitioners, encouraging them to reflect on their experiences and the social structures that constrain their action. As we have read in so many of these accounts, successful, fully collaborative experiences lead to understanding and the possibility of collective action. Yet the literature reports little structural change in the school, in the teaching profession, and little collective action on the part of women teachers.

Zeichner (1992) contends that practices in the current reflective teaching movement hinder rather than foster teacher learning because of its focus on the growth of the individual teacher. He argues:

> Much of the discourse on reflective teaching ignores reflection as a social practice where groups of teachers can support and sustain each other's growth. . . . One consequence of this isolation of individual teachers . . . is that teachers come to see their problems as unrelated to those of other teachers or to the structure of schools and school systems. (p. 299)

Lambert (1988) concurs, adding that teachers have played a passive role in their own development and have failed to take charge of their own profession.

Adding empirical support to Zeichner's argument, Smulyan (1987) reports on an NIE funded action research project involving five junior high teachers and two university researchers. In documenting the development of the project, Smulyan observes a shift in the team's pattern of behavior and goals:

> By year two, most team members no longer believed that changing the school was their primary goal. They focused instead on person growth and their contribution to research on schooling. They were freed from the constraints of designing a project aimed at creating changes over which they had no control. (p. 54)

She concludes the article by observing that the project was a rewarding experience for teachers. It provided an outlet for their feelings of frustration, feelings of collegiality, and professionalism created by working on a project of interest to those outside their own school community.

We have learned, however, to accept these outcomes uncritically as the desirable consequence of a democratic collaborative process. Critical research into school/university collaborations underscores the tensions that exist between the individual and the group in all social organizations. It also reveals the bias toward collective action that inheres in critical research paradigms—a bias that few American teachers seem to share. The tendency of some faculty researchers to filter teacher collaboration outcomes through a Marxist lens is also open to criticism, however. It can be viewed as privileging the researcher's political and theoretical position and perpetuating a view of teachers as unenlightened and resistant. And yet the need to critically examine the norms and outcomes collaboration are vital to better understanding it as a means to educational and societal reform.

CONCLUDING THE CONVERSATION

Collaboration, which is constitutive of our most life-supporting and growth-producing values, offers those of us who care about children and schooling a potentially powerful tool for transforming our environment. It is difficult to dislike the concept of collaboration, of people working collectively to accomplish something that none of them could have accomplished alone. Collaboration is a seductive concept that, as I have discussed earlier, may lure participants into relationships that they are poorly prepared to enter. And because collaboration with real people in real places is so messy—a "congenial paradigm in a cantankerous world" as Oakes and her colleagues (Oakes, Hare, & Sirotnik, 1986) have so aptly termed it—too many would-be collaborators become quickly disenchanted. They retreat to their classrooms and faculty offices, convinced that the rhetoric of school and university partnerships has once again exceeded the reality. It is often easier to work alone.

More than 20 years of action research, collaborative inquiry, and school/university partnerships, however, may be telling us that we are paying a huge price personally and professionally for the convenience of working alone and that we may *have* to learn to work more effectively in groups if we are to learn and grow as a community. That is not to minimize the risks of group behavior. As Houston points out in his 1979 article intriguingly entitled "Collaboration—See 'Treason',", it is only recently that collaboration has taken on a positive connotation. To collaborate with the enemy is to sell out one's community or country for personal gain, a concept not unknown in academic circles today. Collaboration without trust and respect, without open communication, without respect for others as equal partners is exploitation.

Cameron (1984) reminds us that in making art, collaboration is an age-old tradition practiced by many of the great masters. Peter Paul Rubens, one of these masters, would collaborate with lesser-known painters who might specialize in painting portraits, fruit, or backgrounds. "Rubens," Cameron (1984) tells us, "would only hastily paint a pair of figures in the middle distance and then pocket most of the commission, the sale having been originally made on the basis of the artist's far-flung celebrity" (p. 83).

Fox and Faver (1984), focusing primarily on collaboration in scientific research (but sounding a lot like the Flemish art world), point out that there are real costs to collaboration, not only in terms of the process of working with others, but in terms of the outcome. Perhaps the most alarming cost of collaboration is born by the scientific enterprise itself if creativity is inhibited and errors are left undetected because the group itself becomes isolated.

School/university collaborations, as they continue to be more precisely defined, widely experienced, and carefully studied, may become more common, effective, and valued. As we continue to learn about collaboration in a variety of settings, to conduct inquiry on the act of inquiry itself, we may find that collaboration is something that we can learn to do. We may also learn to evaluate and improve it. It may eventually become as easy and seemingly natural as competing for rewards and prizes. Without sacrificing individuality and independence, we can incorporate into our work and our schools the advantages of group affiliation and collectivity. Does it really have to be a question of collaboration or competition?

NOTE

This chapter was written while Cindy was a doctoral student in the Department of Educational Administration at OSU and is published posthumously with the author's permission. Some of the references in this chapter were updated by the editors. The chapter is dedicated to Cindy's daughters, Jane and Elizabeth.

REFERENCES

Appley, D., & Winder, A. (1977). Values, attitudes. and skills. *Journal of Applied Behavioral Sciences, 13*(3), 279–291.

Austin, A. E., & Baldwin, R. S. (1991). *Faculty collaboration: Enhancing the quality of scholarship and teaching.* ASHE-ERIC Higher Education Report No. 7, Washington, DC: George Washington University, School of Education and Human Development.

Bruffee, K. A. (1983). Writing and reading as collaborative or social acts. In J. Hays, P. Roth, J. Ramsey, & R. Foulke (Eds.), *The writer's mind: Writing as a mode of thinking* (pp. 159–169). Urbana, IL: National Council of Teachers of English.

Bruffee, K. (1984). Collaborative learning and the "Conversation of mankind." *College English, 46*(7), 635–652.

Cameron, D. (1984). Against collaboration. *Arts Magazine, 58*(7), 83–87.

Campbell, D. (1988). Collaboration and contradiction in a research and staff-development project. *Teachers College Record, 90*(1), 99–121.

Carnegie Forum on Education and the Economy. (1986). *A nation prepared: Teachers for the 21st century.* New York: Author.

Carriuolo, N. (1992). Rural schools find college partners to overcome isolation. *School Administrator, 49*(10), 18–21.

Clark, R. (1988). School/university relationships: An interpretive review. In K. Sirotnik & J. Goodlad (Eds.), *School/university partnerships in action: Concepts, cases, and concerns* (pp. 32–65). New York: Teachers College.

Clift, R. T., Veal, M. L., Holland, P., Johnson, M., & McCarthy, J. (1995). *Collaborative leadership and shared decision making.* New York: Teachers College Press.

Conner, N., & Sharp, W. (1992). Restructuring schools: Will there be a place for women? *The Clearinghouse, 65*(6), 337–339.

Darling-Hammond, L. (1992). Reframing the school reform agenda. *School Administrator, 49*(19), 22–27.

Darling-Hammond, L. (1994). *Professional development schools: Schools for developing a profession.* New York: Teachers College Press.

Florio, S., & Walsh, M. (1981). The teacher as colleague in classroom research. In H. Rueba, G. Guthrie, & K. Au (Eds.), *Culture and the bilingual classroom: Studies in classroom ethnography* (pp. 87–101). Rowley, MA: Newbury House.

Florio-Ruane, S. (1986). *Conversation and narrative in collaborative research.* Occasional Paper No. 102. East Lansing, MI: Michigan State University, Institute for Research on Teaching.

Fox, M., & Faver, C. (1984). Independence and cooperation in research: The motivations and costs of collaboration. *Journal of Higher Education, 55*(3), 347–359.

Franklin, K., & Mockwitz, T. (1993, Winter). Developing teachers of color: Independent and public school common ground. *Independent School, 52,* 57–61.

Gibson, M. (1985). Collaborative educational ethnography: Problems and profits. *Anthropology and Education Quarterly, 16,* 124–148.

Goodlad, J. (1988). School/university partnerships for educational renewal: Rationale and concepts. In K. Sirotnik & J. Goodlad (Eds.), *School/university partnerships in action: Concepts, cases, and concerns* (pp. 3–31). New York: Teachers College.

Greene, M. (1991). Teaching: The question of personal reality. In A. Lieberman & A. Miller (Eds.), *Staff development for education in the '90s* (2nd ed.) (pp. 3–14). New York: Teachers College Press.

Grumet, M. (1989). Dinner at Abigail's: Nurturing collaboration. *NEA Today* 7(6), 20–25.

Grumet, M. (1988). *Bitter milk: Women and teaching.* Amherst, MA: University of Massachusetts Press.

Hawthorne, E., & Zusman, A. (1992). The role of state departments of education in school/college collaborations. *Journal of Higher Education, 63*(4), 418–440.

Hoffman, N., Reed, W. M., & Rosenbluth, G. (Eds.). (1997). *Lessons from restructuring experiences: Stories of change in professional development schools.* Albany: State University of New York Press.

Hollingsworth, S., & Gallego, M. (1991, December). *Redefining school literacy: Teachers' evolving perceptions.* Research Series No. 210. East Lansing, MI.: Michigan State University, Institute for Research on Teaching.

Hollingsworth, S., & Minarik, L. (1991, July). *Choice, risk, and teacher voice: Closing the distance between public and private realities of schooling.* Occasional Paper No. 134. East Lansing, MI: Michigan State University, Institute for Research on Teaching.

Hord, S. (1986). A synthesis of research on organizational collaboration. *Educational Leadership, 43*(5), 22–26.

Hostetler, K. (1992). Rorty and collaborative inquiry in education: Consensus, conflict, and conversation. *Educational Theory, 42*(3), 285–298.

Hoz, R., & Silberstein, M. (1995). *Partnerships of schools and institutions of higher education in teacher development.* Beer-Sheva, Israel: Ben-Gurion University of the Negev Press.

Huling, L., Trang, M., & Correll, L. (1981). Interactive research and development: A promising strategy for teacher educators. *Journal of Teacher Education, 32*(6), 13–14

Hunsaker, L., & Johnston, M. (1992). Teacher under construction: A collaborative case study of teacher change. *American Educational Research Journal, 29*(2), 350–372.

Houston, W. R. (1979). Collaboration—see "treason." In G. Hall, S. Hord, & G. Brown (Eds.), *Exploring issues in teacher education* (pp. 331–348). Austin, TX: University of Texas, Research and Development Center for Teacher Education.

Johnston, M., and PDS colleagues. (1997). *Contradictions in collaboration:*

New thinking on school/university partnerships. New York: Teachers College Press.

Johnston, M. (1994, Summer/Fall). Post-modern considerations of school/university collaboration. *Teaching Education, 6*(2), 99–106.

Johnston, M. (1990). Experience and reflections on collaborative research. *Qualitative Studies in Education, 3*(2), 173–183.

Kyle, D., & McCutcheon, G. (1984). Collaborative research: Development and issues. *Journal of Curriculum Studies, 16*(2), 173–179.

Ladwig, J. G. (1991). Is collaborative research exploitative? *Educational Theory, 41*, 111–120.

Lambert, L. (1989). The end of an era of staff development. *Educational Leadership, 47*(1), 78–81.

Lampert, M. (1991). Looking at restructuring from within a restructured role. *Phi Delta Kappan, 72*(9), 670–674.

Lieberman, A. (1986). Collaborative research: Working with, not working on. . . . *Educational Leadership, 43*(5), 28–32.

Lieberman, A. (1992). Introduction: The changing contexts of teaching. In A. Lieberman (Ed.), *The changing contexts of teaching,* (pp. 1–10). Ninety-first yearbook of the NSSE. Chicago, IL: University of Chicago Press.

Maeroff, G. (1988). *The empowerment of teachers: Overcoming the crisis of confidence.* New York: Teachers College Press.

Maloy, R.W. (1985). The multiple realities of school/university collaboration. *The Educational Forum, 49*(3), 341–350.

McCutcheon, G. (1981). The impact of the insider. In. J. Nixon (Ed.), *A teacher's guide to action research: Evaluation, enquiry and development in the classroom* (pp. 186–193). London: Grant McIntyre.

McGowan, T., & Powell, J. (1990). Understanding school/university collaboration through new educational metaphors. *Contemporary Education, 61*(3), 112–118.

McGowan, T., & Williams, R. (1990). Communication within school/university partnerships and its effect on curricular change. (Unpublished paper available in ERIC Document Reproduction Service No. ED 319350)

Metzner, S. (1970). School/university partnership: A tale of dichotomous desires. *Phi Delta Kappan, 51*(6), 328–329.

Miller, L. (1991). From the tower to the trenches. *Principal, 70*(4), 22–23, 33.

National Commission on Excellence in Education. (1983). *A nation at risk: The imperative for educational reform.* Washington, DC: Government Printing Office.

National Center for Education Statistics. (1993). *Digest of Education Statistics.* Washington DC: U.S. Department of Education.

Nixon, J. (1981). Introduction. In J. Nixon (Ed.), *A teacher's guide to action research* (pp. 5–9). London: Grant McIntyre.

Noddings, N. (1986). Fidelity in teaching, teacher education, and research for teaching. *Harvard Educational Review, 56*(4), 496–510.

Oakes, J., Hare, S., & Sirotnik, K. (1986). Collaborative Inquiry: A congenial paradigm in a cantankerous world. *Teachers College Record, 87*(4), 545–61.

Oja, S. N., & Ham, M. C. (1984). A cognitive-developmental approach to collaborative action research with teachers. *Teachers College Record, 86*(l), 171–192.

Petrie, H. G. (Ed.). (1995). *Professionalization, partnership, and power: Building professional development schools.* Albany: State University of New York Press.

Profile: Leonard T. Burns, His two hats cover the school-college divide. (1992, November). *School Administrator, 39.*

Reynolds, W. A. (1992). Viewpoint: Partners must be equals in collaborative projects. *School Administrator, 40.*

Saleen, D., & Tyson, C. (1997). African American perspectives on collaboration. In M. Johnston and PDS Colleagues, *Contradictions in collaboration: New thinking on school/university partnerships* (pp. 140–165). New York: Teachers College Press.

Schlechty, P., & Whitford, B. (1988). Shared problems and shared visions: Organic collaboration. In K. Sirotnik & J. Goodlad (Eds.), *School/university partnerships in action: Concepts, cases, and concerns.* New York: Teachers College Press.

Sirotnik, K. (1988). The meaning and conduct of inquiry in school/university partnerships. In K. Sirotnik & J. Goodlad (Eds.), *School/university partnerships in action: Concepts, cases, and concerns* (pp. 169–190). New York: Teachers College Press.

Slater, J. J. (1996). *Anatomy of a collaboration: Study of a college of education/public school partnership.* New York: Garland Publishing.

Smulyan, L. (1987). The collaborative process in action research. *Educational Research Quarterly, 12*(1), 47–56.

Stump, C., Lovitt, T., & Perry, L. (1993). School-university collaboration: A year-long effort. *Intervention in school and clinic, 28*(3), 151–158.

Tikunoff, W., & Ward, B. (1983). Collaborative research on teaching. *Elementary School Journal, 83*(4), 435–468.

Trubowitz, S. (1986). Stages in the development of school-college collaboration. *Educational Leadership, 43*(5), 18–21.

Zeichner,K. (1992). Rethinking the practicum in the professional development school partnership. *Journal of Teacher Education, 43*(4), 296–307.

CHAPTER 2

A Clinical Educator:
Redefining a Teacher's Role

Rhonda Dailey-Dickinson

This chapter describes the rewards and challenges in the experience of a clinical educator. Rhonda Dickinson was one of the first PDS clinical educators and she pioneered the development of this boundary spanning role, a role that stretched between her dual roles of classroom teacher and co-coordinator of a PDS.

In the summer of 1992, the College of Education at The Ohio State University (OSU) posted the following job description:

> Wanted: School-based teacher educator who continues a significant role in the classroom while also assuming responsibility for certain aspects of teacher development, including observation and feedback, program development, and instruction relative to initial teacher preparation, entry year support, and continuing teacher professional development. Service in this role will be directly tied to professional development responsibilities in the College of Education at The Ohio State University, as well as enhance school-based professional development.

I was excited by the possibilities of this position. As a public school educator, I was invited by the college to participate on one of the working committees that conceptualized the college reform efforts. As a master's degree candidate in educational policy and leadership, I knew that the plan to involve school-based teachers in the education of preservice teachers and the continuing education of inservice teachers was part of the Holmes Group agenda.

A PDS CLINICAL EDUCATOR

A Nation at Risk (1983) and other reports described challenges faced by the U.S. educational system, and led to the Holmes Group formation. With a mission to improve the education of prospective teachers, part of the group's plan was to bring talented and experienced teachers into partnership with the university to tap their expertise and wisdom in helping to teach professional courses, supervise student and beginning teachers, and participate in research at schools (The Holmes Group, 1986).

The role of clinical educators was conceived by the Holmes Group and interpreted by OSU's College of Education, but it continues to be defined by teachers who are working as clinical educators in our PDS. In this chapter, I will describe how I have constructed and reconstructed this role and describe some of the opportunities such positions may offer teachers.

What Is a Clinical Educator?

For four years, I have served as the clinical educator at Highland Park Elementary, a PDS in South-Western City Schools, Grove City, Ohio. I work to enhance the professional development of both preservice and inservice teachers. While I remain a full-time school district employee, 50% of my time is reallocated for clinical educator work. The other 50% of my time, I co-teach a class of fourth- and fifth-grade children with another Highland Park teacher, Christy Pearl.

For four years I have constructed my own role around the needs of Highland Park Elementary's inservice teachers and preservice teachers placed there for student teaching. Generally, I see myself as a teacher leader who facilitates preservice and inservice teacher development, stretches the boundaries of what it means to be a teacher, and raises questions and issues from both school and university perspectives. I also work to facilitate school change and improvement, and negotiate the process of sharing my professional classroom practice with a colleague.

What Do I Do As a Clinical Educator?

My clinical educator work fits within three general categories: (1) preservice and inservice teacher professional development, (2) school improvement, and (3) facilitating research and disseminating information about the work of our PDS.

I provide direct inservice to preservice and inservice teachers or facilitate their professional development in a more indirect way. I instruct preservice teachers during professional seminars that I plan and implement as well as conduct periodic teacher meetings and inservices on PDS issues and schoolwide projects. Through presentations to other educators and PDS groups, I impact the professional development of additional inservice teachers. I participate on school decision-making groups and assist with and participate in school-site university course-work with inservice teachers.

As a clinical educator, I also facilitate the implementation of school improvement initiatives. This often means that I arrange opportunities for teachers to work together, locate resources, prepare agendas and materials for meetings and inservice presentations, or create documents or processes for whole school use. I coordinate preservice teacher place-ments at Highland Park, and along with Becky Kirschner, co-coordinate our PDS. As primary recorder for our PDS and Venture School (state school-reform funding) initiative, I maintain a portfolio that documents this work.

In terms of tasks, I do a lot of arranging and recruiting, writing, and talking on the telephone. I check opinion, talk to individuals and groups of teachers and administrators, and confer with university collaborator Becky Kirschner. Generally, I act as a liaison between the school and university.

Both individual and school change within our PDS is facilitated through the process of systematic inquiry. The inquiry model that the EPIC (Educating Professionals for Integrated Classrooms) PDS uses is Ebbutt's model (1985), which views opening the results of inquiry to a public critique as an integral part of the action research process. To dis-seminate information to wider audiences, I help to arrange and make both individual and collaborative presentations to other educators at local, state, and national teacher and teacher education conferences.

A TYPICAL DAY FOR A CLINICAL EDUCATOR

While no day is typical, there is a general flow to my clinical educator work. The day begins by touching base with co-teacher Christy Pearl to finalize plans made the previous day for classroom work. It is important for both of us to know what is going on in our classroom during the days we are not the children's "main teacher" (a term the children began using), so that we maintain continuity in our classroom.

For the next few hours, I often do some of the constant writing that clinical educator work entails. I may be writing a PDS report, a student teacher observation report or recommendation, or struggling with a grant proposal. I also write newspaper and newsletter articles, memos, and email messages to university personnel.

Alternatively, this time might be spent finding or preparing materials to use with student teachers or working with other teachers revising documents for the entire school. Somewhere during this time if I'm working at school, I circulate through our classroom. I want the children in Christy and my class to know that my clinical educator work is still work for them, but in a different capacity.

I use lunch time to talk with teachers while they are available. This might include arranging times for teachers to participate in student teacher seminars, getting information to them about university classes, or meeting to plan upcoming conference presentations. I also write lists and notes to myself and others.

Other days, I am in my car at lunchtime, driving to one of several meetings that are a regular part of my clinical educator work. Twice monthly, I attend clinical educator meetings designed to support and enhance the professional development of clinical educators as a group. If I'm not going to a meeting, I may meet with Becky Kirschner to plan, write, or do a presentation for another PDS group.

If meetings do not consume the rest of the day, I may drive back to Highland Park to participate in a student teacher conference, attend on-site university coursework, facilitate a student teacher seminar, or conference with the parents of a child in Christy and my classroom. Like a full-time classroom teacher, I carry a lot of work home and spend many evenings doing either clinical educator or classroom teacher work.

Opportunities in Doing Clinical Educator Work

Most opportunities have their own particular challenges associated with them, and likewise, challenges met can lead to unforeseen rewards. Early in my clinical educator experiences, I realized that I would be more able to deal with the challenges of a new role if I viewed them as positive opportunities that could lead to enhanced professional development. Reflection on my experiences as a clinical educator has led me to organize my thoughts about those opportunities around five categories: (1) the nature of clinical educator work, (2) my life as a classroom teacher, (3) reallocation of time, (4) collaboration with OSU's College of Education, and (5) professional development and school change.

The Nature of Clinical Educator Work

Working as a clinical educator has provided me with opportunities to develop professionally through communicating with a wider audience, filling a multiplicity of roles, and being challenged professionally. An important part of my experiences is the opportunity I've had to represent Highland Park staff at the university and at teacher and teacher education conferences. Through presentations about our work and collegial interactions at conferences, I have deepened my own understanding of our purposes and increased my ability to articulate it to others. The associated challenge is the constant pressure of preparing for presentations and arranging both my co-teacher Christy's and my schedules to enable my attendance. During the 1993–94 school year, I prepared and delivered two to three presentations each month. Over the course of my tenure as clinical educator, I presented at 17 state and national conferences.

A second component of my work as a clinical educator lies in the variety of roles that I filled. Clinical educator work is more flexible than my work as a classroom teacher. I plan for the use of and account for my own time, as other professionals do. For example, I may teach children in the morning, then participate in a university meeting to restructure the College of Education in the afternoon.

A third component of the work is related to the new challenges that the clinical educator role can provide for an experienced teacher. I do not mean that my life in the classroom is not challenging, but that being a clinical educator has enhanced my professional development in a broader sense, encompassing different areas of our profession. The challenge of this broadened role is that the role itself is fraught with uncertainties. Some clinical educators are unsure about defining roles for themselves, or the role as defined by someone else within their schools and PDS structures. They are uncertain about how they are perceived by colleagues and the support they get at their schools and from the university. There is uncertainty about the future of the clinical educator role from year to year because of university and school district finances. (The college negotiates with each school district separately, so each position is arranged and supported somewhat differently.) As a group, clinical educators also struggle with ways to involve more participants at the university, school sites, and beyond at a time when all arenas of education are being expected to do more with less.

My Life as a Classroom Teacher

The second category of opportunities focuses on my life as a classroom teacher. Because I co-teach a class of children with another teacher, I get the all too rare opportunity to learn from a colleague by teaching with her and seeing her teach on a regular basis. I also gain insights about the children we share by observing them interact with her and by discussing their progress with a teacher who knows them as well as I do. Problems seem less overwhelming and successes are magnified because they are shared between two teachers. The challenging side of this is that co-planning and daily discussions of classroom progress and happenings are quite time consuming.

Through co-teaching, I have strengthened my ability to understand and articulate both my philosophy and practice. Opportunities for reflection about our co-teaching practice abound as we debrief each day's events, our actions and decisions, and the class's progress in learning. The associated challenge is that in negotiating the process of co-teaching, I reinvent my own practice. Together, we co-construct our professional practice, which is neither solely Christy's nor mine, but a subtle blending of the two. It goes without saying that both co-teachers must be willing to open their professional practice to public scrutiny. Because it is new, it brings the added pressure to make it as successful an experience as possible so the opportunity is there for others in the future.

An unforeseen reward for me has been a renewed appreciation and an enhanced sense of the importance of the work that all teachers do with children. When I return to the classroom after two or three consecutive days of clinical educator work, I am more aware of the ways that teachers impact children's lives on a daily basis, and this grounds the work I do as a clinical educator in a practical reality that, for me, is critical.

Reallocation of Time

The third category of opportunity for me has been the reallocation of how I use my time, but new demands have come with new opportunities. Balancing PDS and classroom work is difficult because each is more than a half-time job! Although I now have time designated to work on school improvement, those with whom I work do not. Much still must be done before and after the regular school day.

One role often spills into the other. On classroom teaching days, I often do clinical educator work before school, at lunch, or after school. Finally, there also needs to be time for Christy and me to actually teach together, especially the first weeks of school, to model collaboration for the children, and ensure consistency between the two of us. That must come out of my clinical educator time, too.

The first year of my clinical educator experience, I felt overwhelmed by the many tasks and new roles. The second year was a little more manageable because I was not doing as many things for the first time and felt more comfortable in the role. Entering my third year as a clinical educator, I learned (in theory, at least) that you must balance work and life and that it is OK if you do not get your whole list of "Things To Do" done. I have also learned how to say "no," realizing that life will go on even if I cannot do everything, be everything, and get to all meetings on time. I am, however, uncertain about the length of time one person can or should sustain a role with this multiplicity of demands.

Collaborating With a University

The fourth category of opportunities has been collaborating with a college of education at a major university. Through my interactions with university collaborators around shared interests and concerns, I see the mutually reinforcing aspects of theory and practice and the absolute necessity of valuing and acting from both. Through the larger OSU PDS community, I am witnessing many paths toward excellence in education, ones that can be neither legislated nor mandated, but only created through long-term, painstaking work.

For me, one challenge lies in coping with the pace of university change. For example, time with university collaborators is constrained because most PDS work is done over and above regular university responsibilities. As mentioned in the introduction, the university is only now beginning to address the structural changes that will enable the work which it maintains is necessary, in order to improve teacher education. Just learning the university structure, culture, and bureaucracy has been a daunting task.

Another challenge is coping with the disparate time lines and cultures of the university and schools. For example, my first-year appointment as clinical educator, although done well before the university quarter began, gave me only one week before school began to find a co-teacher and reinvent my classroom and professional practice to accommodate the co-teaching situation. Likewise, the mechanisms for decision making and the channels through which decisions are conveyed are different at the university and in schools. School-based educators are used to decision-making time lines that are relatively fast, practical, and action oriented. The university culture values careful deliberation and is also constrained by university structures and traditions.

Reflections on the Role of Teachers in School Change

As clinical educator, part of my time is designated for enhancing teacher professional development and fostering schoolwide initiatives. In this role I have coordinated school improvement initiatives such as the redesign of our school's assessment procedures and documents. Working with groups of teachers, I have facilitated the transition to methods of assessment and reporting which are consistent with our school's philosophy and practice. I have co-authored a successful grant proposal that is enabling teachers to plan and implement classroom inquiry projects designed to enhance classroom practice and improve student learning.

As a professional development site, Highland Park staff are exploring ways to expand the role of teachers in planning and implementing change. We are expanding our roles in the classroom, school, and beyond. At the classroom level, we engage in inquiry and have revised assessment procedures, explored shared teaching, and contributed to curricular changes which have increased the developmental appropriateness of our instructional practices.

At the school level, our roles as teachers are also expanding. We are engaged in researching, developing, implementing, and revising an assessment program, implementing site-based decision making, coordinating school improvement efforts through a collaborative committee, and implementing multigrade classrooms.

Our roles are expanding beyond school boundaries as well. As teacher-researchers who publish and present our research findings in professional journals and at professional conferences, we are adding to the body of knowledge about teaching and learning.

CONCLUSIONS

Acknowledging the different levels of expertise in the teaching profession is becoming a reality through the National Board for Professional Teaching Standards licensure process and also in state revisions to teacher certification and licensure. It is time to stop the fiction that all teachers are identical in their professional abilities, interests, and aspirations and start viewing our differences as potential strengths rather than liabilities. It is necessary to recognize and fully utilize those with differing areas of expertise in order for our profession to grow.

Teachers can play important roles in school improvement at their school sites when they are enabled to do so. Through positions such as the clinical educator, teachers can contribute significantly to school improvement. So often, teachers have wonderful ideas, yet lack the time or support to follow through on them because they are always with children, and there is literally no time to do anything else. So just the naming of a position such as clinical educator with time designated to work toward school improvement and teacher professional development is an important step in redefining the scope of what teachers can achieve.

I am privileged to work in a school district, South-Western City Schools, and be part of an education association, South-Western Education Association, that both work to promote teacher professional development. I and many others have helped to create this and other opportunities for teachers, yet we need to continue pushing for structural changes at all levels, that will enable more teachers to play significant roles in preservice and inservice teacher professional development and school change efforts.

The clinical educator position was envisioned as a role which would not be held indefinitely by one teacher. Therefore, it is important to me to work in such a way that other teachers will have the opportunity to fill and expand this role after my four-year tenure. Through my work as a clinical educator, it is my goal to raise the visibility of teachers and their potentials to both effect and affect change in the profession.

The "want ad" for the clinical educator role that began this chapter needs to be modified significantly. Here is my own version:

> WANTED: Experienced teacher (who has no other life interests or commitments) wanted to define his or her own role in teacher preparation and school/university change. Must be able to live life at warp speed and to perform multiple tasks simultaneously in a loosely defined environment with differing rules, expectations, and cultures. Should be able to tolerate a high degree of ambiguity and enjoy taking risks on a minute by minute basis. Much of your time will be spent planning, speaking, teaching, writing, and traveling between schools, meetings, seminars, and conferences. You will be responsible for facilitating the learning of children, teacher education students, and colleagues, often on the same day. You should enjoy working longer hours for no increase in pay. PS: This is a halftime position.

Would you answer this "ad?" I did, and incredibly, knowing what I know now, I think I would do it again.

REFERENCES

Ebbutt, D. (1985). Educational action research: Some general concerns and specific quibbles. In Robert Burgess (Ed.), *Issues in educational research: Qualitative methods* (pp. 152–175). London: Falmer Press.

Holmes Group. (1986). *Tomorrow's teachers: A report of the Holmes Group.* East Lansing, MI: Author.

National Commission on Excellence in Education. (1983). *A nation at risk: The imperative for educational reform: A report to the Nation and the Secretary of Education.* Washington, DC: Author.

CHAPTER 3

The Missing Voice of the Principal in School/University Collaboration

Don Cramer and Marilyn Johnston

The authors for this chapter collaborate to offer a principal's voice. To develop this chapter, they did what they do best, that is, what their institutional roles of principal and university professor support—Don talked and Marilyn wrote. Don was not interested in writing for publication, but he had many things to say about what he learned as a principal in their school/university project. Marilyn tape-records a lengthy conversation and then writes it up for this chapter. In this way, they use their separate expertise to discuss the role of the principal in a PDS.

The principal's voice is often missing from the literature on school/university collaboration. In our database on collaboration including some 420 books, journal references, and conference papers, very few deal directly and solidly with the role of the principal. Many articles mention principals briefly, particularly to advocate how important they are, yet few deal with the principal's perspective specifically or include principals as a separate group of subjects/participants in research studies. Three references include extensive discussions of the role of the principal, but they speak from the author's point of view, not a principal's perspective (Goodlad, 1987; Lieberman, 1990; Metzner, 1970). One excellent chapter (Stevenson, 1995) in Hugh Petrie's book *Professionalization, Partnership, and Power* argues for specific kinds of preparation for principals involved in PDSs. In Marsha Levine's edited book on *Professional Practice Schools*, administrators are only mentioned in one small section in one chapter and then only related to how rarely they are part of the conversations:

> Experiences with pilot professional development school programs in Massachusetts and an early version of the mentor program in Connecticut suggest that, in most cases, the principal's role in restructured schools . . . is not part of ongoing discussions. (Neufeld, 1992, p. 141)

Only eight research projects studied the principal's role directly: two reported on their perceptions of their role and participation (Gentry & Peele, 1992; Putnam, 1992); three surveyed their attitudes related to school/university collaboration (Moore & Hopkins, 1993; Putnam, 1992; Rosen, 1993); one identified three approaches used by a principal in a middle school collaborative project (Williams, 1990); one considered the principal's role related to institutionalizing PDSs (Bowen & Adkison, 1996); and an earlier study by Bowen (1995) identified stages in principals' assessments of the impact of PDS participation in their schools. In one further study, Dolbec and Savoie-Zajc (1996) reported on a Ministry of Education study in Quebec where they developed a bottom-up approach with 37 principals interested in learning about action research. The principals experimented with new ways to work with their teachers and their leadership practices changed through several action-reflection cycles during their research initiatives. Some studies of school/university collaboration outside the context of PDSs arrangements have looked at the implications of principals related to, for example, school-shared decision making (see the Collaborative School Improvement Program [C-SIP] at Eastern Michigan University, Hackmann & Schmitt, 1995). Our conclusion from the literature to date is that the principal's perspective on collaboration is not well represented in the literature on school/university collaboration.

A PRINCIPAL'S PERSPECTIVE

Don and I worked together in our PDS for five years. He was the principal of one of our initial PDS schools. He has continued, since retiring, to be one of our strongest supporters as well as a helpful critic.

As representatives of our separate institutions, the schools and the university, we initially exhibited the stereotypic differences extolled in the literature (Cuban, 1992; Haberman, 1971). Don's perspective was practical and demanded that the project support positive outcomes for the teachers and students in his urban school. He wanted assurance in the beginning that our collaboration would not be at the school's expense. In particular, he was concerned that we were not just going to use them for our research purposes. My concerns were predictably more theoretical, partly because I was apprehensive about how to make school/university collaborations work at a practical level. I kept asking

Don about his goals for the school, the things he thought might interfere with developing collaborative relationships, and the changes that might be necessary to make collaboration work. Don was not much interested in the topic of collaboration and, as we started working together, the talking necessary to make collaborative decisions was frustrating to him. "If we ran school this way," he would tease me, "the whole place would fall apart. We don't have time for all this talking, we have to *do school*."

But talk we have, and a lot of it. The 45 teachers from seven elementary and middle schools and university faculty and doctoral students who make up our PDS, called the Educators for Collaborative Change, have been meeting after school on Thursdays for eight years.

In addition we have committee meetings, we go to conferences and make presentations, and we've written a book together (Johnston, 1997). Don has been the only principal who regularly attended our Thursday meetings. While other principals have attended sporadically, Don was the consistent administrator's voice in our group while he was a principal. He often raises questions that the rest of us would have ignored, for example, the principals' concerns with parents and district policies, political issues for administrators, the challenges to principals of teachers assuming more authority and voice in school decisions. Through many conversations, we have learned much from each other.

Our conversations increased even more during the year we worked together as co-coordinators (with a teacher colleague) of the 13 PDS projects. This new role pushed us to think about the larger issues related to school/university collaboration that extended beyond our individual PDS. To take on this added responsibility, Don was made a clinical principal and was released from his school responsibility half time. A retired principal took care "of school" while he was at the university doing co-coordination work.

Writing This Paper

For Don, like the other principals in our PDS, writing was not a priority although he had strong feelings and much to say about the role of principals in school/university collaborations. We agreed during a four-hour drive home from making a PDS presentation at another university, that Don would talk and Marilyn would run the tape-recorder.

Marilyn edited the conversation into a text to make it smoother for reading, but most of the text is verbatim. Even though we have had many conversations, Marilyn was impressed with the insights and articulate wholeness of these extended reflections.

The Challenges to Principals in PDS Work

There are many reasons why some principals are just not interested in PDS or lose interest after becoming a PDS principal.

It's difficult and hard work.   PDS work is really difficult. Principals are overworked and their agendas are already full. I don't think principals need another agenda item and this is one they can easily say no to. The school district is not mandating PDSs much less understanding them, it's a choice. The district is generally supporting PDS, but it doesn't go much further than that. PDSs are a choice not a mandate.

It's open-ended.   Once you get involved, there are many demands and a lot of detail work. In PDS work there aren't many big decisions that can be made that are then finished decisions. It's not like moving lunch from 12:00 to 12:30, and that's the end of it. It seems like when you solve one problem, it just creates another. It's never ending. I think that's a real frustration to a lot of principals. There is no closure on teacher education and professional development work. Every student and every situation brings its own problems. Most of these problems are not critical to the working of the school, so I think a lot of principals say, why bother?

It's not valued by others.   The principal's work in PDS is also not valued by either the school district or the university. It's not a factor in the benefit category in terms of salary structure or evaluation. So why spend the effort? Why bust your tail for something that is not going to be appreciated by the people you work with? Principals are not necessarily appreciated by the university either. Many university people don't understand the critical role of the principal and what he or she has to do to make a PDS work.

There's a parallel lack of appreciation or knowledge, almost counterattack, from one's peers as to what you're doing with the university. For some, it borders on jealousy in the sense that I've become a part of a community that many would like to be a part of (but they have not been willing to make the effort to make it happen). For others, it's more a question of how higher education is positioned in relation to the field. The universities have been out of touch for so long, they question why I'm associating with that group. In the district, there has also been a history of people who were not competent in the schools moving to the university; they couldn't cut it in the field so they got jobs at the university. There have only been a few of these cases, but we all know them. They don't remember the quality people who may have also moved to the university. It may just be a way of rationalizing their own jealousy or whatever. I get a lot of cynical remarks, like how's the old PhD doing (even though I was not actually pursuing one)? Or, how are things going on those two days off? Some of the principals think I am setting myself up for a position after I retire.

It's like having two staffs.   The way our PDS is organized (some teachers are participating in PDS and others are not) presents another set of problems. It's like having two separate faculties with different agendas. It never was a problem at Gables, but I know it was a problem in some schools. Principals are not looking for more problems in their building. It is difficult enough to get solidarity in a normal situation.

It's hard not being the king.   The professional development focus of the PDS may seem like a threat to some principals, especially new principals. With professional development work comes the idea of fostering teacher leadership, and unfortunately a lot of principals are uncomfortable with the concept of teacher leadership. I think principals have to admit that they can't do everything—the king is dead. You have to be willing to say that you can't do everything and that teachers are going to need to take on some of the leadership to get everything done. Some principals may try it and it doesn't work, or they are uncomfortable with it because of their own leadership style or beliefs about the principal's role. I think this approach takes an experienced administrator, and someone who is secure in what he or she is about in the school.

It requires risk-taking.   For new principals, there are other considerations. You're concerned with salary increases, evaluations, buying houses, raising kids, and getting kids through college. PDS requires a lot of risk-taking. You have to maneuver, you have to massage and twist the regulations, you may even have to break some of the rules. I call this creative administration to make things work. I'm not so sure I would be willing to take those risks if my kids were young and my job security was at risk. Maybe that's a spot on my own personality, but I think it's real.

It means people are around asking questions.   In the traditional student teaching plan, students came into the school for 10 weeks, left, and no one asked any questions. I often did not even know the students' names. Now students are here for the year. They ask a lot of questions. University faculty and doctoral students are around and they know a lot about what's going on. Sometimes it's a challenge to defend what schools are about. The school community is not used to being questioned from within. We're used to parents questioning, but that's different. Questioning from within may actually expose bad practice and no one wants that. I think that's one of those troubled nerves that is out there, and that may make principals anxious about PDS.

So why do it?   So, if the system doesn't appreciate what you're doing, the university doesn't appreciate or understand what you do, you get grief from your peers, it creates problems in your school, you have to develop a new leadership style, and people are around asking questions, you might ask why anyone would want to be a PDS principal?

Are the Positive Aspects Worth It?

I think in the beginning I was interested in PDS because it was a bit of an ego trip. I felt it was an honor to be involved at the cutting edge of something new, even though we didn't know exactly what it was. I felt my staff was unique and they could contribute to a new way to educate new teachers. We put in a lot of time in the beginning. We saw this as a feather in our cap, as a way to show off what we were doing. There's a period, like in Trubowitz's first stage of collaboration (Trubowitz, 1986), when you're on a high. We had been asked to become a real part of university work. Never before had someone come from the university and said take a look at us, and help us change. I can remember the dean saying that. I can remember the staff saying that if they were not able to change the university in this partnership, then they were going to get out of it. If the university was sincere in wanting to help us, and also in us changing themselves, this was a new deal and a new way of doing business.

Of course, there was a downside to all of this. It started to cause friction in the staff when they found that the university wanted to use a collaborative decision-making approach. Some of my staff were uncomfortable making collaborative decisions. I can remember a couple of them getting so frustrated; it was so chaotic. This is not the way we do things in school. We don't have time for all that talking. Collaboration was uncomfortable to me and a lot of my staff. We spent hours and hours and hours talking about things. At that point we lost some people and gained others.

Why Aren't Principals Used to Working Collaboratively?

This may sound strange, but there's very little in schools that is done collaboratively. I don't know whether it's because we do schools the way we traditionally do, or maybe it's because we're a large school system with many system procedures. One day the teachers and I started jotting down the things they wanted me to do, things they didn't want to be bothered with. There were some things that they wanted to work out collaboratively, but actually very few. Maybe that was because things were going okay in the school. Maybe if there had been a lot of problems, it would have been different. It took us two years before we had this conversation. It was an enlightening and important discussion.

It's hard to go back and look at it the way it was in the beginning. I'd like to think that I always worked collaboratively with my teachers, but I think I became more collaborative because of the PDS. I certainly never got any of this in my administrative preparation program. For a while there was a lot of self-reflection. I used to write these morning bulletins asking myself if I was just making a bunch of edicts. The teachers got sick of my raising these questions. It got to the point where I wasn't allowed to say the "C" word (C collaboration). They were just tired of it.

You Have to Live It to Understand It

From a principal's point of view, the university initially seemed insensitive to the routines and needs of the school that a principal has to manage. They were not in our schools and seemed not to appreciate the schedules and pressures that teachers and principals have, especially the time pressures. For example, the university wanted our interns to be out in schools the day that school started. But that's the beginning of school. You have to get people into their places. We don't have much time to be explaining things to the interns. As university participants have spent more time in schools, they have become more sensitive to these issues.

I also don't think that university participants always consider the important role parents play in the school. The principal is on the front line related to parents, their questions and complaints. The dynamics of parents, community, and teacher relationships is very powerful. Traditionally, student teachers didn't get to see much of this, they were primarily focused on their one classroom. In the PDS, we do a much better job of getting them ready for their first jobs. They see the entire workings of the school and how schooling is embedded in the community and the politics of the school system. I'm not sure the university at large has as clear an understanding of all this as the interns are getting.

Sensitive Issues—Talking About School in School

In the PDS, everything is visible and gets talked about. Everybody knows what's going on with everything. I've seen faculty or students who bring up situations in schools that are not particularly good practice and this becomes a major topic of discussion for a longer period than it should. At least, longer than I think it should. Maybe it's okay to use these incidents later on, but these discussions of current incidents can really destroy the foundations of a partnership and cause some bad feelings. I don't know how to deal with these problems, but they are real. The issues can't be ignored and yet talking about them so much can cause a lot of problems. It can cause people, again, to say, "I don't need this." I can see how it's a beautiful example from the university's point of view, but it's something that would never be discussed openly in the school with the principal and the teachers. Yet, all of a sudden, the students, graduate students, and some of the teachers are talking about the incident in Focus Group (weekly meetings with MEd students in the school). Maybe these things were talked about before at the university, but then we didn't know each other so well and we didn't know what was going on at the university.

In the course of a day, we've all done stuff we didn't want to do. Luckily schools are pretty forgiving places. And yet, to an observer, it becomes the case study of the month. It doesn't warrant that much attention, and yet it happened. When I talk to parents, I openly say, "This is not a perfect place here, when you work with kids, it is not perfect. There are going to be some mistakes made just as there are in family homes." You try to make sure they don't happen again, and keep on going.

When there are bigger issues, we don't always have good ways to deal with them. We don't have a good way to talk about them among ourselves, we don't have an overt agenda about these things. These are difficult issues. What's bad practice to one student, or one faculty is not the same for the next. It's pretty subjective. Maybe PDSs are about learning to talk about some of these things and learning to appreciate different kinds of good practice as well as talk about the problems. Maybe as we try to deal with some of these issues we will learn better ways to deal with them together.

Having a Student Teacher—
A New Level of Professional Commitment

I used to look at regular student teachers as a way to provide my own staff a little bit of support, a way to reward good teachers by giving them assistance, giving them a break, giving them planning time. For the teachers, it used to be viewed as four weeks with no responsibilities—smoke in the lounge, especially spring quarter, "Yes! I want a student teacher spring quarter." Principals used to dole out placements as a kind of reward. For me, it was also a way of seeing new teachers who were close to graduation that I might want to hire. In the traditional teacher education programs, I would not have ever known the preservice teachers. I don't think I had any conception that this was a professional responsibility. That has only come about through the PDS. It's a new way of looking at teacher preparation.

I now see the whole PDS program and related issues as professional development for myself and the teachers. Anytime you put teachers in long-term mentor relationships, it helps support them in questioning their own practice. I don't think we did much of that in the past. In a 10–week period, there's not time for that. Year long placements energize the staff, helps us reflect on what we do, and question our practice, which is healthy.

The other important aspect of the PDS is what it does for the elementary students themselves. No one has really done a study of this, but I think the achievement of our kids is probably at a higher level because they've had interns for the last 3 years. The data is all there, you could look at the children who have been exposed to more resources. Anytime you put more interested people in front of students, particularly kids who have a lot of needs, it's going to be beneficial.

There is also an intangible part in terms of making teachers feel important, in making them feel that they are leaders and mentors. In the PDS, teachers are given the responsibility of being a teacher educator aside from just teaching kids. It's a step toward developing teacher leadership, a next level of professionalism. It puts teachers at a different level. I've seen a lot of interesting dynamics, for example, parents who were proud that their children were in mentor teachers' rooms who had been given the responsibility to train our future teachers. This attitude was not a coincidence. We all worked hard to help parents understand the benefits of PDS, which included having extra hands in the classroom.

I might get in trouble for this next item, but I think the association with the university provides in-kind resources that school districts don't understand or appreciate. Professional development of the teachers is supported by the university and these resources are unaccounted for by the school district because you don't know how many dollars you're talking about. School districts go out and pay thousands of dollars for consultants to do professional development and many times very little happens as a consequence. In PDSs you've got commitment from a university to do continuous work in classrooms, there's no charge at all, and the impact on teachers and the school is significant.

We'll Help You Change if You Help Us Change

The whole way of going about the business of being a principal has changed for me. I've changed, and this is true for teachers as well. We've been put in a position of responsibility to help change the university and to help reform teacher education. This is an intangible. We are looking at how we can change the university in terms of the needs of our kids, particularly in the urban context. We have kids living in poverty, they are hungry, they come from single-parent families, from violence and crime, and many have to deal with all kinds of conflict situations. Very seldom were these kinds of issues explored when we were trained at the university. Now we have an opportunity to make sure that these issues are addressed so that *we* can learn as well as the preservice teachers. Specifically, this has helped me and our staff to look at what we are about, as compared to what we thought we were about before we got involved in PDS. It's a kind of reexamination of our own agendas and a wider set of goals that includes the academic as well as the social needs of our students.

Professional Development Sparks Change

All but three of our teachers have participated in PDS at some time or another. We view PDS as an important part of what goes on in our school related to teacher education and our own professional development. It goes on at the same time as other things. It's a little laboratory where some our teachers have dedicated themselves to working with preservice teachers. It's a sidebar that moves alongside other school agendas. I don't find it divisive. I've worked hard and directly to integrate it into the wider school goals. It's a resource and a strength to the larger school. All PDS announcements go into everyone's box whether they are in PDS or not. Some get tired of all the paper, but my response is that it's an important Gables school project, and everyone needs to know what's going on. There may be a time when they want to be involved.

PDS activities have been the key to our school reform. I don't think our Venture Capital Grant ($250,000 over a five-year period) or any of our formalized reform would have happened without PDS. For one thing, it put us in touch with resources and made us aware through various university channels that these things were available. For example, we had been notified through the school system about Venture Capital grants, but it was really pushed through the university. I threw the stuff from the school district away. If it hadn't been for Marilyn Johnston, Nancy Zimpher (college dean), and the university, we wouldn't have done it.

The other thing PDS has done is magnify and develop the concept of teacher leadership, which is central to our school reform. I don't think that ever would have emerged. I don't think I was negative about it, I just never thought much about it until I started reading some of the things Ken Howey, Nancy Zimpher, and others have written (for example, Howey & Zimpher, 1989; Howey, Matthes, & Zimpher, 1987). I think I had always believed in it and practiced it to some degree, but I hadn't formalized it in my own leadership style. Reading and talking in the PDS helped me to recognize it and make it more formal. We began to talk about leadership so that my own style could evolve, and I could admit that I needed the teachers. In many ways, I'm pretty autocratic about things. On the other hand, I don't have any problem with giving my authority to people who I feel can be responsible for things. I think it legitimatized my role along with the teachers. I don't think that would have ever happened without PDS.

Teacher leadership is also related to issues about urban schools. Education in urban schools has become so complex that you come to a point where you realize you'll go down the tubes without help. You realize that teacher leadership is essential, that you can't do it alone.

What Have I Done for My Profession Lately?

I did not think about my role or responsibility to help out my profession until I got to the end of my career. I started to wonder where the profession was going to be when I'm gone. I think that's important. I wish this had come to me earlier. I can remember saying the last five years, that I wanted to dedicate my last few years to insuring the future of the profession. I wonder if that's something that comes with age.

MARILYN'S PERSPECTIVE

I was a classroom teacher for 15 years before taking a university position, but never a principal. As a teacher, I had little sense of what principals did, and as a professor (before PDS), I had less contact and little interest in what principals do. I knew they were important, of course, and when soliciting schools to work collaboratively with the university, I talked with the principals first.

In our PDS, we have worked with a wide variety of principals. Some principals have been continuous, others were transferred in and out. Some schools have been in the PDS since the beginning, others left. Of the seven schools that have been in our PDS for more than two years (four of them since the beginning) plus four other schools that participated for one year, we have worked with 16 principals. Two of our long-term schools have had three principals each during this five-year period. The number of principals in our project has provided us with a wide sample of attitudes and varying degrees of support.

As a group, our principals have not been full participants in the PDS, except for Don. Several continue to be very supportive and attend meetings occasionally, others are less supportive, a couple have been overtly or covertly negative about collaboration, both in the PDS and in their schools. Our Thursday night meetings have not held sufficient interest to keep principals regularly involved. We have puzzled about this and only recently come to realize, partly through Don's insights, that teachers' and principals' concerns are very different. Because teachers make up the majority of our PDS participants, the goals and decision making have focused primarily on teacher issues. We rarely dealt directly with the challenges and problems principals face with PDS.

PDS adds yet another set of demands and people with whom principals have to contend. In our PDS, university participants and interns are in their buildings continually. They ask questions, make demands on scheduling and resources, and interrupt the normal flow of programs. Seldom do these extra people provide support; rather, they add to principals' workload and responsibilities.

Don has also helped me to become sensitive to the multiple contexts in which the principal is excluded. Beginning with our first trip to the national Holmes meeting the first year of our PDS (where no one was talking about principals), Don continues to be my conscience related to administrative concerns. Time and again he points to situations in which the importance of principals is extolled and their concerns are ignored. In the PDS, they are expected to do many things for which they were not trained, and are given new responsibilities and programs to implement with little support.

In a truly collaborative fashion, Don and I have had a significant influence on each other, and as a result we have expanded our horizons of both the problems and possibilities of school/university collaboration.

REFERENCES

Bowen, G. (1995, August). *The role of the principal in the professional development school.* Paper presented at the annual meeting of the National Council of Professors of Educational Administration (NCPEA), Williamsburg, VA.

Bowen, G., & Adkison, J. (1996, August). *Institutionalizing professional development schools: Supporting the principal.* ERIC document: ED 409–623.

Cuban, L. (1992). Managing dilemmas while building professional communities. *Educational Researcher, 21*(1), 4–11.

Dolbec, A., & Savoie-Zajc, L. (1996, April). *Collaborative inquiry with principals to implement a continuous learning culture.* Paper presented at the annual meeting of American Educational Research Association, Washington, DC.

Gentry, A. A., & Peele, C. C. (1992). Urban school/university collaboration: The Boston Secondary Schools Project. *American Secondary Education, 20*(4), 24–29.

Goodlad, J. I. (1987). Schools and universities can—and must—work together. *Principal, 67*(1), 9–15.

Haberman, M. (1971). Twenty-three reasons why universities can't educate teachers. *Journal of Teacher Education, 22*, 133–140.

Hackmann, D. G., & Schmitt, D. M. (1995, Fall). School improvement through school/university collaboration: The C-SIP model. *Journal of Staff Development, 16*(4), 22–26.

Howey, K. R., & Zimpher, N. L. (1989). *Profiles of preservice teacher education: Inquiry into the nature of programs.* Albany: State University of New York Press.

Howey, K. R., Matthes, W., & Zimpher, N. L. (1987). *Issues and problems in professional development.* Elmhurst, IL: North Central Regional Educational Laboratory.

Lieberman, A. (Ed.). (1990). *Schools as collaborative cultures: Creating the future now.* London: Falmer Press.

Metzner, S. (1970). School-university partnership: A tale of dichotomous desire. *Phi Delta Kappan, 5*(6), 328–329.

Moore, K. D., & Hopkins, S. (1993). Professional development schools: Partnerships in teacher education. *Contemporary Education, 64*(4), 219–222.

Neufeld, B. (1992). Professional practice schools in context: New mixtures of institutional authority. In Marsha Levine (Ed.), *Professional practice schools: Linking teacher education and school reform* (pp. 133–168). New York: Teachers College Press.

Putnam, J. (1992). *Professional development schools: Emerging changes in educators and the professional community.* ERIC document: ED 370 890.

Rosen, M. (1993). Sharing power: A blueprint for collaboration. *Principal, 72*(3), 37–39.

Stevenson, R. B. (1995). Critically reflective inquiry and administrator preparation: Problems and possibilities. In Hugh G. Petrie (Ed.), *Professionalization, partnership and power: Building professional development schools* (pp. 199–216). Albany: State University of New York Press.

Trubowitz, S. (1986). Stages in the development of school-college collaboration. *Educational Leadership, 43*(5), 18–21.

Williams, R. O. (1990). Partners for educational progress: A university/school middle grades project. *Contemporary Education, 61*(3), 161–172.

PART II

Elementary and Middle School PDSs

CHAPTER 4

LEADS:
An Evolving Program

Patricia Enciso, Becky Kirschner, Theresa Rogers, and Barbara Seidl

This chapter weaves a complicated story. It begins with the evolution of an historic teacher education program moving into a PDS project and then joining forces with a new PDS. Together they form a project focused on literacy education and diverse settings in the context of elementary and middle school teaching and learning.

The university leadership for this evolving PDS has changed hands and each university co-coordinator(s) has worked with various school-based educators to provide the leadership necessary to keep the program vibrant and innovative. With changes in leadership came changes in focus, style, and accomplishments. Pat Enciso begins the story with a history of the EPIC (Educational Programs for Informal Classrooms) teacher education program, then Becky Kirschner describes the way this project became a PDS. Later she works with Terry Rogers for two years to merge the EPIC PDS with another PDS (Urban Professional Partnerships School or UPPS) into the LEADS program. The next year, Terry Rogers and Pat Enciso work together in LEADS, and then Pat and Barbara Seidl take over the leadership. Barbara describes the PDS in its most recent iteration. Each author writes from her perspective and her particular work in the PDS. In this narrative you will see both continuity and change.

This chapter tells the story of how two Professional Development School projects, each with its own rich history, came to be the current Literacy

Education for Diverse Settings (LEADS) program. The diversity of the program itself, and of its participants (up to 90 at any given point), has kept the process lively, frustrating, and nearly impossible, yet we have collectively prepared hundreds of teachers, many of whom are now our professional colleagues.

It is a complicated story to tell, and we have succeeded only in telling it from our own perspectives as university faculty and from moments and perspectives that we felt were salient. Much of the story is left out, or is told by other members in other places (see listing of our publications at the end of the book). What we provide are brief histories of the two original programs and a picture of the present program with all its complexity and need for careful tending. In writing this chapter, we have tried not to leave out the most troubling issues and challenging aspects of those histories, complexities, and communities.

Taken together, these various iterations reveal a PDS as a moving target that has to be constantly tended and reformulated in order to maintain communication and continuity of purpose. As we carve out our shared goals over time and among a diverse group of people with differing understandings, needs, and expectations, we are ever mindful that we need to remain both alert and flexible in response to changing conditions. At the same time, our work—which consumes so much of our academic lives—is not always supported, or even understood, by our university colleagues. Yet the PDS lives on through sheer commitment by those who have seen the improved quality of teaching at all levels, and the ways that the results of our work ultimately find a place into the lives of children in our schools.

EPIC: THE BEGINNINGS

Pat Enciso

This story begins with EPIC, a teacher education program conceptualized and initiated in 1972 by Drs. Charlotte Huck and Martha King of The Ohio State University. EPIC, the acronym for Educational Programs for Informal Classrooms, was founded on Deweyian principles of open, democratic education. At the time EPIC began, Dewey's educational philosophy had long since lost support in public education.

Huck and King observed the revival of Dewey's practices in British primary schools and, with the support of a federal grant, set out to establish a teacher education program at Ohio State that would bring preservice and inservice teachers together to study and develop teaching that would: (1) be responsive to children's interests, (2) place learning of skills in meaningful contexts, (3) value and develop children's learning through talk and literacy across integrated curricula, and (4) be reflective and informed about the purposes, theories, and observations that guided decisions and actions with children.

The EPIC undergraduate program was designed in blocks of cross-curricular study, over a three-quarter period, with students moving through three different school settings as they worked toward student teaching. Central to their work at the university were frequent opportunities and encouragement to explain and explore ideas through different artistic media, especially through drama, writing, and visual arts. Thus, students' and teachers' learning involved movement away from conventional curricula and school-like forms of representations and testing toward exploration and representation of complex questions that required cross-disciplinary knowledge, extended time and effort to be involved in inquiry, and time to analyze and reflect on relationships between past and future directions for learning.

EPIC continued as an undergraduate program for more than 20 years prior to the introduction of Ohio State's MEd program. EPIC has come under pressure, both from changing demographics and more visible scholarship in multicultural education, to consider the goals and methods of the program in light of the demands of a more diverse society. EPIC was not a program that actively sought multiple cultural perspectives or pressed students to develop curricula that were culturally relevant or informed by issues of social justice and equity. Although its founders were aware of Dewey's philosophies of equity in education and were attuned to the political climate in Columbus surrounding desegregation, very little of these social issues were integrated into the life and perspectives of the program.

The PDS that evolved out of the EPIC program (EPIC/PDSC— EPIC/Professional Development School Community) and the Urban Professional Partnership School (UPPS—Urban Professional Partnership School) both responded to these issues. The EPIC/PDSC includes only EPIC schools, while the UPPS works primarily in urban schools but continued the EPIC orientation to curriculum and instruction. Both of these programs initially involved similar orientations to curriculum and instruction since they both emanated out of the same academic program, and they both moved to graduate level certification in line with Holmes Group recommendations and restructuring within the College. After a year or two as separate PDSs, they decided to combine their efforts and became the LEADS (Literacy Education in Diverse Setting) PDS.

We continue with the separate stories of EPIC/PDSC and UPPS and then discuss our joint efforts.

THE EPIC PROFESSIONAL DEVELOPMENT
SCHOOL COMMUNITY

Becky Wendling Kirschner

The EPIC Professional Development School Community (PDSC) was initiated as an inquiry-based PDS by the teachers, staff, and principal at Highland Park Elementary School in South Western City Schools. After their selection in 1991, Highland Park asked me, a member of the graduate reading faculty and coordinator of the EPIC Preservice Program, to become co-coordinator of their PDS along with Rhonda Dickinson, a fourth- and fifth-grade teacher. They also invited three other schools associated with the EPIC program to join them in forming a professional development community in which they could reflect on their practice and expand their already active role in the EPIC Program. In 1992, the single-site PDS expanded to include Indianola Alternative Elementary School, Columbus City Schools; Wickliffe Informal Alternative Elementary School and the Informal Program at Barrington Elementary School, Upper Arlington City Schools; and faculty and graduate students in the graduate reading program.

Reflection and inquiry have been central to our work. To address the Holmes Group's goals, we adopted a systematic model of inquiry that can be visualized as a spiral of problem framing; planning; acting; monitoring through observation, reflection, rethinking, discussing, replanning, understanding, learning, evaluation, and analyzing; and critiquing.

History and Context

In becoming a PDS, the four EPIC schools formalized and expanded on their 20-year cooperative relationship with the EPIC program and the graduate program in reading. Informally organized as a community of learners, the school-based and university-based educators associated with the EPIC program share a common philosophy of teaching and learning, commitment to informal education and to teaching using thematic units, and dedication to preparing career professionals capable of implementing classroom environments in which children and adults can actively engage in learning.

To intensify the levels of reflection and inquiry being carried out in the schools and to become more systematic in our thinking about our practice, the teachers and I co-planned a workshop on reflective inquiry. In the summer quarter 1992, participants from the four EPIC PDSC schools came together in the workshop to (1) define what it means to be a reflective practitioner; (2) learn about action-research models and methods; (3) design an action-research project to be carried out in the classroom during the 1992–1993 academic year; (4) establish a support network for those doing action research; and (5) identify audiences with whom the findings from the action research projects could be shared and critiqued.

Three forms of inquiry have shaped our work: *inquiry AS teaching and learning* to provide a theoretical framework for conducting our day-to-day work; *inquiry INTO teaching and learning* to improve our practice; and *inquiry ON teaching and learning* to assess the outcomes of our efforts.

Inquiry AS Teaching and Learning: A Theoretical Framework

EPIC PDSC participants define both teaching and learning as inquiry. Guided by the belief that all participants associated with the schools and university are continuous learners, educators in these settings use inquiry-based pedagogy to engage learners in authentic activities to construct, understand, and use knowledge. Children in these schools conduct inquiry-based projects and are expected to constantly question what is learned and why. During their professional year, preservice teachers are introduced to inquiry-based pedagogy and are asked to constantly reflect on and question what they learn in their university classes and the schools. Inservice teachers are thoroughly involved in their own professional development. Working in the *self-monitoring inquiry mode* (Ebbutt, 1985), they regularly reflect on their practice, implement action steps, informally collect and analyze data, and incorporate their findings into their practice.

Inquiry INTO Teaching and Learning: Improving Learning

EPIC PDSC participants engage in *inquiry INTO teaching and learning* to determine how they can improve student learning and promote the professional development of preservice and inservice teachers. As members of a community of learners, school-based and university-based educators work collaboratively to frame research questions, systematically seek answers, use findings to inform practice, and relate their findings to others who have similar interests.

Classroom level inquiry.   At the classroom level, EPIC PDSC teacher-researchers work in the *self-evaluation action-research mode* (Ebbutt, 1985). They regularly reflect on their own practice, systematically implement action steps, request help from consultants or critical friends, systematically collect and analyze data and generate hypotheses, write reports open to public critique, and systematically incorporate reflections to change practice.

Teacher-researchers in the EPIC PDSC have used inquiry into teaching and learning to improve student learning by studying instruction and assessment. Janet Brown and Carol Stowe (1995) designed and implemented a spelling program consistent with a whole language, developmental philosophy to study their students' spelling development. Tracy Bigler (1995) systematically listened to children's talk about literature to gain insights into their learning. Intermediate teachers systematically studied the action steps they took to (1) implement techniques and methods they had learned at conferences and workshops to improve math instruction by using concrete manipulatives, (2) integrate math and literature, and (3) make science and literature connections. Two fifth-grade teachers worked with professors in The Ohio State University Medical School to develop and pilot a curriculum on human growth and nutrition. They monitored their teaching and their students' learning, evaluated the results, and shared their findings with the medical school faculty.

Two intermediate teachers studied how students' nonfiction writing was improved when they used CD-ROM technology and word processing. Four teachers working in a satellite facility with no library facilities, studied how they and their students could use CD-ROM technology to support children's inquiry on topics of interest. A teacher and tutor of learning disabled children studied how they might use technology to give their students fuller access to research materials and processes. They investigated how they might use a CD-ROM computer and software with their students to help them successfully locate, read, and use information that would otherwise be inaccessible. They then introduced students to the equipment and software and studied the effects its use has on children's learning.

In one of the earliest projects on assessment, Nancy Bryant and Jenny Gee (1995) studied the process they and their students engaged in when portfolios were used in their classroom to assess literacy development. A Severe Learning Disabilities (SLD) teacher and tutor investigated ways to better assess the achievement of learning disabled children. They used data from the assessments to develop Individual Educational Plans, share students' progress with parents, and plan for instruction.

Teachers have also used the self-evaluation action-research mode to restructure and gain insights into teachers' work. Beth Swanson and Jenny Hootman (1995) combined their two classes of children; shared the teaching responsibilities for all of the children; they studied the process they engaged in to restructure space, time, and classroom interactions; and they studied the impact the new structure had on students' learning. An intermediate teacher, who was job sharing, studied the processes she engaged, in order to co-teach her class and to identify the advantages and challenges in restructuring her work (Pearl, 1995). Rhonda Dickinson (Chapter 2) studied her role as a clinical educator within the EPIC PDSC.

School-level and PDSC-level inquiry.   At the school and PDSC levels, we have used the *classic action-research mode* (Ebbutt, 1985) to improve classroom instruction, assessment, and teacher education. Teacher-researchers working collaboratively, approach reflection systematically and seek to add to the knowledge base of educational research. They work in their own classrooms, meet in groups regularly, systematically reflect on their own practice, and implement action steps. They use consultants or critical friends and systematically collect data. As part of a group, they systematically analyze data and generate hypotheses, write separate and joint reports open to public critique, and systematically incorporate reflections. They change their practice and also work toward improvement by testing hypotheses at the institutional level.

Teacher-researchers at Highland Park used the classic action-research mode to develop schoolwide spelling instruction consistent with a whole language philosophy. A team of five teachers worked together to address what they perceived as a lack of consistency in (1) word study experiences that children have as they progress through the grade levels, (2) messages being sent to parents about what constitutes good spelling practice, and (3) spelling practices and Highland Park's building philosophy in other curriculum areas. They gathered data about building-wide spelling practices, studied spelling as a developmental process, studied word study strategies, and developed an action plan for integrating the strategies into their spelling program.

The Highland Park learning community also conducted a schoolwide authentic assessment project to redesign assessment practices to make them more consistent with the school philosophy. The action plan included three major components: a child's portfolio, a teacher's working portfolio and revised assessment procedures, and a student's progress report to communicate to parents. To develop the student progress report and a handbook for parents explaining how to use it, the Highland Park staff and I engaged in three action-research cycles (Howlett & Kerstetter, 1995). Insights gained from implementing each revision have been used to develop subsequent versions of the form.

PDSC-Level Inquiry.   We have also used the classic action-research mode to restructure the formal and informal components of the EPIC preservice teacher education program to better prepare teachers who have a deep understanding of children, engage in interactive teaching, are critical thinkers, and possess a penchant for inquiry. Focusing on our goals to (1) make explicit the EPIC program philosophy of teaching and learning; (2) facilitate preservice teachers' reflection on teaching and learning; (3) encourage preservice teachers to take ownership of their learning; and (4) provide a structure to support preservice teachers' learning and development, we revised the scope and sequence for the methods courses and developed new course assignments to connect course content with school-based experiences; planned an orientation retreat designed to build community and stimulate preservice teachers' reflection on themselves as learners; and designed field-based assignments that would promote reflection on practice and dialogue between mentors and preservice teacher.

To evaluate the action steps, we monitored our actions through systematic observation and documentation. To open our findings to public critique, we shared what we had learned in written reports and presentations (Kirschner, Dickinson, & Blosser, April 1995; Kirschner, Dickinson, & Blosser, February 1995; Kirschner, Dickinson, & Blosser, 1996). Insights gained from our collaborative action research were used to develop a supervision model for the LEADS MEd Program.

Inquiry ON Teaching and Learning: Evaluating Outcomes

To assess the outcomes our PDSC's efforts have had on student learning, teacher education, and professional development, EPIC PDSC members have used the classic action research mode to conduct *inquiry ON teaching and learning* .

School-level inquiry. Teacher-researchers at Wickliffe, Barrington, and Highland Park have engaged in multiple action research cycles to conduct outcomes-based assessments of student learning and teacher development.

To receive accreditation form the North Central Association, Wickliffe and Barrington used classic action research to engage in a three-year outcomes self-study accreditation process. Focusing on student success, efficiency, and quality-with-equity programs, this process required schools to document the success with which the schools were achieving specific learning outcomes they had established for themselves. Wickliffe's target area was progressive education. They looked at student growth within an integrated curriculum and developed a Holistic Thematic Assessment tool to consistently measure both cognitive and affective growth on a continuum and to assesses student learning in reading/writing, mathematics, appreciating and using the arts, and understanding and awareness of multicultural issues. Barrington studied student decision-making in the informal classroom from the teacher and children's perspectives. Using teacher and student surveys they identified areas of need, established objectives, gathered baseline data and developed an improvement plan to increase and assess students' ability to articulate reasons for making decisions and teachers' ability to support students' decision-making skills.

Over a five-year period, Highland Park used classic action research as one method of assessing the school improvement efforts they undertook as a part of their participation in the Ohio Venture Capital Grant Program. They identified indicators of success, documented their progress toward meeting goals with informal and formal assessment approaches, and wrote reports on their progress.

PDSC-level inquiry. At the PDSC-level, university-based and school-based educators used the classic action research mode to study the outcomes of our restructured teacher education program. In keeping with Richardson's (1994) guidelines for conducting formal research on practical inquiry, we analyzed all of the data collected for the action-research project. In addition, we conducted in-depth interviews of six preservice teachers and analyzed transcripts of the interviews, the six preservice teachers' portfolios, videotapes of their portfolio presentations, and an audiotape of a presentation two of the six made at a meeting of all OSU PDSs.

Analysis took an ethnographic stance and used interpretation as a framing prospective. All nineteen reached the highest level of development (consolidation), were able to engage in interactive teaching, demonstrated a deep understanding of children, displayed an ability to think critically and to critique their own teaching, and demonstrated a penchant for inquiry. Detailed analysis of the six focal students revealed that while each approached the process in her own unique manner, all used the continuum and goal sheets to monitor development and facilitate dialogue with mentors and college supervisors; engaged in reflective inquiry into their practice; used their portfolio to document growth; and developed and could articulate a philosophy of teaching and learning consistent with the EPIC program.

Conclusion

While we have successfully used the self-evaluation and classic action-research modes to conduct *inquiry INTO teaching and learning* and *inquiry ON teaching and learning*, our work has not been without difficulties. Like others who have worked to grow a PDS, we have struggled with the personal and institutional issues of building trust, defining and redefining roles, and finding the time, resources and support to further our work (Berkey et al., 1990; Darling-Hammond, 1994). Fortunately, we found early on that the model of inquiry we had adopted supported the sustained conversations we needed to engage in to insure that all participants had a voice in framing problems and in analyzing and critiquing outcomes (Kirschner, Dickinson, & Blosser, 1996). Using inquiry as a basis for our PDS, we have woven together multiple perspectives and furthered our goals to improve student learning, teacher education, and educators' professional development.

THE URBAN PROFESSIONAL PARTNERSHIP SCHOOL: A BRIEF HISTORY

Theresa Rogers

As with the EPIC program, The Urban Professional Partnership School (UPPS) program began as an undergraduate teacher training program focused on preparing K–8 teachers for urban settings. It was becoming clear that while we were experiencing increasing numbers of diverse, economically disadvantaged, and non-English-speaking students in our schools, the teaching force continues to be dominated by White, middle-class women. To truly experience reform, we felt a need to prepare teachers who would be responsive to this evolving social context and who would be responsive to broadening their own cultural perspectives.

After one year, in 1992, the co-coordinators of the program (myself, an assistant professor of literacy education, and a reading teacher and doctoral student, Mari McLean) and four Columbus Public schools, applied to become a PDS.

Our earliest list of mutually defined goals for the preparation program included: (1) familiarizing interns with a variety of teaching strategies; (2) emphasizing the overall importance of integrating authentic reading and writing activities throughout the curriculum; and (3) combining practical knowledge and theoretical bases in order to enhance the development of informed, reflective, and flexible practitioners in urban public schools. We later added a fourth goal: promoting a multicultural perspective in terms of content and pedagogy, with a focus on race, class, and gender. We also co-developed an interesting if somewhat idealistic political agenda, as written in our mission statement (1992): "As a group of people concerned about improving teaching and learning in urban schools, we will all consider ways to counter the public's misconceptions and negative attitudes about urban schools that result in damaging news stories and punitive legislation."

The program began in the early 1990s, when, once again, as a nation, we were confronting issues of the inequalities of our educational system, and when the notion of "urban education" was becoming an acceptable term, and, indeed, a field of inquiry. Books such as Kozol's *Savage Inequalities* (1991), Freedman's *Small Victories* (1991), and Kotlowitz's *There Are No Children Here* (1992) told vivid stories of these inequities. These books were being widely read as our program was just beginning, and they became required readings for all of us.

We also read academic works by critical theorists, such as Peter McLaren's *Life in Schools* (1994), work of African American educators, such as Lisa Delpit (1995) and Gloria Ladson-Billings (1997), and with work done by those who had been engaging in school partnerships (e.g., Darling-Hammond, 1994a; Cochran-Smith & Lytle, 1990). Together these influenced our thinking about how to engage in a kind of teacher preparation that would help our largely White and middle-class female interns prepare for what we were calling the "realities and possibilities" of urban public school teaching. We now see that we were, in many ways, naive about the struggles we would encounter as we asked interns to deal with identity and difference, and with issues of race, class, and gender, in more explicit, open, and honest ways. We were also just beginning to experience not fewer, but a greater onslaught of negative depictions of urban schools and teachers, and more legislation that privileged and enacted new calls for standards, testing, and accountability in our schools.

Creating a Partnership

Our UPPS "leadership team" consisted of teachers, principals, university faculty, and undergraduate students. Some of the leadership team's early conversations have been captured on audiotape and reflect struggles around discourse issues, working toward mutual agendas, and defining ourselves as a partnership. Early on, we spent much of one meeting discussing the word "urban." What was surprising then, but much less so in retrospect, is that we had different understandings of the word, and that the word itself seemed to serve as a mask or as a code word for the existence of high numbers of "minority," especially African American, and poor children and families, rather than for a sense of diversity. As such, it led to conversations about who was "more urban"—who was in the center and who was at the "suburban edge" of the city, who had higher counts for free and reduced lunches, and who was not within the Columbus Schools' guidelines for racial balance (more than 20 percentage points away from the overall ratio of White to non-White students).

From this exchange, and others like it, we learned much about school-university partnerships. My first response was to view the discussion as divisive and to dismiss it as not helpful to our goals as a new community. But what I came to learn, from conversations with my co-

coordinator, Mari McLean, who saw her role as a "boundary spanner," is that the very touch points of tension need to be acknowledged and understood, as much as possible, from the perspective of those who feel those tensions the most.

Later conversations that dealt with college-level reform initiatives served to help teachers and principals see the types of tensions that existed for faculty members who are seen as more autonomous, yet experience some pressures related to the tenure system. In one case, the dean had suggested that two of the four schools in UPPS participate in a grant to engage in collaborative restructuring of urban schools. As a group, the UPPS wanted to push back against perceived power differentials and decided that to participate, all schools would attend with less funding rather than create divisiveness in the group. As part of that discussion, the untenured university faculty expressed their concerns about the politics of "talking back" to their own administrators given the nature of university tenure policies and politics. Conversations such as these served to help us understand what many educators engaged in professional development sites came to see as the "cultures" of schools and universities.

In our local site, these kinds of issues and conversations became part of our "3 Rs" of struggle—roles and relationships, reform, and research; within the "3 Rs" lurked issues of power, time, and culture. At one PDS conference, we attempted to address these issues with humor to break some of the underlying tensions that everyone was feeling. In terms of time, we argued: "nobody has enough, but they have more; we need commitment and tenacity to make this work, and longer lives; and please release me." We addressed issues of power by pointing out that love may mean never having to say you're sorry, but in PDS power means having control of the budget and the meeting agenda; and we addressed issues of communication by asking, "Excuse me, are we talking about the same thing?" "Clinical what?" "What is a cohort, anyway?" and "I'll tell you what a PDS is if you tell me what site-based management is." We also wondered aloud why many of the more productive PDS conversations took place in hallways and bathrooms. The humor was cathartic for us in the PDS and seemingly also appreciated by the audience.

Creating a Teacher Education Program for Urban Settings

The teacher education component of UPPS continued to grow and develop out of conversations among all the participants. We wanted to create a program that emphasized child-centered and holistic instructional practices coupled with sustained immersion in urban settings (interns entered the classrooms on the first day, and often stayed in the same classroom for the entire year except for prolonged partner school experiences), and an emphasis on reflective teaching. We had decided to admit interns who had an expressed interest in working in urban settings, and at the same time, selected teachers based on stated commitments to urban teaching. We soon found out, however, that these commitments are based on an array of assumptions of what it means to be an urban teacher.

We knew that up to 50% of those who begin teaching in urban schools quit or fail within five years (Haberman, 1995), and many others are at risk for leaving (cf. McLean, 1994). There are, no doubt, many reasons for this failure rate, but it is interesting to note that several researchers point to underdeveloped belief systems of these teachers; specifically, their beliefs related to social issues, cultural difference, and social justice (e.g., Ladson-Billings, 1997; Haberman, 1995; Cochran-Smith, 1995). These belief systems, coupled with a lack of sustained experience in urban settings with successful mentor teachers seem to provide insufficient training for teaching diverse populations.

In contrast, research on successful practicing urban teachers paints a picture of a teacher who is on the one hand professional and realistic about her work, and who, on the other hand, is clear and explicit in her understanding of social issues and in her critique of social injustice. Haberman's work (1995), spanning over 35 years, notes that what he calls "Star" urban teachers have a "coherent vision" of teaching. For instance, they recognize societal conditions that contribute to children's problems in schools, but at the same time they feel a responsibility for engaging their students in learning. These teachers also have a professional orientation toward their students—an orientation of respect rather than a relatively naive need to "love" or "save" all the children they teach.

According to Ladson-Billings (1997), successful teachers of culturally diverse students (i.e., culturally relevant teachers) help their students recognize, understand, and critique current social inequities; but, as she points out, that presumes that the teachers themselves recognize social inequities and causes—that they have what she calls a "socio-political or critical consciousness" (p. 483). Ladson-Billings also notes that many studies claim that teacher preparation students not only lack these understandings, but they also reject information that might foster them.

In our own work in an urban teacher education program, we found that many of our interns did come with some sense of social justice and desire to make changes through teaching (and a specific desire to teach in urban settings) but that their assumptions about social issues and about culturally diverse children and families were often, in fact, simplified, overgeneralized, and unexamined. And, as we came to find, those who did have more sophisticated and experience-based knowledge of social justice issues, may not have necessarily openly shared their insights or their frustrations with others in the program.

We agree, then, with Cochran-Smith (1995) who argues that "prospective teachers need opportunities [within teacher preparation programs] to examine much of what is usually unexamined in the tightly braided relationships of language, culture, and power in schools and schooling" (p. 500), and that without such opportunities they may not develop their sense of social justice or deepen their understandings of cultural difference and privilege.

We provided these opportunities to reflect on cultural diversity and social inequities throughout the program and in specific forums, such as the collaborative seminar that included teachers, principals, interns, and outside speakers. Topics in these seminars included an analysis of the Goals 2000 in which interns questioned:

1. How realistic the goals were and whether they were more political than supportive of educational initiatives.
2. The ways in which the media exaggerates the problems in urban schools and do not share the positive aspects and outcomes.
3. The relationships of race and power to schooling and inequities, including a teasing out of the effects of race versus school funding on school segregation.
4. The importance of training teachers specifically for urban settings and the usefulness of that training for any context.

An interesting exchange resulted when a student said he would not even consider working in a nonurban setting. A teacher responded that there are problems everywhere in our society: "You don't know where you will end up if you want to practice your craft, and you may find that youngsters there sorely need your skills and your insights and nurturing." During these seminars, the interns had many questions about how to keep up their own spirits when simultaneously dealing with issues in their classrooms or schools. They struggled with how to be advocates of urban schools while dealing with constant public criticism of education.

Another place for such reflections was in an initial course on school and society. One conversation in this course was riveting and memorable. That year our cohort consisted of 20 White interns and five African American interns. Oftentimes, the African American interns were put in the awkward position of having to speak for a group, rather than simply for themselves. In this conversation, a White intern said she was tired of having to walk on eggshells when talking about race, to which an African American student responded, "Well then my feet are full of cuts." This exchange became a kind of turning point for the groups' understanding of differing perspectives, and we have found that it is, in fact, often in single moments that the enormous progress is made in terms of understanding others.

Recreating a Partnership: Moving toward LEADS

Defining ourselves as a partnership was a continual process and was revisited as LEADS was formed. Teachers with a long tradition of informal teaching philosophies and those whose approaches ranged from more traditional to more informal, but were connected by a commitment to teaching in urban settings, came together to form a new program. Much time was taken early in that planning year to find out what philosophies were shared across a diverse group of teachers (such as emphases on child-centered and literacy-based teaching, and teaching as inquiry and reflection) and where the tensions might arise (such as meeting the needs of diverse students through a range of approaches, and acknowledging difference). As Barbara Seidl describes below, this process is still occurring as the LEADS program is in its third year.

During our first year as the LEADS program, we tried several approaches to involve interns in discussions of literacy, culture, and difference as these issues relate to schooling. We asked them to explore the communities in which they would be teaching and to write about their own literacy assumptions. Early in the year we all shared our own "social injustice" stories, which were later rewritten in relation to a backdrop of works on equity and justice in education. Interns wrote about being passed over for promotion for jobs because they were women, or being Jewish in Gentile society, or not being able to play with certain children when they were younger for mysterious (to them) reasons. An African American intern wrote that his mother always told him that he had to be better than other students—good was not good enough. We hoped these stories would heighten our awareness of unfairness and difference, an awareness that could be carried with us as we became what we hoped would be more passionate and engaged teachers of all students.

We continued these conversations through book groups, focusing on issues of race, gender, and inner-city children and teaching. Many of the stories initially raised in the social injustice papers resurfaced in new forms during these discussions, providing evidence of a deepening understanding of how they, their students, and their colleagues position themselves and others in our schools and society. A continuing struggle is to engage in these discussion in the larger LEADS community.

Today, LEADS schools are, for the first time in 20 years, segregated again by neighborhood, while the program is infused with the scholarship on multicultural education and culturally relevant pedagogy. The history of EPIC and UPPS places the current program (LEADS) at the center of two opposing national trends in educational reform. The first is influenced by a desire to open and rejuvenate the meaning and forms of learning. The second is influenced by a desire to prescribe and set normative standards for teaching and learning. Both trends are also informed, in part, by heightened awareness that schooling has failed disproportionate numbers of children who are African American and Latino/a. How do we educate preservice and inservice teachers at these crossroads?

NURTURING A CARING COMMUNITY

Barbara Seidl

As a new faculty member at OSU, I assumed the role of co-director for an MEd program within an already existing PDS network. I was very committed to nurturing the strong and productive relationships that had been built within this community and to continuing the solid work that had come before me. I was also interested in creating learning experiences for our interns that would prepare them to be exemplary teachers with the skills and talents necessary for creating powerful learning configurations for children from diverse communities.

The literature on PDS work (Epanchin & Wooley-Brown, 1993; Rushcamp & Roehler, 1992) as well as my own experience had contributed to my awareness of the challenges in creating successful PDS communities. I was prepared to continue to create opportunities that would allow both public school faculty and university faculty working within the network to build both personal and shared visions while striving toward common goals. However, what I discovered in actually assuming the role of co-director was a community of people much more diverse than the university/public school differences typically described in the literature.

The different needs, goals, and aspiration of multiple groups within the LEADS PDS became apparent very quickly. For example, we believed it was necessary for our interns to engage in long-term experiences and dialogue around teaching in diverse contexts. To do this we were building a new relationship with Mt. Olivet Baptist Church, an African American church within the Columbus community. Members of the Mt. Olivet community had committed their time and energy to help our interns learn about education within a specific sociocultural context. The needs of this new member of the LEADS community were particular and distinct. Our MEd interns also had needs that were urgent and particular to them as they began this five-quarter, intensive master's program. Additionally, the needs of the mentor teachers within the PDS demanded careful attention as the solid professional relationships that had already been built between mentor teachers and OSU faculty were centrally important to our efforts.

While there are many definitions and configurations for PDSs, building a "community of learners" (Holmes Group, 1990) is a goal central to the concept and one that is unarguably necessary if schools and universities are to work together to create powerful teacher education programs and improve schools. Thus, a focus on shared goals within PDS work is important. However, any community is also comprised of people with diverse learning needs, goals, and aspirations and the health of the community is dependent upon caring for these diverse needs. Early efforts in PDSs illustrate the complexity and difficulty of building such communities when these divergent interests are not addressed (Pugach & Pasch, 1993; Zeichner, 1992); misunderstanding, distrust, and withdrawal are often the results.

My university colleague and co-coordinator (Pat Enciso) and I began to discuss what it would mean to accept responsibility for the health and growth of this diverse community. While the groups within our community shared common goals: preparing exemplary teachers for diverse classrooms and improving education for all children, they also had different motivations for becoming involved, came to the community with different needs, and brought distinct and individual goals to their involvement. If individual growth and development were inextricably linked to the health and success of the shared goals of the community, as we believed they were, then we needed to be about the business of building a community where diverse needs could be met and where diverse interests and goals could be sought within the context of shared goals.

Drawing heavily from the work and literature of a caring ethic (Noddings, 1984, 1986), Pat and I began to do two things. First we attempted to recognize the different groups within the LEADS program and identify what it would mean to care for, or attend to the growth and well-being of each of these groups. Second, we began to think about the structures that would support growth and enhance our abilities to care for others. We were interested in organizational structures that would allow us to become engrossed, to know the concerns, motivations, and hopes of our members, as well as structures that would promote dialogue and create opportunities for the confirmation of the talents and abilities of our diverse community.

Caring for Our Diverse Community

There are twenty-eight students in the LEADS MEd cohort. These students are placed in schools within the LEADS PDS network with teachers who mentor them for the entire school year. Most of the course work is delivered by a cohort of OSU faculty and clinical educators on the OSU campus. Doctoral students, called PDS Educators within our program, work closely with the teachers within schools as well as supervise and mentor the MEd interns placed there. The MEd interns fulfill part of their coursework requirements through a community education placement at Mt. Olivet Baptist Church. They spend two hours every week working with children involved in one of the Church's educational programs. The adults from the community who organize and operate these programs work closely with our interns. Identifying the distinct groups within our community helped us to become more aware of these needs and goals and, thus, build organizational processes and relational links necessary for nurturing the growth and well-being of the many individuals within our community.

The LEADS MEd Interns.   The interns in our MEd program are involved in an intensive, demanding, and highly stimulating year. Heavy demands and high expectations are placed upon them in regards to commitment and growth. Thus, the interns need clearly established expectations. They also need continuous supportive mentoring from their teacher mentors as well as from the university faculty.

PDS Educators from OSU work very closely with the MEd interns. Every other week they observe interns in one school, hold a meeting with the group of interns in that school, and read and respond to journals. This structure allows for PDS Educators to develop close and supportive relationships with interns. Placing MEd interns with LEADS mentor teachers for an entire year also allows for significant and supportive mentoring relationships to develop. Finally, efforts to reduce ambiguity and establish clear expectations for interns include using PDS Educators as a direct communicative link with interns, communication through electronic mail, and the formalization of procedures and expectations within a LEADS Student Handbook.

Mentor teachers.   Teachers choose to become mentor teachers within the LEADS community for a variety of reasons and come to the community with different skills and talents. Some teachers need support in becoming good mentors for teacher education interns. Others have developed this expertise and seek different challenges such as opportunities to collaborate around teacher education curriculum, plan teacher education experiences, and co-teach teacher education coursework. In addition, because PDS communities are environments where teachers are engaged in ongoing inquiry around their teaching and the work of the school, teachers must also be provided with support for inquiry.

Most direct support for mentor teachers comes through the PDS Educators who meet regularly with groups of teachers in each school. These meetings, held every other week, allow PDS Educators to answer questions, provide support with consistent opportunities to discuss MEd interns' progress and growth. In addition, PDS Educators support teacher inquiry in their assigned schools, and share their own expertise with teachers. Mentor teachers are further supported in their inquiry efforts through large group LEADS PDS meetings that allow for sharing across schools and through release time supported financially through the LEADS' budget. Finally, every attempt is made to allow those teachers interested in teaching or team-teaching courses or acting as clinical PDS Educators to do so.

PDS educators.   The PDS Educators within the LEADS program are either doctoral interns or teachers within one of the PDSs. PDS Educators are assigned to mentor no more than six interns in no more than two different schools; one, in which they have sole responsibility for mentoring teachers and interns and for supporting teacher inquiry, and another, in which they share those responsibilities with another PDS Educator. Because many of the PDS Educators are involved in doctoral work, they need support to engage in inquiry or research around their work.

Weekly meetings are held with PDS Educators. These meetings allow for discussion around student progress, mentoring issues, and provide an opportunity to share and help in support for inquiry. A formal course of study around teacher education will be provided during the winter quarter of the academic year. Weekly meetings will also be focused around supporting the PDS Educators in research and inquiry of their own.

OSU faculty.   For those in teacher education, the conceptualization and decision making around the curriculum and teaching/learning experiences for interns is a source of intellectual, professional, and personal interest. The OSU faculty members who work with the LEADS MEd program are committed to teacher education and the expertise and talent they bring to the program is underused if there are not opportunities for discussion and critique of the curriculum.

Decisions in our program often need to be made on the spot and in response to particular and immediate needs. Thus, it is easy for decisions regarding curriculum and program to become too centralized. When this happens, interest is undermined and faculty tend to teach their one course and have little further involvement. Meetings held every other week with teaching faculty are intended to provide opportunities for discussion as well as support inquiry and scholarship around our work.

Mt. Olivet community.   The Mt. Olivet community has welcomed the LEADS community and extended their already scarce resources and time to include the valuable work of preparing teachers for diverse classrooms. Tending to the needs and interests of the Mt. Olivet community means maintaining a critical awareness of the strengths, needs, and challenges faced by community-based organizations. For example, because resources are scarce we are currently involved in identifying ways in which resources from OSU can be extended and shared: involvement in technology course work is a high priority for the Mt. Olivet teachers. Money for other professional development pursuits such as engagement in inquiry is also set aside in the LEADS budget.

Elementary and middle school students.   We can never forget that our energies are ultimately directed at ensuring that students in schools are cared for, that they are provided with exemplary teachers, and that their classrooms are caring environments where there is continuity of people responsible for nurturing their emotional, physical, and intellectual growth. The structure of our teacher education program and the work of the PDS community must be congruent with these goals and any decisions made regarding our work must foreground what it means to care for these students.

PROCESSES THAT BRING US TOGETHER

Tending to the diversity within the LEADS community is important to maintaining the health of the community and the overall success of shared goals. We are a strong community. As we continue to grow we'd like to maintain that strength and ensure that voices will be heard and respected. We are in the process of initiating what we call the LEADS PDS Community Council. Representatives from the diverse groups within our community will have a seat on the community council. These representatives will be responsible for bringing to the table the opinions, suggestions, and feedback from the groups they represent. The community council will act as a clearinghouse for ideas and serve as a vehicle through which decisions will ultimately be made.

Communication is also a challenge within a community as large and diverse as ours. What we know without a doubt is that lack of effective communication undermines efficacy, erodes commitment, and eventually results in half-hearted participation. This year we have centralized our communication processes within an office and a role. Designating one of our graduate students as the LEADS Project Assistant has allowed time and energy to be directed toward formalizing communication and committing expectations and procedures to paper.

Nurturing the growth and well-being of a community as diverse as the LEADS community is challenging and rewarding. Approaching the health of this community through a caring ethic and nurturing the group processes that promote broad participation and commitment have helped us in conceptualizing our work as co-directors. While we do not have the final answers, we are confident that we are doing all that we can to nurture individual needs, goals, and aspirations within the context of the shared goals of our community.

REFERENCES

Berkey, R., Curtis, T., Minnick, F., Zietlow, K., Campbell, D., and Kirschner, B. W. (1990). Reflections on reflection from a collaborative research/staff development project. *Education and Urban Society, 22*(2), 204–232.

Bigler, T. (1995). Learning to listen. In B. W. Kirschner (Guest editor), *Ohio Journal of the English Language Arts, 36*(1), 21–28.

Brown, J., & Stowe, C. (1995). The Monday–Friday spelling cycle: It can be broken. In B. W. Kirschner (Guest editor), *Ohio Journal of the English Language Arts, 36*(1), 35–40.

Bryant, N., & Gee, J. (1995). The long and winding road: From here to portfolio. In B. W. Kirschner (Guest editor), *Ohio Journal of the English Language Arts, 36*(1), 58–62.

Cochran-Smith, M., & Lytle, S. L. (1990). Research on teaching and teacher research: The issues that divide. *Educational Researcher, 19*(2), 2–11.

Darling-Hammond, L. (1994a). *Professional development schools: Schools for developing a profession.* New York: Teachers College Press.

Darling-Hammond, L. (1994b). Developing professional development schools: Early lessons, challenges, and promises. In L. Darling-Hammond (Ed.), *Professional development schools* (pp. 1–27). New York: Teachers College Press.

Delpit, L. (1995). *Other people's children: Cultural conflict in the classroom.* New York: The New Press.

Ebbutt, D. (1985). Educational action research: Some general concerns and specific quibbles. In Robert Burgess (Ed.), *Issues in educational research: Qualitative methods* (pp. 152–175). London: The Falmer Press.

Epanchin, B. C., & Wooley-Brown, C. (1993). A university-school district collaborative project for preparing paraprofessionals to become special educators. *Teacher Education and Special Education, 16*(2), 110–123.

Freedman, S. (1991). *Small victories: The real world of a teacher, her students, and their high school.* New York: Harper Collins.

Haberman, M. (1995). *Star teachers of children in poverty.* New York: Kappa Delta Pi Publications.

Holmes Group. (1990). *Tomorrow's schools: Principles for the design of professional development schools.* East Lansing, MI: Author.

Howlett, S., & Kerstetter, K. (1995). Bringing practice into line with philosophy: The development of an alternative reporting document. In B. W. Kirschner (Guest editor), *Ohio Journal of the English Language Arts, 36*(1), 62–68.

Kirschner, B. W., Dickinson, R., & Blosser, C. (1995, February). *Restructuring student teaching through collaborative action research.* Paper presented at the annual meeting of American Association of Colleges of Teacher Education, Washington, DC.

Kirschner, B. W., Dickinson, R., & Blosser, C. (1996). From cooperation to collaboration: The changing culture of a school/university partnership. *Theory into Practice, 35*(3), 205–213.

Kirschner, B. W., Dickinson, R., & Blosser, C. (1995, April). *Using collaborative inquiry to restructure preservice teacher education.* Paper presented at the meeting of the American Educational Research, San Francisco.

Kirschner, B. W., Dickinson, R., & Blosser, C. (1995, April). *Widening circles: Teachers engaged in action research.* Symposium paper presented at the meeting of the American Educational Research, San Francisco.

Kirschner, B. W. (Guest editor). (1995). Teacher-researcher: New voices and multiple perspectives (theme issue). *Ohio Journal of the English Language Arts 36*(1), 5–10.

Kotlowitz, A. (1992). *There are no children here: The story of two boys growing up in the other America.* New York: Anchor Books.

Kozol, J. (1991). *Savage Inequalities.* New York: Crown.

McLaren, P. (1994). *Life in schools: An introduction to critical pedagogy in the foundations of education.* New York: Longman Publishing.

McLean, M. M. (1994). The role of a boundary spanner in school-university collaboration. In *What is Different, What has Changed?* First annual theme issue of the Professional Development School Publications Series. Columbus, OH: The Ohio State University College of Education.

Noddings, N. (1984). *Caring: A feminine approach to ethics.* Berkeley: University of California Press.

Noddings, N. (1986). Fidelity in teaching, teacher education, and research for teaching. *Harvard Educational Review, 56*(4), 496–510.

Pearl, C. (1995). A break with tradition: Sharing a job and teaching cooperatively. In B. W. Kirschner (Guest editor), *Ohio Journal of the English Language Arts, 36*(1), 48–53.

Pugach, M., & Pasch, S. (1993). The challenge of creating urban professional development schools. In R. Yinger & K. Borman (Eds.), *Restructuring education: Issues and strategies for communities, schools, and universities.* Norwood, NJ: Ablex.

Richardson, V. (1994). Conducting research on practice. *Educational Researcher, 23*(5), 5–10.

Rushcamp, S., & Roehler, L. R. (1992). Characteristics supporting change in a professional development school. *Journal of Teacher Education, 43*(1), 19–27.

Schon, D. A. (1983). *The reflective practitioner.* San Francisco: Jossey-Bass.

Swanson, B., & Hootman, J. (1995). Collaboration in action. In B. W. Kirschner, (Guest editor), *Ohio Journal of the English Language Arts, 36*(1), 53–68.

Zeichner, K. (1992). Rethinking the practicum in the professional development school partnership. *Journal of Teacher Education, 43*(4), 296–307.

Small Beginnings to a Collective Takeover: Collaboration, Integration, and Change in Our PDS

Francee Eldredge, Kathleen Ibom, Marilyn Johnston, Lisa Maloney, and Mike Thomas

The ECC PDS was one of the initial PDSs. This group of diverse schools and university faculty participants defined a set of goals that was initially beyond their reach. They saw each of these goals as a rather separate agenda and worked away at each one in a deliberate way. What they come to see some time later, is the interdependence of these goals and the ways that collaboration, teacher education reform, professional development, and inquiry are mutually supportive of their learning as well as of their interns. The collective takeover is their way of describing this move from separate to integrative purposes. Written in many voices, this chapter reflects what these PDS participants have learned from each other within this seven-year PDS project.

The Educators for Collaborative Change/Professional Development School (ECC/PDS) has been an organization for seven years. We are a group of 45 teachers and principals from eight elementary and middle schools from two school districts (one urban and one suburban), and 10 doctoral students and professors from Ohio State.

We were initially a group of five schools that were working colla-boratively with Marilyn and some doctoral students on a funded curri-cular project related to the Columbian Quincentenary. We had been involved in this project for about a year when the college issued a call for PDS proposals. Because we were already working collaboratively, we decided to write a proposal to become a PDS. Our proposal was accepted.

Since we became a PDS, we have worked with eight cohorts of ele-mentary and middle school MEd certification students. These students are in a five-quarter graduate program that begins in June of one sum-mer and is completed in August of the next year. The school and uni-versity participants in our PDS meet as a group on Thursdays after school.

Since its inception, our PDS has had four guiding purposes: (1) col-laboration between the schools and the university; (2) reform in teacher education and urban education; (3) professional development of our members, and (4) inquiry into our programs and teaching practices. In the early years of our PDS these purposes were separate and distinct. We tended to focus on our interns, on our own learning, *or* on inquiry pro-jects, but seldom did we see ourselves working on more than one of these simultaneously. Over time, though, work has become more inte-grated, more of a single piece. In fact, we now find it difficult to talk about any of these purposes without talking about all of them.

We began working in small ways in separate areas. The collective takeover occurred as each of our goals became a part of the other. An account of this transition is in many ways the story of our development.

A fuller account of the development of our PDS would require accounts of our students' development and the learning of students in our public school classrooms. Other chapter-length accounts would be required for these topics. Overall, however, we consider our efforts to have been fruitful in both these areas. Evaluation of our certification graduates clearly demonstrates that they are different from students who came out of our non-PDS certification programs. They are more widely prepared, they demonstrate a wider range of professional responsibili-ties and attitudes, they feel prepared to teach, and are more aware of the complexities and political realities of teaching (see Johnston & Thomas with PDS participants, 1997).

WRITING IN DIFFERENT VOICES; LEARNING AS WE WRITE

This chapter integrates texts from various people and sources (journals, conference papers, research interviews, etc.). We write in a collective as well as individual voices. We try to represent both what we have learned collectively and how this has evolved in the lives of particular people. We think this is important because we have not all had the same experiences even when we were in the same meetings. Different things are important to us as individuals and our separate histories and contexts are the diversity out of which our collective story has developed. We try to capture both individual stories and collective learnings, and acknowledge that there is an uneasy tension here that characterizes our collaborative endeavor as a whole. We also acknowledge that not everyone's voice is present, and some points of view are absent. It is a partial story as well as a continuing one.

In the process of writing this chapter, we have come to see more clearly how integrated our goals and learning have become. Not only are they dependent on each other, but the interaction between them provided fruitful cross-fertilization, and consequently, change and growth. We decided to call this transition from separate to integrated goals a collective takeover, and it is the story of this takeover that follows.

FIRST GOAL: COLLABORATION

In the beginning, collaboration seemed like a process useful to promote reform and to counter the hierarchical norms and structures of both schools and universities. We thought we would use collaboration to support our reform agenda and promote professional development. It had both formal and informal aspects, formal in the sense that we agreed on it as a central purpose. Informal in the sense that it undergirded the way we tried to build relationships and attend to persons as well as our reform agenda. Collaboration in general was a means to other ends (our reform initiatives) and confined primarily to constructing new kinds of relationships within our group.

Creating these kinds of new relationships and individual understandings has not been easy, but it has been endlessly intriguing. Kathy Ibom writes about our beginning this way:

> Only as I sit here trying to remember the early days of our collaboration do I realize the tremendous changes our group has undergone. I did not initially know what it meant to collaborate, and I did not understand the endless talking in our Thursday night meetings. I can remember expecting that the university was going to show me how to become a better teacher by bringing in speakers and "collaborating" with teachers from other schools. I now realize that it's me, not an expert, who will make me a more competent teacher. So I began this project hoping someone would "fix" me—and I felt, although I never shared these feelings with others, that I was in dire need of fixing.

> After a few quarters of collaboration I was thoroughly frustrated but intrigued. We seemed to talk nonstop and never make a decision about anything. But the talk would stay in my head long after the meeting, and I was beginning to connect the talk to my practice. For me, I liked the "talk" and that was enough to keep me going.

Marilyn Johnston was the only university participant at the beginning of the PDS project. She had a particular perspective on collaboration seen from her university position. She thought collaboration required relationships that defied the hierarchical associations typical of schools and universities, but was uncertain how to create them.

> Marilyn: School/university collaboration was new to all of us. As a university participant, I was particularly concerned that this did not become another collaborative project in name only. As a classroom teacher and university professor, I had seldom experienced anything that approached the kind of mutuality, parity, and respect for differences that were discussed in the literature on collaboration (Clark, 1988; Holmes Group, 1990; Hord, 1986; Oakes, Hare, & Sirotnik, 1989). I wanted this collaborative project to be different and tried to keep us talking about what it meant to be collaborative. This often meant examining my role as a university participant and asking why I was so often positioned in a place of authority, and why others were unwilling to actively take on responsibilities and leadership roles. We were used to working in particular ways with each other, and it was hard to change, but slowly it did.

One of the most striking things to occur as we learned more about collaboration was that it began to influence other parts of our professional lives. We began to want faculty meetings, classroom decision-making, school district initiatives, and even our personal relationships outside of school to be more collaborative. Francee Eldredge describes this influence.

> Francee: I had had some experience with collaboration before I came into the PDS. I worked collaboratively with two doctoral students who did their dissertation studies in my classroom.
>
> When the first dissertation started, I was a very direct instruction teacher using a skills-based approach to teaching reading. As a result of Katie doing her dissertation in my classroom, my teaching moved to the other end of the continuum. Katie would say, "What would happen if you tried this?" and the next day I'd try it. I was trying to find answers and the collaboration with Katie helped me to do that. By the end of the year, I was thoroughly committed to a whole language approach to teaching reading.
>
> Two years later, Joan did her research in my classroom. Joan wanted to look at curriculum development in the classroom and the

way children direct the curriculum. My involvement in these dissertations gave me a sense of what collaborative research was all about, but I didn't have a sense of collaboration in education more generally.

In my second year in the PDS, I became a clinical educator. In this position I was learning a lot about collaboration and how to work in my school as a facilitator of teacher development and change. Then suddenly I was transferred to another school. It was very difficult. I was devastated. However, I'm a survivor. I decided to just throw myself back into my teaching. It was a lonely role, however, because I didn't have the kind of collaborative support I was used to.

I eventually found ways to collaborate in my new school. The teachers were very receptive to some of the ideas I had, but they weren't used to working collaboratively. Then we got a big federal grant and the principal put five of us together to plan for the professional development in the school. Many of the teachers who had been teaching for some time, however, were not interested in change or collaboration.

In the PDS I had learned how to work collaboratively and how to provide some leadership to make it work. We established a trust level and made collaborative decisions together. I learned not to get upset when there were different ideas expressed, and how to value everyone's opinion. Without my PDS experience, I wouldn't have known how to do this, or that it was even possible.

The group of teachers at my new school eventually became interested in PDS because of our work together. Collaboration was intriguing enough to keep them involved and now we've joined the PDS as a group.

What I am learning in PDS has infiltrated everything I do as an educator. I work as a team with my MEd interns rather than tell them what to do. It seems that collaboration has taken over my life. It's not just something that happens in PDS, but it's because of what happened in the PDS that I have come to value collaboration.

The collective takeover of collaboration evolved as we learned to work together in new ways. As we gained experience with collaboration in the PDS, it often led to working differently with our students and colleagues outside the PDS. Our classes became more collaborative as we learned to work more collaboratively with each other. As we became empowered to make decisions, we began letting our students make more decisions in our classrooms. As we experienced the feeling of being in charge of our own learning, we began to want our students to also have this kind of control.

Collaboration is a fragile process. Because it is based on relationships, when the group changes in membership, the ways we work together take on new forms and new challenges emerge. Collaboration is an ongoing process of negotiating relationships. Seen in this way, collaboration has come to permeate all aspects of the PDS and many facets of our teaching and learning.

SECOND GOAL: TEACHER EDUCATION REFORM

We were designated a Professional Development School (PDS) Project in May 1991, and our first cohort of MEd certification students started their course work at the university in June, and their field placements in our schools in September. In our first summer planning meetings, we talked about the problems of teacher education, in general, but were forced by our time line to make rather practical and immediate decisions. Even though we, as teachers, were included in these kinds of programmatic decisions and participated in implementing the reforms, it took a long time before we felt like we had ownership of the program in general.

Eventually, we began to trust that we could have a significant voice in decision making, and we saw that our input was valued. University professors were willing to juggle field placement schedules, even when it meant holding classes at odd times and in strange places, like in schools. As we began co-teaching university methods courses, we found that constructing good methods courses was more difficult than we had anticipated. We became less critical of professors and they of us as we struggled together to develop courses that truly connected theory and practice.

Most of us now feel that this is *our* program. We feel jointly responsible for our interns' development and success. From small beginnings, where we made tentative decisions about practical things, to a sense of fully collaborative decisions about the total program, the collective takeover moves us into shared ownership of this teacher education reform.

One aspect of this takeover is related to the role of the cooperating teacher. Most of us before the PDS saw supervision as something we did for the university and for the student teachers. Besides, student teachers were rarely in our rooms long enough to have much impact except maybe to create a little short-term chaos. Now our interns are with us for an entire year. Cooperating teachers and student teachers (now called interns) work collaboratively to plan, teach, and evaluate the learning that takes place in the classroom. Interns are a permanent fixture in the classroom and are seen by students and parents alike as another teacher in the classroom. Interns ask questions, challenge the way things are done, and experiment with new things in the classroom. Teachers not only become different kinds of mentors but often learn a great deal as well.

Who's Teaching Who?

Kathy Ibom's narrative—entitled "Who's Teaching Who?"—describes her transition from a "trainer" to a learner.

> Kathy: As I try to make sense of who I am as a teacher and what I want to bring to a classroom, I have changed the way I mentor our yearlong interns. Through their struggles, I see my weaknesses. Just as each child teaches me about myself as a teacher and more importantly about me as a person, the interns have had this same effect on my practice.
>
> With my first intern I wanted to appear that I was always in complete control and well prepared to teach. I felt that if my intern would be successful if I modeled teaching techniques and complimented her on her strengths and creative nature. I felt that perhaps it was my fault if she was having problems. I also knew that I did not have answers for many of the problems. What was the point of bringing up problems if I had no solutions? I wanted it to appear that I had everything under control.
>
> The second year I had a huge challenge dropped in my lap. I had an extremely bright but troubled intern. He was constantly journaling with me about gender issues, class interactions, and discipline philosophies. I had never journaled with anyone before and his comments were often very personal and sometimes I felt embarrassed to respond to them. He was very well read, which made me reflect and question my practice, but this was not a comfortable situation for me. This young man also had a difficult time dealing with children in conflict and became so upset he was unable to complete student teaching. I silently felt like this was a reflection on my teaching and I felt that I had let both of us down.
>
> My third intern was a quiet, reflective perfectionist. She sat back and observed for a very long time, but one day she walked into the room and stated that she was ready to teach. After watching my intern fail the year prior, it was important to me that this one do well. She was wonderful to work with and became a good friend, which made it easier to talk about the class. I was able to admit that I did not have all the answers. I saw problems ahead for her, but I was not able to become a "critical friend."
>
> My fourth year was one of escalated professional growth for me. I became a clinical educator and I began working on my master's degree. I started going to meetings where ideas and opinions were out in the open and my views were welcomed and nourished. I also started sitting in on focus groups (weekly meetings with the interns in our school) where a graduate associate (GA—doctoral student from the university) and the interns would meet and discuss strategies and struggles. I watched as the GA working in my school gave feedback in very direct ways and the interns seemed to welcome this discourse. I was amazed that the interns would ask me practical questions and that I

was often able to explain what I had done in similar circumstances. I was also doing observations of all of the interns in our building and seeing that most were dealing with the same issues. This made me feel that it was not my fault if my intern was agonizing with some aspect of teaching. As a clinical educator, I gained a new appreciation for the interns and their struggles. My intern and I were journeying together. I now inquire about both of our practices. I ask a lot from both of us, knowing that we both have much to learn.

Seven interns have come through my classroom door with different learning styles, different life experiences, and different emotional intelligences that mold them into different types of teachers. Some have had very painful experiences that have led me to critically look at my teaching practices and realize that being a "critical friend" is just as important as being supportive and caring. I need to push the questioning even when they are not ready to give answers. "What do you want the children to learn?" "What will you do the next time Billy responds to you in such a negative manner?" "Did you realize that you misspelled three words on the chart today while taking dictation? What can you do about your spelling problem?" "How can you work with a small group of children and yet maintain a sense of the large group?" "How can you help children in conflict without appearing to take sides?" After getting feedback from the five interns who have gone on to find employment, I have a better sense of their struggles but am uncertain how to help. How can I push them toward critical thinking skills and urge cooperative learning approaches when their evaluators may not give them the time, noise factor variance, and support needed for such processes? Will they be in environments that support questions, seeing them as promoting growth, not revealing weakness? Will they be allowed to treat children as individuals and not a group where "fairness" is "sameness?" Is it OK to nurture philosophies that they are not ready to institute on their own? I want them to carry on these approaches, yet I cannot continue to support their growth because each year I have a new intern to mentor. Will asking the tough questions start and maintain their own reflection?

I had to ask tough questions of myself before I was able to ask them of others. I have gone from too easy and too much praise to perhaps too demanding. I know what lies ahead for them and I want to prevent someone else from negatively judging them with different values and perspectives than mine. I want them to be ready for these barriers.

The interns have made me question my practice. Their questions fuel my inquiry. Developmentally our questions are not the same but hopefully our observations can support each other.

For many of us, like Kathy, our teacher education goals have expanded to include our own learning as well as that of our interns. The collective takeover of this goal involved being teachers and learners together rather than a more hierarchical model where we know the answers and our interns have to work themselves through our check-sheets and evaluation requirements.

THIRD GOAL: INQUIRY

Research began in a small corner of ECC. We thought of research, at that time, as something that was done separately from the main work of our teacher education responsibilities. But this conception of research has changed and so has our methodology.

When we began, few of us had any secure sense of what a genuine school/university collaboration would look like, so the university participants wanted to study how it evolved. Marilyn and four graduate students interested in this research question invited teachers to join the research "team."

We began having these very interesting conversations about collaboration. Rather than the drudgery of collecting and coding data (the teachers' perception of research), we were talking about the problems of working collaboratively. There were many things happening in our schools and in our larger group as we tried to work without the traditional leadership roles (or imposition) of the university participants. It took many incidents of slipping back into "traditional" roles and ways of doing things before we began to recognize patterns and places where we could make things more collaborative. We tried to continually ask ourselves, "Is this a collaborative way to do this?" The smallness of the research group was an ideal laboratory for practicing new ways of relating to one another as we practiced the very processes while we studied them.

> Lisa: As teachers in the research group we did not consider ourselves researchers, but we were willing to learn. We watched while the university participants tape recorded and documented everything we did in our group and everything that happened in the larger project. We rarely, however, got around to using (or coding) these data in typical ways. Mostly we just talked. In this talk, we were learning many things about ourselves. We were learning to trust each other with our problems and concerns, and to learn from each other across schools and across the traditional divides of schools and the university.

The kind of talk we have come to call dialogue now permeates much of what we do in ECC. However it is difficult to sustain, and sometimes even more difficult to get started. It depends on trust and the willingness to take risks. We try to make dialogue happen as often as is possible. But, how does one keep this sense of risk and learning occurring in a long-term project?

Marilyn: Dialogue, for me, seems to happen most often when we are genuinely perplexed by some issue or situation, and particularly when we feel some kind of risk or uncertainty associated with it. It doesn't seem to matter whether it is a theoretical or practical issue, but it must include some uncomfortableness. This is a fruitful starting point for inquiry because inquiry starts with a question. Sometimes our inquiry takes us out of our comfort zone, other times we must push ourselves toward the edge. Individual commitments have to be shared in ways that critique and self-reflection are possible. We not only have to be willing to say what we think, but we have to be willing to have our most cherished commitments shared and compared with the ideas of others.

From this kind of exposure through dialogue, we learn about ourselves and others. Margaret Drabble (1969) describes the sudden insight and power that follows from this kind of learning:

> Learning was so dangerous: for how could one tell in advance, while still ignorant, whether a thing could ever be unlearned or forgotten, or if, once known and named, it would invalidate by its significance the whole of one's former life, all of those years wiped out, convicted of one blow, retrospectively darkened by a sudden light? (p. 70)

Drabble's description of learning captures my experience of inquiry through dialogue—it is both uncertain and irreversible.

In a dialogue focused on inquiry, our most cherished ideas and commitments may be called into question. We gravitate toward the possibility of this kind of dialogue even as we feel a sense of risk. We search out the possibilities of this kind of learning even as we are afraid of what it might bring. It is hard as individuals and as groups to continually be in a place where we can embrace this kind of exposure and openendedness.

My experience in our PDS, however, is that one can become addicted to dialogue. Rather than feeling a sense of risk, I have come to feel disappointed when it doesn't occur, when we spend too much time describing, complaining, or focusing solely on practical problem solving. All of these are necessary in an ongoing project, and dialogue can emerge in the context of any of them, yet I fear the long-term success of our PDS may work against dialogue. As we become institutionalized and routinized, we rarely talk about collaboration as we did in the beginning. University-based participants too often run the meetings, and their suggestions or points of view rarely get questioned. The doctoral students who work with us have fallen into traditional supervisory roles and rarely come to weekly meetings. They feel little responsibility for the direction or evaluation of the program. The teachers, particularly new teachers, have started calling Thursday night meetings a "university class," which may indicate that they feel obligated to someone else's requirements for university credit rather than to direct their own self-defined professional goals.

Maybe we can't fight the system long term. Maybe dialogue eludes us because we are not calling into question the basic assumptions that ground our work together.

Just as we were feeling these disappointments, we began last spring quarter to talk about them. There was a kind of energy that resulted from dealing with difficult questions, from wondering about why things had changed, and new plans for doing some things differently. Dialogue is elusive, but this kind of inquiry into our assumptions and actions is what keeps me coming back to this group and to our struggles to figure out what it means to be collaborative across schools and universities.

Keeping critical questions in front of us represents the way in which dialogue as inquiry has become a pervasive part of our work together. To support this, we have instituted project groups as part of our weekly meetings. Some groups depend heavily on dialogue as inquiry, other groups use more formalized approaches like action research. Overall, inquiry, once a separate goal, has become a pervasive aspect of our work together.

FOURTH GOAL: PROFESSIONAL DEVELOPMENT

Our fourth goal, professional development, was something we initially decided to put on hold. We had pressing needs to plan for our MEd interns and our research project to study collaboration was underway. We did not anticipate the way our work on the teacher education and research initiatives would promote professional development.

Lisa's narrative shows how her beginning involvement in the research project influenced her classroom teaching and promoted professional development that she did not anticipate. What began as an interest in garnering some university credit prompted significant changes in her understandings of research and her teaching practice.

Lisa: I don't remember how I got started in the research group, but the initial meetings intrigued me. It was the conversations; they didn't fit into my definition of research. The conversations were very interesting. They focused on our issues related to collaboration, things that were happening in our schools.

I had never before taken a course where I learned for the sake of learning. The learning in the research group was connected directly to what I was interested in exploring. It was truly emergent. I learned things as I needed them. I read things because I need to know something to understand something else, rather than read something and then find a way to make it relevant. It met my needs.

For the first time, I was learning to learn. I could transfer what I was learning into the classroom, but no one was telling me how to do it. In the process, I was changing. For example, I used to think that every student should be engaged all the time. I remember when Marilyn came to teach in my classroom the first time I expected her to have all the kids just wrapped around her little finger. I thought they were going to be in awe of everything she said. But the kids were the same for her as they are for me. Having experiences in the research group taught me that it doesn't have to be "light my fire" everyday all day in order for it to still be good. Besides, I think there needs to be times when kids are struggling, when they don't quite get it. Especially the bright kids, they don't have enough struggling, and the challenged kids have too much. Finding those balances is important to me now.

Things are much more complex to me than they were before PDS. There's always another perspective to think about. There are many sides to every issue. Actually it has made life more difficult because it's hard to make decisions when there's always something else you need to think about. I used to go home and think that I knew when I did something the "right" way. Now I go home and say, "Well I did these things that worked out okay, but there are these consequences from making those choices." I have learned to live with ambiguity and dissatisfaction.

I was bored with teaching before PDS. Seven years of teaching in the same school district at the same grade level. Now I have new things to think about. I think students' social development is intriguing; I never really thought about that before, at least thought about it as a central part of the curriculum. I used to teach where everyone did the same task at the same time. Now I want everyone to be working on open-ended projects so individuals don't feel compared to others by having to meet the same requirements and accomplishing the same level of learning (especially for my inclusion students).

Another part of my professional development has been to learn about how the university operates compared to how schools work. I sat in on discussions at the university where people argued about ideas, really having an intellectual conversation. By contrast, in schools it is more important to "go with the flow" and "not to rock the boat." Divergent thinking is not acceptable. I often found myself in trouble if I disagreed with an idea or presented a new way to think about something. I have learned how to be careful about what I say in my school, and I've gotten better at not talking as often, but trying to say more important things.

My experience with the university built my confidence because people asked questions about things I know about that they wanted to know. The last presentation we made, a professor asked me for my email address. I was amazed. In my school, no one ever asks me about anything I'm doing.

Co-teaching a methods course has also promoted professional development. Co-teaching makes you walk the talk. It makes me think and I have to justify my practice. Co-teaching keeps pushing me to think more deeply. The issues we were talking about in the Research Group, like power and hierarchy, were also issues for co-teaching. So there were many connections. I started thinking about the influence of hierarchy in my classroom.

In my co-teaching experience all the aspects of PDS—collaboration, teacher education reform, and research—come together. They've really always been together, but I don't think we could understand their relatedness, until we looked at them separately. I don't think I intentionally separated them, but initially it was easier to think about them one by one. I initially only intended to "buy into" the research portion, but I ended up with that plus a whole lot more. I bought one and the rest was free.

PDS has opened up my professional world. It's a bigger place with different people doing all kinds of things. Once you see the big picture, however, you have to step back and look at the parts. In looking at a picture, you may recognize things as a whole, but you have to then look at the particulars. That's how I learned about the PDS.

PULLING IT ALL TOGETHER

This chapter has introduced stories of transformation. Each of these stories begins with individuals or groups embracing one of the goals—collaboration, reform in teacher education, professional development, or research—only to find that goal spill over into others. This gradual integration—the capacity to see all of our purposes as related—is characteristic of a kind of development that has happened repeatedly, if not universally, in our PDS.

The fact that we can document this movement in some of our members and not in others, however, leaves us with two important questions: (1) Why do we not see more of this kind of transformative change in our PDS? and (2) What comes next for those who have undergone these changes? Mike Thomas, a half-time clinical educator for two years and a full-time clinical educator for three more years, writes about these two questions.

Mike: We have thought and talked a lot about these questions over the last couple of years and have arrived at some tentative answers. We see at least two categories of answers to the first question—Why do we not see more of this kind of transformational change in our PDS? One deals with how this kind of change is perceived from the outside, and the other with the influences that provoke and support this kind of movement.

With respect to the first category, it is important to understand that this kind of transformative change may not look terribly attractive from the outside. As people grow to see themselves differently, their relationships with everything and everyone also change. In many cases, these changes are perceived as a loss. From the outside, the question becomes: Is a more complicated and equivocal life a better one? Is being authentic really more important than getting along? Are the changes I see in this person changes that I want to accept? These are all valid and important questions, and all of them make the prospect of change a daunting one.

The second set of ideas focus on the actual process or context of change. The people represented in this chapter all found themselves in somewhat unusual positions. They were both embroiled in difficult circumstances (a demanding master's program, co-teaching a university course, or loosely defined clinical educator role) and also provided space and supportive relationships to deal with these circumstances. None of these people set out to change themselves. Instead they engaged questions of purpose that put past understandings at risk. They found themselves in circumstances that would not allow them to remain who they were. Most of us do not willingly enter into such ambiguous territory. In the case of these educators, it was the attraction of new understandings and the support of similarly engaged colleagues that outweighed the fear and anxiety. Other members of our PDS have either not been given the opportunity to step into such circumstances, or they have chosen not to take this difficult step. This kind of change cannot be done alone, but each person must make an independent decision to begin this journey.

What comes next? The forecast is no more certain. What we know about developmental processes is that while each movement provides new perspectives and new possibilities for action, each also presents problems and challenges of which we were not previously aware. This is the double-edged sword of development; no vantage point solves all problems or resolves all conflicts. Each new place to stand leaves us knowing more, but also knowing more about the inadequacy of all individual perspectives. Paths toward enlightenment that once seemed straightforward and finite are revealed as convoluted and equivocal. But oddly enough, what appears on the outside to be frustrating is in fact a movement toward peace. By seeing the world as complicated and equivocal, we are gifted with tolerance, patience, and acceptance. The truth is not out there. It is who we are in whatever circumstances we may find ourselves.

CONCLUSION

The story of our PDS is one of change and integration. We began our collaborative work together with a set of separate goals (school/university collaboration, reform in teacher education and urban education, professional development, and inquiry) initially imposed from the college's association with the Holmes Group and its teacher reform initiatives. Nevertheless, these included enough shared interests to form the foundation of our project.

It was not until we had worked together for some time that we could see the influence that each of our separate goals was having on each other. Slowly we began to realize that working collaboratively (our initial goal) was influencing how we structured our classrooms (professional development goal). Inquiry on collaboration (research goal) helped us to think about ways to make our relationship with students more collaborative (professional development goal). Working with interns (teacher education reform goal) pushed us to think about our own teaching (professional development goal). As Lisa said earlier, she bought into one goal (research), and got the other three free. As a group, we bought into four goals and the collective takeover was free. We got more than we initially bargained for or expected.

A web of relationships among our initial goals has helped us to see the connected nature of our work. Before PDS, teachers supervised student teachers for the university, went to workshops and university courses to get "professionally developed," and considered research as the job of university professors. In the PDS, everything is collaborative and these once separate activities feed our growth as we actively work to influence the future of education and its future teachers. Our integrated goals now shape some shared attitudes that form an integrated whole within which we talk and question ourselves as we work together.

REFERENCES

Clark, R. (1988). School-university relations: An interpretive review. In K. A. Sirotnik & J. I. Goodlad (Eds.), *School-university partnerships in action: Concepts, cases and concerns*. New York: Teachers College Press.

Drabble, M. (1969). *The waterfall*. New York: Alfred A. Knopf.

Holmes Group. (1990). *Tomorrow's schools: Principles for the design of professional development schools*. East Lansing, MI: Author.

Hord, S. (1986). A synthesis of research on organizational collaboration. *Educational Leadership, 43*(5), 22–26.

Oakes, J., Hare, S. E., & Sirotnik, K. A. (1986). Collaborative inquiry: A congenial paradigm in a cantankerous world. *Teachers College Record, 87*, 545–561.

CHAPTER 6

Middle School PDS:
Moving Beyond the Canvas

Patti Brosnan, Diana Erchick, and Holly Thornton

Chapter 6 tells a story of the evolution of how the middle school concept was implemented in one school. The learnings from this one intensive student-driven curriculum project were then shared with an additional seven schools and forty-four teachers. The question that drove our inquiry was, would the redefinition of middle school teacher and student roles result in positive substantive reform? A metaphor of teacher as artist and students as paints is used throughout to provide the reader an expression of the feelings of passion that permeated this project.

If one accepts the idea that the necessity of role admits students as legitimate participants in the process, then reform efforts tend to violate every proposition for successful change with respect to young people.

—Corbett and Wilson

Too big, too small, too much, too little, who am I? Where am I? Why am I here? What do I intend to do in life? What is important to me? Where do I fit in? These are concerns and questions that both early adolescents suffering from the "terrible toos" and middle grades institutions have in common. As awkward as a 13-year-old, the middle school struggles with its own identity crisis. Am I a little high school? Am I an elementary school with class changes? Am I student-centered? Am I

109

content-centered? Where do I belong? How do I fit in?

To address the unique needs of early adolescents and the varied differences in philosophies between elementary, middle, and high school cultures, as middle school advocates, we gathered together in a PDS.

This chapter begins with a description of the prehistory of our Middle School Network PDS. It also describes the inception and development of the PDS, as well as the PDS's subsequent <re>formation. The Middle School Network PDS is rooted in the Middle School concept found in the middle school literature over the past 100 years. Here is our story.

TRADITIONAL SCHOOLING:
WHAT'S WRONG WITH THIS PICTURE?

Typically, in middle school, teaching issues center around control. Maintaining behavior and achieving academic order are primary goals. Bells ring and students and teachers move obediently to them; those resistant suffer from the consequences of tardiness. The students work quietly, saving their socializing for after/outside school. Schedules tell everyone what to teach and learn at what time. Time periods are claimed for specific curricular areas, and boundaries around those periods are rigid. Curriculum guides tell teachers and parents what is to be taught. Tests tell what has been learned.

As partners in this PDS, we wanted to know how better to support student needs in a middle school environment. We saw this as a support to help us move away from rigidity and a move toward intellectual and social freedom. For us, liberatory education was a viable means toward this end.

Tradition as Teachers

We found that our experiences in middle school reform parallel those of many artists. For us, the goal of the teacher as artist is to create art, and she/he is attempting to do so within the confines/expectations of the art community. The community has an established outlook regarding the meaning of art, and a belief about how the process of creation is correctly carried out.

We think here about the teacher. *An artist sets out her tray of paints, each neatly isolated in its own space, sitting, waiting, hoping that she will dip her brush into them. They wait for her to bring them meaning and life. She dips the brush in, careful not to drip, careful not to let the colors mix. Order is the epitome of good management. She controls the movement of the brush as she carefully fills in the lines. Who designed the project does not matter, as long as her painting comes out, like all of the others who used the same kit. Her work is to do, not to question. She and the paints must conform to the will of the expectations of the kit.*

Tradition as Students

The middle school student knows that it is not simply the two-year-old who experiences the restrictions of adult control. It is the school-aged child who is voiceless, and who is reminded, "You will do what you are told because you are the child." It is the quiet student who is the good student, and when the complicit student emerges with learning that looks, acts, and talks like a well-educated student, then everyone knows that she or he has learned well.

As the students wait in their isolated seats and rows, *the individual bottles neatly arranged in the paint tray set up below the cardboard canvas,* they do not get to move outside of their space. *They do not have the opportunity to mix with other colors, to have a turn at controlling and directing the brush. They see not the picture, but only the brush dipping down from on high, casting a shadow over them, bending them to its will, directing them to their spaces within the lines, lines not only determined by others, but confined by a frame,* a curriculum that limits the scope and shape of the work. *Some paints are seen as the* ugly *colors, they are used rarely if at* all, children who wait to become a part of the painting. As they wait, they begin to *dry and harden.* Over time they can no longer be reached or made useful.

Tradition as Teacher Educators

When reform comes along in education. It is expected to produce higher-achieving and thus better-prepared teachers; teachers equipped to contribute to the needs of society and to function within the system. The goals of reform become production and efficiency. Teacher preparation programs, obliged by the perceived needs/demands of society, participate in reformation plans to produce and place interns in re-formed schools. Our middle school PDS, too, participated by accepting interns in their school.

The teacher educator readies her classroom for her new interns. *She places a tripod at every station mounted by a cardboard template readied with the training sketch.* As the interns enter the class, *the master painter hands each a new brush and assigns them a tray of paints.* As class begins, the familiar opening remark is made, *"Today you will learn to paint within the lines of the sketch."* The enthusiastic novices listen *carefully while they follow their instructions to the letter making sure to*

stay between the lines while painting the picture that the painter chose.
During the interns' experience in the PDS classroom, they take numerous courses at the university. The interns study curriculum and how to choose the best kits. They also study teaching, concentrating often on issues of control, *learning how to handle the brush. The interns learn, too, about children. They learn to identify the brightest paints, the most reliable, those that should be placed first according to the numbers. They learn about the paints that are the most difficult as well as those that work well. The interns learn how to manage the drips and errors, to scrape, remove, whitewash, and make invisible. They also learn how to close out, seal away, cover, snap the cap over, or dry out the paints they cannot control.*

THE NEED FOR CHANGE

The state department of education in Ohio mandated all school districts to write curricula at all levels in compliance with the state model curriculum developed from recommendations from national professional organizations. This mandate occurred after the state proficiency tests showed very poor achievement results. As school district personnel scurried to make necessary changes, our collective discussions revealed many concerns at the middle school level.

The Need for Change: Students

As adolescents work to develop self-esteem and negotiate peer pressures, they need opportunities to explore, to experiment, to make mistakes, and to succeed at defining themselves.

Some adolescents, often the ugly ones, tire of waiting for opportunities to become themselves. In the classroom, they tire of waiting to contribute to the discussion. They want to see the picture, to change it, to own it. But more than this, they want the teacher not to move them, but to move with them. Experience, however, has taught these students that this will not happen. *The picture will remain unchanged.* Some students resist. They disrupt the culture. *They drip onto the tray, into other colors waiting there, and across the neatly defined lines of what is a predefined drawing.*

The Need for Change: Teachers

Prior to forming a partnership, our PDS teachers felt controlled by the educational system. The old ways, the teachers had been told by reform agents at the top, are not effective. There are re-formed ways to teach, ways that effectively make the children into what they are supposed to be. The teachers are needed in these reform efforts; *after all it is they who do the painting.* They are needed to enforce the changes; they are needed in their complicity.

The teachers are rewarded for complicity, recognized for skills in fulfilling the administrators' mandates. Their students become the successful products they are meant to be. They know the right answers to the test questions; they pass the tests. *They paint in the right spaces with the right colors.*

The Need for Change: <Re>forming Reform

The artist approached a still flat, untextured, white canvas, a canvas with the same predetermined dimensions, but now without the lines. The tripod, including administrators, art gallery personnel, brokers, and critics all knew what was best for the artist and the paints. They knew what needed to be painted, what size and shape the canvas had to take. They knew the limitations of the artist and the paints in creating art.

They recommended taking away and using a different brush, one that is thicker, wider, one that can accomplish more at once. Recommended re-formed techniques included wider, thicker brushes, that integrated curriculum, applied alternative assessment techniques, and implemented individualized or computer-assisted instruction in open classrooms. *Artists used less time to paint more space, the essence of progress, efficiency. Some considered making even more radical changes, intermixing wide and thin brushes, perhaps using a sponge.* Even though these changes are viewed as significant differences in the methods of the art of teaching, there is more to reform than merely using another type of brush.

When the Middle School Network PDS began, teacher and university participants had been trying some popular reform ideas. The university experts supported this path toward a better product, *a better work of art.* For the participating teachers, teaching and learning had taken on a new, re-formed definition through a new process. (New to them, but familiar to the middle school reform literature.) They had gone to bigger brushes and broader strokes, and had already decided, after many earlier reform efforts that nothing substantive really changed.

The Need for Change: The "Experts"

The teachers, university deans, and faculty regularly attend annual *art shows, gallery hops,* and education conferences. After one year's hop, the dean discussed with her faculty the similarity between and among all the art in the shows. They discussed how much of what was being produced in schools was no longer needed in society. *Even though some of the paintings were treasured and hung in family rooms, others were placed in attics, garages, and basements or were simply thrown away. The artists felt that the work was too valuable and too important to end up devalued or invisible, too important to be flat and lifeless and lost in sameness.*

So, in came the experts. It is the duty of university personnel to create new knowledge and to be leaders in educational change. *Firmly in hand are their packaged brush and sponge sets, with their step by step "new reformed painting" kits. They realize that they still hold the brushes and all is well. There is some comfort as they teach others how to paint in the new ways. Of course it is a new and improved painting process and technique.* But it is still a method. *The brushes are different, the process is new, but the products as usual, all look the same.*

MOVING BEYOND TRADITION

When it became apparent that the products still had not yet changed, the university dean (Nancy Zimpher) requested *a collaborative re-viewing of community art submitted by area schools. This new show included not only displays but also proposals for change. The invitation drew small groups of participants who had shared beliefs, experience, expertise, and vision for what art could be.*

At the *art show* and proposal review, a dynamic exchange between school and university faculty revealed areas of common concern. This is where Holly Thornton, a middle-grades language arts teacher, and Patti Brosnan, a professor of mathematics education, discovered their mutual beliefs and philosophies regarding middle school education. This convergence became the underlying strength of our PDS.

Together we began to talk to the teachers on Holly's middle school team. They were discouraged about the unchanging nature of their work, even in the midst of reform. More importantly, they began to wonder about the paints. Their concerns were lulled by a sense of security and control that the experts gave them. But still nothing really changed. *The surface, the fabric, and the frame have changed little. The product, and the roles of those creating it, are essentially the same.*

Holly's middle school team identified the sameness and the lack of student-centeredness as what was making them uncomfortable. That was when we decided that the focus must be on the paints, not the brush, not the canvas, not the painting, but the paints. It was within this context that the one team of teachers (Holly Thornton–language arts, Laura Lindsey–math/science, and Phil Cordea–social studies), their principal (Doug Gillum), and university participants (Patti Brosnan–mathematics education and Diana Erchick–doctoral student in mathematics education) formed their PDS partnership.

The First Year

To move beyond tradition requires creative thinking not bound by current structures. James Beane's book, *From Rhetoric to Reality* (1986) was the source for the conceptualization of substantive change. Time together reading and discussing books and articles about change helped us to plan a student-centered program. Our PDS plans were informed by theory, best practice, and a research-grounded knowledge base. It is, however, still the actions of the teacher and ultimately the interactions of the teachers and students that define learning in each classroom.

As the artists reflected on their work, they wondered about the paints, paints still sitting in their isolated spaces. The artists proposed using a pallet instead of a tray of bottles. On the pallet the colors can see that there are other colors like them as well as many more that are different. They can see up into the picture being painted, to see where they are heading in the picture, how they might become part of it, how they might self-control, flow, and make themselves fit. They begin to ooze about on the pallet, intermingling at the edges.

Change is scary even for risk-takers. Change takes time, courage, integrity, and commitment. The first year of the Middle School PDS was a time for tending to reading, searching, planning, and <en>visioning. All participants committed themselves to collaboration. School faculty committed to implementing group ideas; university faculty committed to supporting the implementation of new strategies and providing opportunities for professional development; the administrator committed fiscal and administrative support; and graduate students agreed to serve as human resources.

Having a common philosophy was the lifeline of this partnership. We agreed that providing students with opportunities to define their own learning path was simply the right thing to do. We knew that trying to recreate a middle school using guidelines suggested by middle school literature, including Beane's book (1986), would require lots of trial and error.

The artists/teachers knew how different and problematic this all could be. Where would there be order? Too much change at once is overwhelming. *What to do with these new intermingled shades and colors? Should it be controlled somehow? If the painting becomes too different, the risk may be too great. Would the artist return to the tray and bottles of paints or would they persist?*

The Second Year

The second year of our PDS was one of implementation. Our PDS was a single team of teachers led by Holly Thornton who pioneered the student-driven integrated curriculum project. For this project to be successful, teachers had to relinquish control of the classroom. Students were empowered by playing an active role in making decisions regarding what they would study and how they would structure their time.

"Who are you?" "Why are you here?" "What is important to you in life?" What is interesting is that not only did these middle schoolers discuss what was important to them, but they somehow felt as though they would be able to do something about it. They were concerned about big issues such as the environment, apartheid, racism, sexism, classism, starvation, and other things that were wrong with the world.

During this year, the three teacher participants adhered to the "new" ideas until it came time for the annual achievement tests. To prevail in achieving lasting reform, one must persist even in the eye of a storm.

Using the pallet leads to a fear of a loss of direction, a loss of control over the painting. The artist grasps the brushes even more firmly to make certain the paint doesn't take over too much control. She pushes them harder on the canvas, upsetting the old balance. The tripod begins to tip, its support is questioned.

Our teachers struggled with how to assess more open-ended projects. The teachers changed their assessment procedures with state department permission, giving grades of P for Proficient and I for In Progress. The students faced less fear of failure by being given an opportunity to re-work their own projects. Teachers became facilitators, advisors, and peer learners rather than controllers. The "A" students were angry at the system. They wanted more "A"s. However, they gained respect for their previously less-successful peers. The less successful students were able to shine. Students started respecting each other for their different intelligences rather than for what they received on tests.

The benefits included not being judged by letter grades, having a voice in what and how they learned, deciding how to use time in meaningful ways, experiencing curriculum thematically rather than in separate pieces, and developing individual student-conducted parent conferences. During these conferences the students explained what they learned, why they learned it, and how they went about learning. Many said that they felt they had the power to help make the world a better place.

As part of the reform, we placed teams of interns with teams of middle school teachers. Using the same philosophy with the interns, they learned what liberatory education was all about and how different things could be for middle school students when provided the opportunity.

To promote the professional development component of our PDS, we wanted teachers to participate in critical thinking and liberatory education for themselves. Results showed that the participating students made gains toward becoming independent learners, problem solvers, and critical thinkers. Teachers felt more comfortable with their role as facilitator because of how the students performed.

The Third Year and Beyond

The network evolved out of the successes of our pilot middle school team. Because things were progressing well, we extended an open invitation to other middle schools and immediately added seven schools and 44 teachers to our middle school PDS now named the Middle School Network PDS. The added participants benefitted greatly from our learnings. Our university supervisors and cooperating teachers worked with 24 interns each year placed with teams of teachers. Our PDS intern graduates were hired at a faster rate than those interns not placed in our PDS, for having such a rich experience.

RESISTANCES/RESOLUTIONS

Since successes did not occur immediately, some nonparticipating school colleagues criticized the participating teachers for working so hard for no obvious benefit; they scoffed at the student-driven curriculum. They thought that the district curriculum would never be covered. As it turned out, that negative speculation was laid to rest when the end-of-the-year curricular inventories showed that not only did they "cover" the curriculum, they surpassed its boundaries. Because the students were pursuing their own lines of inquiry, their questioning often led to learnings well beyond tradition.

After the first couple of years, some of art work in the local showing was noticed and talked about. They were the pieces that were found in the midst of the more conventional showings. They didn't look like the rest. These were surreal, abstract, different in substance and in the techniques used to produce them. Some artists, critics, and art dealers looked at them with confusion or disdain, wondering how to critique them, asking what the works were supposed to be. "Do you call that art?"

Monthly meetings and annual retreats across the 6 years of our partnership served as vehicles for the participants to remain a critical mass to draw from the confidence within the group to generate renewed energies to continue the great fight. Partners remained as critical friends to ensure continuing risk taking and reform.

During years three, four, and five, Holly Thornton, Diana Erchick, and Patti Brosnan co-designed and co-instructed summer and yearlong courses for the newly recruited teachers from all the schools now participating in our PDS. Because of the great successes by our middle school students, graduate students from the university were intrigued and wanted to study the student-centered curriculum phenomenon. Three dissertations were completed during years three, four, and five by Kay Martin, David Erickson, and Holly Thornton respectively. Grants were written, interns were placed, and many "outsiders" visited our original site to see what middle school could be when students and teachers redefined their roles.

Progress was not always smooth; reform seemed to hit its limit at times. Some of the new sites did not realize some of the benefits because there were barriers such as the organization of the school or the structure of the schedule. Some in our new sites did not believe that their students could take responsibility in their own learning. Neither did they believe that in-class decision making should be shared. For these resistant teachers, under the current constraints of school, the students remained in traditional student roles.

STUDENT ROLE REDEFINITION

Student role redefinition is central to our school change efforts. The issue for students is not whether they know how to do what they are expected to do, but whether what they are expected to do is appropriate and a valuable aspect of being who they are as people. This redefinition of student role allows us to share the change process with students, to establish new relationships, to change together, to move beyond the canvas that used to confine/define our thoughts and actions.

The artists began to take more risks with their paints. In their studios, the colors were allowed to freely intermix, to blend, to create new colors together that did not exist before. The artist let the colors run together on the canvas, to blur the boundaries, to erase and challenge them. The paints began to control the decisions along with the artist. The artists let the paint create, become something that was not there before. Layers, textures, subtle blendings, bold new shapes, colors and feelings began to emerge. The paintings took on meaning and depth as the colors created it and brought it to life. The artist became more excited and more involved in her/his work. The paints splashed about and moved across the canvas. The activity and intensity began to shake the tripod. More support was needed or all would come to an abrupt and messy end.

Once these previously-perceived-as-ugly colors were provided an opportunity to show their true color, they shined. These colors were able to open doors to new ways of thinking and viewing art, to ways of creating new colors, brighter, braver, and deeper. The other colors took note and wanted to be a part of what could be and were pleasantly surprised that so much good could come from the unexpected.

BEYOND THE CANVAS

In our PDS, we wanted our students to feel that they are accepted for who they are without conditions and reservations. It is this intimate level of relationship, that may be a key missing ingredient in moving beyond our current limitations in school change. The student/teacher relationship that is generally characterized as one of a quest for teacher approval should be replaced by one of mutual acceptance, an acceptance that includes an unconditional positive regard for the learner that enables the learner to drop defenses and open up to possibilities. Students need opportunities in risk-taking and venturing into the uncertainties of change and growth, of authentic learning, as opposed to "doing school." However, the system continues to contain barriers to a practice that matches our beliefs. Some barriers are structural; others are grounded deep within ourselves.

By re-thinking our roles, the classroom became a different place. Students and teachers question together, think together, and work together toward understanding and changing what is. The acquisition of knowledge and skills takes on new meaning, far beyond memorization and application. An ethos of caring about others' feelings, ideas and beliefs fosters appreciation of difference and opportunities to think and grapple with issues in an atmosphere of trust. Difference, controversy, and conflict are embraced as positive, as a means to broaden thinking and deepen understanding. Anything becomes possible.

Now, the free spirit paints can come to life, they can be set free by the artist to jump off the palette, mingle with other paints, make new colors, add texture, add a new dimension, or even take on new art forms. They can go with the flow, become what they want to become. They can get what they want out of life, and make what they want of their world. They can become an active part of their world. They do not have to stay within the lines, or be like everyone else. Never again will they harden, dry up, or be used up. They are now free.

EPILOGUE

Sustaining a PDS as was originally envisioned is nearly impossible. The only consistency in education is change. The Middle School Network PDS experienced two major changes during and at the end of its six-year tenure. The first major change was in year two when the student-driven curriculum was first implemented. This change was not only exciting but it changed the school culture to something that built community between and among all involved. Change occurs constantly, but changes happen quickly when PDS leadership changes. This occurred at the end of the six-year stint when Holly Thornton completed her PhD and took a university position elsewhere as did Diana Erchick. Patti Brosnan was recruited by the dean to work on a different project and handed the middle school gavel over to a new faculty member. Though the Middle School Network PDS still exists, the clientele has experienced almost 100% turnover and has re-conceptualized itself as defined by the new membership.

For those of us who placed our hearts and souls into this project, questions remain such as, What will happen to all of our innovations? What will be the residuals? Will there be regression back to the traditional ways? Are there any regrets? But wait. The paintings are still here, and yes, the paints, the paints will last a lifetime . . .

REFERENCE

Beane, J. (1986). *A middle school curriculum: From rhetoric to reality.* Columbus, OH: National Middle School Association.

PART III

Secondary PDSs

CHAPTER 7

After the Honeymoon Is Over: What Eight Years of Collaboration Have Taught Us About School/University Collaboration in Social Studies and Global Education

Sue Chase and Merry Merryfield

Can university professors and experienced teachers work together to integrate theory and practice in social studies teacher education programs? In this article a classroom teacher and university professor analyze what they have learned through 8 years of school/university collaboration in the preparation of preservice teachers, the professional development of experienced teachers, and the process of working together. The authors also speak directly to teachers and professors about issues that need to be considered in long-term school/university collaboration in social studies and global education.

Before PDS:

> The problem with the methods classes is that they're too much theory. They didn't prepare me for actual teaching in Columbus schools. And my cooperating teacher just laughed when he saw the unit plan I got an "A" on in methods. He said that's just for the ivory tower, because real social studies teachers don't teach like that. (Evaluative comments from a student teacher, March 1989)

After PDS:

> PDS methods was at times overwhelming, but the seminars and school experiences really prepared me to teach. The different methods and

handouts from the field professors and Merry during seminars were very helpful, and I had support when I tried them out during methods and student teaching. I think the best part of PDS is spending two quarters actually learning from teaching real kids. (Evaluative comments from a student teacher, March 1994)

Our goal in writing this chapter is to share what we have learned about the process of developing and nurturing school-university collaboration in the preparation of preservice teachers and the professional development of practicing teachers. In this paper we bring together our perspectives as a field professor (Sue Chase) and a university professor (Merry Merryfield) in an examination of school/university efforts to improve teacher education.

THE DEVELOPMENT OF OUR PDS NETWORK

Our PDS network grew from teacher/professor relationships that began during 1988–90 through several overlapping school/university connections. First, problems with student teachers and one university supervisor led to ongoing conversations between Merry and Keith Bossard (Columbus Alternative High School), about problems in the Ohio State program and possibilities for improvement. Second, several relationships developed through school-based research projects on teacher decision-making in global education as Jim Norris and Connie White (Linden McKinley High School), Shirley Hoover (Upper Arlington High School), and Steve Shapiro (Reynoldsburg High School) shared perspectives with Merry on teaching and learning one day a week over an entire school year. Third, Bob Rayburn (Eastland Career Center), Barbara Wainer (Independence High School), and Merry got to know each other through course work in Ohio State's graduate program in global education, school district inservice presentations, and our local social studies council. Finally, Merry and Sue became friends through a mutual colleague, Jeff Cornett, who had worked with Sue extensively during his doctoral program at Ohio State. Some of us had been active in global education since the early *Columbus and the World* (Alger, 1975; Alger & Harf, 1986) curriculum projects of the Mershon Center in the 1970s. Others of us had studied the theory and practice of global education through the work of Lee Anderson (1979), Robert Hanvey (1975), Willard Kniep (1986), and Angene Wilson (1982, 1983).

In a brainstorming session at Merry's home in 1991 we agreed on the problems that needed to be addressed: (1) the relation between courses on campus and the realities of the schools, (2) the need for reflective teacher education that prepares teachers for cross-cultural teaching and learning with multicultural and global content, and (3) the lack of time and support to change our institutional structures, reward systems, and roles. We recognized that intensive, long-term school/university collaboration was absolutely essential.

We began to meet more formally to plan how to improve preservice teacher education. We became a team of seven teachers and one professor as we worked together to develop new goals for preservice teacher education that were driven by the knowledge and skills that we collectively viewed as essential for beginning teachers. We planned a new field-based methods course that would focus on teacher reflection and exemplary practice in social studies and global education. We spent a considerable amount of time developing 20 team-taught seminars on methods such as cooperative learning, group research projects, simulations and role-playing, decision-making strategies, and approaches to teaching controversial issues and multiple perspectives. We also addressed skills in cross-cultural interaction and higher-level thinking skills. We began to design assessment tools such as rubrics, reflective journals, portfolios, and teacher-written cases (Shulman & Colbert, 1988).

Our preservice teachers are required to have field experiences in several school settings before entering the methods classes. We decided, however, that they should be placed in the same schools for methods and student teaching to provide high-quality mentoring and continuity in their knowledge of students and the school culture. We wanted our preservice teachers to think of themselves as teachers instead of college students and trained ourselves to use the term preservice teachers. We decided to use the term "field professor" for teachers who took on the new roles of designing programs and methods courses, team-teaching methods, mentoring the preservice teachers and researching the progress of the program and its participants.

We team taught our first field-based, four-credit-hour methods course during autumn quarter 1992. It met on Tuesdays and Thursdays after school for two hours. Each year since, we have extended and improved the methods courses and concurrent field experiences. In Autumn 1993 we added a new middle school component and new middle school field professors, Tim Dove (McCord Middle School, Worthington Schools). We also collapsed two separate methods courses into an eight-credit-hour methods "block" so that the preservice teachers could spend three hours every day teaching secondary students under the guidance of their field professor. We had learned our first year that the preservice teachers' learning increased dramatically when they began actual teaching as they learned methods. We have identified immersion in the same school culture during methods and student teaching to be a critical component in closing the gap between theory and practice. When preservice teachers begin to teach during the first week of methods and know that every lesson and unit plan they develop for the methods course will be actually taught to students under the supervision and assessment of the same teachers who are their methods instructors, they tackle significant issues in the relationships between teaching and learning.

In 1993 we also moved our seminars off-campus into the PDS schools and rotated from school to school to make it easier to include other teachers, administrators, and at times, even middle and high school students. We also began to offer annual workshops for all the practicing social studies teachers in PDS network schools. These professional development days are times for the sharing of interests and expertise across eight schools in six school districts. Principals have willingly provided substitutes for the teachers as part of their contribution to our PDS each year. Our professional development component has increasingly included presentations at professional meetings, articles about what we are learning (Levak, Merryfield & Wilson, 1993; Merryfield & White, 1996) and the development of our own instructional materials for preservice teachers (Shapiro & Merryfield, 1995).

In 1994 we added an additional two-credit-hour field experience to the eight-hour methods block so that the preservice teachers could spend another six clock hours each week with a second field professor in a different kind of school environment (urban/suburban, middle/high school). In 1996 we began to require that all preservice teachers participate in our PDS listserv, an electronic community of our graduates, other social studies teachers, and resource people.

LESSONS LEARNED ABOUT THE PREPARATION OF PRESERVICE TEACHERS

Over the years we have learned a number of lessons about the preparation of preservice teachers in social studies and global education. We have found that congruence, the modeling of competence, time, high expectations, reflection, and caring are critical factors in our preparation of preservice teachers.

Developing Congruence

A major strength of our PDS is the congruence between what our preservice teachers learn in the methods seminars, read about in articles and books, and see practiced day-to-day in their field experiences. Because the nine field professors and one university professor who teach methods are the same people who mentor and supervise the preservice teachers in their field experiences, there is no school/university chasm. When Jim Norris and Keith Bossard choose readings and demonstrate alternative approaches to cooperative learning in seminar, their ideas are reflected in the teaching methods that the preservice teachers see in other field professors' practice. When Barbara Wainer and Keith Bossard share different strategies they use to develop student research skills and manage students' inquiry projects, they explain how their choices are based upon their professional knowledge and experiences and their students' abilities, interests, and knowledge. They often get in a friendly debate about sequence or method or ways they assess student achievement. Preservice teachers are encouraged to explore other approaches to building students' research skills and managing projects through their own field professors and other teachers in their schools.

Modeling Competence

Perhaps the most important lesson learned is how important it is that classroom teachers and university professors, model the thinking, the teaching, and the learning of outstanding practitioners in social studies and global education. Modeling includes demonstration of attitudes, knowledge, skills, and participation in multicultural and global education. Most of our preservice teachers are White males (about 30% are female, about 5% African American or Asian American) from small towns in Ohio. Many have had very limited experience with people different from themselves, especially African Americans or people with limited English proficiency. Given these demographics, we must pay special attention to modeling behaviors that will help our preservice teachers learn about people different from themselves and work against prejudice and inequities over race, gender, and class. Most of us have extensive cross-cultural experiences, and we all share a commitment to diversity and equity.

Extending Time

We learned that one quarter of field experience in the same school is not enough. A major factor in the success of our PDS is the extensive experiences our preservice teachers have in getting to know their students and working with them from September through the end of March. We expect our preservice teachers to study the cultures of their classrooms and learn about each student as an individual. By the time they begin their full-time student teaching in early January, they have had several months of learning and teaching with their students and know them as individuals.

Expecting High Standards

We find that high expectations bring about a high quality of performance. We focus on the PDS methods block as the beginning of their careers as professionals, not just a college course to be taken for a grade. Although many preservice teachers are initially overwhelmed by the workload and responsibilities of their field professors, most rise to the occasion and greatly improve their interpersonal, organizational, and teaching skills and their content knowledge from one week to the next.

Unlike the years before PDS, most of our preservice teachers get beyond the survival stage of teaching and are able to use student teaching to expand upon their initial repertoire of teaching skills and look more deeply at the complexity of student learning. Based on mentoring experiences with first-year teachers, we find an overall maturity and reflectiveness in our PDS graduates that we rarely see in even experienced teachers. They think about the process of what it means to be a teacher.

Reflecting on Practice

Many of our preservice teachers come to us with a vision of social studies teaching as the lecture/discussion method of their own high school experiences or the lecture/recitation methods of their college professors. Reflection influences their thinking. We use multiple approaches to reflection to meet the needs of each individual. Journaling, constructing cases, seminars and small group discussions, portfolios, rubrics for self-assessment, conferences with field professors, and the writing of synthesizing essays are used to bring together what is learned in seminars, schools, and readings.

Caring

A central factor in our success with preservice teachers is caring—caring a great deal about our own middle and high school students and a shared concern that our program develops outstanding beginning teachers. Preservice teachers are given considerable individual attention every day, supported according to his/her individual needs. When a preservice teacher is not excelling, many people work with the preservice teacher. At times we have met as a group to develop interventions. The effects of our team approach in bringing about positive change in a preservice teacher's performance are similar to those effects of our interdisciplinary teams in improving the work of our middle and high school students.

LESSONS LEARNED

Long-term professional growth and the development of relationships among teachers across schools and districts are important benefits of our PDS collaboration. Our work together has allowed us to learn first-hand about many different approaches to improving schools and social studies. Two of our schools are members of the Coalition of Essential Schools, and one school has gone totally to double-blocking (all periods are two hours long and teachers have no more that 60 students a trimester). Four of our schools have social studies teachers teaming with teachers in language arts, science, math or art. One school is an English as a Second Language magnet school for Columbus. Eastland Career Center is the educational technology center for our county, and at Columbus Alternative High School all tenth, eleventh, and twelfth graders work one day a week off campus in service learning projects. Our schools have benefitted from our sharing of ideas, materials, and experiences and our construction of courses, seminars, and assessments. Our program research shows that the diversity of our teachers and schools, the development of new roles and opportunities, and changing of the status quo have contributed to the professional development of experienced teachers.

Creating New Roles and Opportunities

We are doing much of the supervision, mentoring, and the making of connections between educational theory and classroom practice that once were left to university supervisors. Now we, as field professors, are the university teachers in our schools. Our professional development includes presenting and writing about our PDS work. In the last eight years, we have made more than 30 professional presentations at state and national meetings. We did not know some of these organizations existed before PDS, and we have found new knowledge and networks through these meetings. In 1995–1996, we had a grant to write about what we have learned together (Dove, Norris & Shinew, 1997; Levak, Merryfield, & Wilson, 1993; Merryfield & White, 1996; Shapiro & Merryfield, 1995). In 1995, Steve Shapiro spent two months in Poland teaching Polish educators about school/university collaboration. In 1997, Steve, Barbara Wainer, and Tim Dove worked with eight Indonesian teacher educators to help them prepare for school/university collaborations at IKIP Bandung and IKIP Malang.

We developed several eight-hour workshops in consultation with our colleagues. Topics in the last workshop included the construction of rubrics for student assessment, a discussion of teacher-written cases of actual problems with preservice teachers, and our sharing and critiquing of new instructional materials in social studies and global education. The inservice workshops play a major role in creating a shared vision for the PDS and in providing a time and place for us to discuss concerns and learn together.

Challenging the Status Quo

We are the teachers of our preservice teachers and our responsibilities are to interact intensely with them about every aspect of teaching. We want them to question what we are doing. We want them to become reflective about their practice, and in the process of doing that, we are forced to look more closely at our own practice. This intense work with preservice teachers and extensive scrutiny of our own practice goes against the status quo, and some teachers are not comfortable with such challenges. PDS work exposes our own vulnerability. Just as not all college students are cut out to be preservice teachers, not all educators are able to work effectively with preservice teachers.

We have essentially had to "sell" PDS collaboration through its benefits to both preservice and practicing teachers. What we are advocating is a much higher level of professionalism and reflective practice for all. We are also promoting the concept of a "learning community" for teachers. Many teachers are used to working in virtual isolation, and we have to convince them that they will benefit from learning and sharing with others.

THE PROCESS OF SCHOOL/UNIVERSITY COLLABORATION

When we began our work together all of us had personal and professional commitments that filled our lives. PDS become an additional commitment that required time and energy. Consequently, we have learned to work together in a very efficient manner (as few meetings and as little paperwork as possible, well-defined responsibilities and time lines) with an understanding that although PDS is important, our families and our own students come first. Merry's role in coordinating and communicating across the nine sites has served as a glue to hold us together between meetings. A shared vision, a feeling of control and ownership by those who are doing the work, and tangible achievements are major elements in the success of our PDS Network. We are still working on the compensation, rewards, and recognition that must be in place for institutionalization of a professional development school.

Building Trust and a Shared Vision

The foundation for our work was laid in our early meetings through the development of mutual respect and trust, a growing commitment to creating a better way together, and a shared vision of our long-term goals (see Tim Dove's section in the book conclusion for a further discussion of these goals). When differences of opinion arise (and they always will), we try to learn from each other and resolve them in ways that are productive for our own professional growth. For example, we have spent considerable time trying to understand why some of us are more comfortable with portfolio assessment than are others, and how these differences in experiences and attitudes about assessment should play out in our work with preservice teachers.

"Growing Our Own": A Situated Approach

We believe in teachers and professors building school/university collaboration from the ground up to meet the needs of their particular contexts. Unlike many PDSs, we did not have a structure imposed by a university or by a school district. We began our collaboration to address some serious problems in the preservice program. Some of us have studied the literature on teacher education reform, the Holmes Group, and other professional development schools. Our strengths, however, come from our assumption that *the people who actually do the day-to-day work in a PDS should be the people who develop the goals, courses, and assessments.* We believe this "grow your own" approach situated within a specific context is essential, as long-term school/university collaboration is very difficult under the best of circumstances. Classroom teachers and university professors who create, experiment, and assess their own work feel ownership and responsibility for success.

Working Within Institutional Frameworks

However, a PDS that differs considerably from others at the same university may have problems with college support because of its unique character. We have experienced two major problems with our institutional framework. First, because our PDS originated and developed differently from all the other professional development schools associated with Ohio State, we did not receive formal recognition as a PDS until February 1995 and did not receive cash stipends for the field professors until the fall of 1995. Soft money grants from a private foundation paid the field professors $15,000 from the fall of 1993 through winter 1996. Ohio State's College of Education has provided fee waivers to the school districts as part of our exchange of services agreement, but fee waivers have little meaning to field professors who, for the most part, have many hours beyond their master's degrees. Currently our field professors are receiving cash stipends (approximately $15,000 divided among all the field professors who work with our social studies cohort each year). Although this sum is relatively small given the hours in planning meetings, teaching seminars, and working with preservice teachers, it is an important step in financial compensation.

The other problem is more complex and difficult to overcome. We as teachers have found meetings with some Ohio State professors and administrators to be frustrating, demeaning, unprofessional, and elitist. The conflicts arise because of conceptual and programmatic differences and are intensified when university professors and administrators say they know what is best for teachers. Our temporary solution is for Merry to take on the role of dealing with the Ohio State bureaucracy and meetings with other OSU PDSs at our request.

Coordinating the Network

Finally, a PDS network with many schools and school districts needs someone to coordinate activities and communication. Merry has served this role with help from field professors who offer their homes and schools for meetings and help out as needed in other tasks. We see the coordinator being responsible for finding times and places for us to meet, taking detailed notes and circulating them in memos after each meeting, and keeping our "archives" up to date. Our archives serve as a database, currently including every memo and letter written (to teachers, administrators, funders), each year's course documents, readings, and evaluations, notes from all brainstorming and planning sessions, focus groups, and debriefings, and copies of all presentations, papers, and published work.

IMPLICATIONS FOR TEACHERS AND PROFESSORS

In the "notes" that follow, Sue speaks to practicing teachers and Merry to social studies professors.

Sue's Notes to Classroom Teachers

I have been a classroom teacher for more than 30 years and involved with student teachers for a long time. There is no question in my mind that our PDS Network has vastly improved the preparation of preservice teachers. It has changed the perspective of preservice teachers because we have begun to bridge the gap between theory and practice. It has changed the perspectives of cooperating teachers because their practice is placed under much greater scrutiny and because they have been asked to take responsibility for the quality of the preservice experience. Maintaining the high standards that we have set and working cooperatively across several school districts requires much time and effort. In this section I outline my ideas about the factors that have influenced my colleagues and me in our work with the PDS Network and discuss some considerations for teachers who are thinking of becoming involved with PDS work.

Opening your practice to scrutiny and discussion.   Classroom teachers should enter PDS relationships because they want to grow as professionals and believe they have something to contribute to the profession. The opportunities for growth have been considerable as we have become professors of a college methods class. We have presented at state and national conferences and published our work in books and journals. We have opened our instructional decision making and classroom practice to the intense scrutiny of preservice teachers and colleagues in our building and five other school districts. Do you want to learn from the practice of others and be part of a learning community that values reflective practice? Do you have the confidence to explain your practice not only to preservice teachers but also in seminars with some of the best teachers in your community?

Making a time commitment.   It takes many full-day sessions and after school meetings for a diverse group of teachers to plan a college methods class, and many afternoons are spent in teaching and assessing it. Each teacher has determined an area of "expertise," chosen readings and assignments for those topics, and prepared two-hour seminars for the preservice teachers. Because we work collaboratively, we have spent time with other teachers deciding what and how it would be taught.

Much more time is spent daily with our preservice teachers as we reflect with them about our practice and their practice. We observe and debrief after lessons are presented. We spend time showing them how we plan, grade, develop ideas, manage our classes, and share every possible experience that can expose them to the realities of teaching. Are you willing to spend that kind of time in planning and teaching? Are you willing to stay in the classroom when your preservice teacher is teaching and accept a serious mentoring role?

The most significant time commitment may be over the long term. PDS work is not something that can be accomplished in a year and then dropped when the novelty wears off. We have changed social studies teacher education at The Ohio State University because we have improved and refined our work over several years. PDS means long term, intense relationships with other teachers and university professors. When we began our intensive planning in 1992, Merry asked us for a three-year commitment. Could you make a three- or five-year commitment to a PDS?

Collaborating across schools, districts, and the university.   An important component of the structural change in our PDS has been our willingness to work across several different school cultures. For me this has been both the most challenging and among the most rewarding parts of our PDS. The social studies departments of the nine schools in six different districts operate differently. We have learned to appreciate each other's contexts and provide some flexibility in our methods course and student teaching in order to provide similar assignments and assessments for our preservice teachers.

For example, one of our assignments calls for the creation and teaching of a unit plan. In traditional school structures a unit plan usually means a one to four week plan of 45–55 minute lessons each day. But some of us are in settings where we teach each class two hours every day and complete a year's course in one semester. Others of us are part of interdisciplinary teams with flexible scheduling determined by a team, not a single teacher. Others are in schools with long (6–8 week) units that culminate in exhibitions or other authentic assessments. Do you want to work within a multischool environment? Can you adjust to a number of different types of structures and different demands? Will you appreciate differences as well as similarities in social studies programs? Can you overcome the tendency to think you or your school has the one "right" way to do something?

In PDS work we not only work across schools but we also work with the university. For many of the field professors, one of the most challenging cultures we have had to adjust to has been the university environment. Although our own PDS work with Merry has been quite rewarding, we have had a number of negative experiences when we have interacted with other professors (associated with other College of Education PDSs) and Ohio State administrators. We have left several meetings feeling devalued as classroom teachers. Let me illustrate this point.

We are often treated like guests at meetings of all the OSU PDSs, "almost relegated to student status" according to some of my colleagues. We do not want to be treated as guests, visitors, or observers, but as team members with equal status in PDS discussions. Yet Ohio State administrators have not even put us on the roster. Recognition of our roles could be as simple as our names appearing in a faculty directory, access to faculty parking stickers, or having a place on campus to conduct our PDS business.

One field professor received a letter from the president of the university. He was pleased as he opened it up because he assumed it was to recognize his role as a field professor in the our PDS Network in Social Studies and Global Education. Alas, the letter was to thank him for his devoted service as an usher at Ohio State football games! This paradox (recognition for being an usher, no recognition for being a field professor who made a major contribution to building a superlative preservice teacher education program) illustrates our frustration with the lack of recognition.

A last illustration will show our frustration with the culture of university meetings with other PDS professors and college administrators. Along with another field professor and Merry, I attended an Ohio State meeting that was to serve as formative evaluation for all OSU PDSs. We were placed in groups of PDSs to share experiences and ideas with others who are working in similar contexts. Our group consisted of all the secondary level PDSs—Secondary English Education, Project TRI (focusing on school restructuring), and the Reynoldsburg PDS (focusing on Coalition of Essential School reforms). This meeting seemed like an excellent opportunity to share and learn from others. However, in our group the English Education professor began by apologizing for her need to attend another meeting and announced she would need to go first and leave. She hurried through her program description and left. Immediately the coordinator of Project TRI also noted she had to go out of town, spoke quickly, and left. This left my colleague, Merry, and me to "share" our experience with the two people who remained. The message I heard from these busy folks was the same—what you have to say isn't important. Are you prepared to deal with university culture? Can you handle the potential lack of respect from university people?

Rethinking roles and procedures within your school.   Entering into this new relationship with colleagues across school boundaries and the university also impacts our relationships with the members of our own department and our interdisciplinary teams. We have found different levels of enthusiasm from our fellow teachers. A few resent us for becoming "field professors," teaching a university course, and supervising preservice teachers. They see us as "showboaters." For a PDS program to work effectively, it needs broad-based support within each school, and each field professor needs the cooperation of colleagues.

In the past, many cooperating teachers opted for student teachers during spring quarter. Now there is no choice as PDS methods takes place autumn quarter and student teaching during winter quarter. One field professor said that a colleague chose not to participate in our PDS because "he only wanted a student teacher during spring quarter."

Changes in the structure and roles may cause some resentment among department members. Most field professors, who reported an initial lack of support from department members, have said that when their colleagues saw the improved quality of the student teachers, they wanted to become involved. One field professor commented, "Our teachers are more into it [working with preservice teachers]. . . . They want to do a better job. They used to think nobody really cared."

We are also asking more of cooperating teachers. They are expected to work extensively with their preservice teacher and get involved in portfolio and other alternative assessments. Preservice teachers are looking more closely at the practice of their cooperating teacher and probing deeply into the "whys" of teacher decision-making. This scrutiny has resulted in what a cooperating teacher said was "a good deal of soul searching and reflection." Are you willing to change your work with preservice teachers? Do you want to work with your colleagues so that they will contribute to PDS collaboration? Can you justify the additional demands that will be placed on your colleagues?

Through all the time and hard work, my PDS experience has been one of the most gratifying experiences of my professional life. In the very competitive world of social studies positions, my school has hired two of my PDS student teachers. I see everyone winning with this approach. We are truly bridging the gap between theory and practice. Social studies teachers can improve our profession through school/university collaboration. Stop criticizing teacher preparation programs and create a better one!

Merry's Notes to Professors of Social Studies

Although PDS has profoundly improved our program's preparation of our preservice teachers, and my collaboration and team-teaching with the field professors has been one of the most meaningful learning experiences of my career, I have come to believe that PDS is no panacea. Long-term collaboration between teachers and professors requires a special brand of cross-cultural learning and interaction that many college professors are unable or unwilling to embrace. Let me outline some ideas about the university professor's role that the field professors and I see as factors in our work.

Respecting teacher knowledge.   The university professor enters the PDS relationship recognizing that he or she has much to learn from teachers. Teachers have the authenticity of current practice because they are involved every day in the teaching of students and the cultures of school and community. Classroom teachers have perspectives, knowledge, skills, experiences, and personal theories that university professors rarely possess. Do you want to work with and learn from outstanding teachers? Do you recognize they have specialized knowledge that you may not possess? Will you value their knowledge as much as your own?

Trusting the group process.　In setting up school/university collaboration as in a methods course, the professor must trust the judgment of the teachers and share control and ownership of the course in equal status with the teachers. Initially the majority of the decisions will be in the hands of the teachers since a professor cannot ask teachers to help revise a course and then reject their ideas and expect "collaboration" to continue. Although I have always expressed my ideas and opinions freely, I am one voice among the nine of us, and as we work toward consensus no one person dominates our decision making. Are you willing to share control and ownership in your course or program? Are you willing to trust the judgment of the teachers and the process of group decision making?

Finding time and building interpersonal skills.　As with any long-term collaboration, PDS requires a significant time commitment, and it requires attention to building and nurturing cooperative interpersonal relationships. Setting goals, planning a course or inservice workshop, and developing assessments all need more time when a group of nine is working to consensus than when one professor works alone. Are you willing to take the time that is needed to work collaboratively with teachers? Are you able to develop long-term interpersonal relationships with teachers based on equality and collaboration so that they will want to continue to work with you?

Considering one's university context.　Professors also need to reflect on their career goals and the contexts in which they work as they consider PDS relationships. Such work may not be valued within a department, college, or university. When I was preparing my dossier for promotion and tenure a few years ago, no one could tell me where to put my PDS work. My department committee didn't see PDS work as "counting." Even in the college committee meeting (on how to prepare one's dossier) there was a notable lack of interest in what I saw as one of my major contributions to improving teacher education in our program. Just as with teachers, college professors are not necessarily rewarded for collaboration. Within our college, school, and section communities, many professors look down upon those of us who "work in the schools" as somehow not doing the work expected of university professors. Will your PDS work be valued by your colleagues and institution? How will the quality of compensation or rewards affect your interest or work in PDS?

Although PDS collaboration does require much time and work, we see our efforts pay off with every preservice teacher. Feedback from other teachers and principals has been 100% positive as the combination of better-prepared preservice teachers and professional development for inservice teachers has become evident. I find my own teaching has become more grounded in the language, worldviews, and personal theories of my field professor colleagues.

CONCLUSION

Dona Kagan (1993) has studied how high school social studies teachers and university methods professors perceive the gap between what is taught in methods courses and actual classroom teaching. She concludes that what is missing in teacher education is attention to teacher-student interactions. She quotes Jim, the high school social studies teacher, as she speaks about the importance of a teacher's personality, interpersonal skills, and commitment:

> Above all, it has to do with the sense that the teacher is there for the students . . . the rapport between a teacher and his or her students. It's an aspect of teaching virtually ignored by university course work. The university never teaches candidates about being sensitive and relating to pupils. (Kagan, 1993, p. 113)

The field professors not only provide real-life modeling of building rapport and developing interpersonal skills during field experiences, they also teach the preservice teachers why such connections are important during seminars and assessment sessions.

A PDS Network also affects the development of inservice teachers. Often teachers are resistant to "teacher education" that is perceived as coming from outside the school, from experts who are not "in the trenches." Ken and Barbara Tye (1992) have written of the difficulties of working with inservice teachers in global education when the teachers perceive teacher education as something that comes from the university, not the schools. When teachers in the school play dual roles—practicing teachers and teacher educators, there are new opportunities for all.

In closing we note that although our work together is not without problems, those of us who have created a PDS Network in Social Studies and Global Education cannot imagine ever again working with preservice teachers in isolation from a learning community.

NOTE

Sections from earlier versions of this chapter have been published in Chase & Merryfield, (1998) and Chase & Merryfield (1997).

REFERENCES

Alger, C. F., & Harf, J. E. (1986). Global education: Why? For whom? About what? In R. E. Freeman (Ed.), *Promising practices in global education: A handbook with case studies* (pp. 1–13). New York: National Council on Foreign Language and International Studies.

Alger, C. F. (1975). *Columbus and the world.* Columbus, OH: Mershon Center, The Ohio State University.

Anderson, L. (1979). *Schooling for citizenship in a global age: An exploration of the meaning and significance of global education.* Bloomington, IN: The Social Studies Development Center.

Chase, K. S., & Merryfield, M. M. (1998). How do secondary teachers benefit from PDS networks? Lessons from a social studies and global education learning community. *The Clearing House, 71*(4), 251–254.

Chase, K. S., & Merryfield, M. M. (1997). Bridging the gap between campus and school. *The Inside: Perspectives on PDS Work, 1*(1), 17–19.

Darling-Hammond, L. (Ed.). (1994). *Professional development schools: Schools for developing a profession.* New York: Teachers College Press.

Dove, T., Norris, J., & Shinew, D. (1997). Teachers' perspectives on school/university collaboration in global education. In M. M. Merryfield, E. Jarchow, & S. Pickert (Eds.), *Preparing teachers to teach global perspectives: A handbook for teacher educators.* Thousand Oaks, CA: Corwin Press.

Hanvey, R. G. (1975). *An attainable global perspective.* New York: Center for War/Peace Studies.

Kagan, D. M. (1993). *Laura and Jim and what they taught me about the gap between educational theory and practice.* Albany: State University of New York Press.

Kniep, W. M. (1986). Defining a global education by its content. *Social Education, 50*(6), 437–466.

Levak, B. A., Merryfield, M. M., & Wilson, R. C. (1993). Global connections. *Educational Leadership, 51*(1), 73–75.

Merryfield, M. M., and White, C. (1996). Issues-centered global education. In Ronald Evans & David Warren Saxe (Eds.), *Handbook on teaching social issues* (pp. 177–187). Washington DC: National Council for the Social Studies.

Shapiro, S., & Merryfield, M. M. (1995). A case study of unit planning in the context of school reform. In M. M. Merryfield & Richard C. Remy (Eds.), *Teaching about international conflict and peace* (pp. 41–123). Albany: State University of New York Press.

Shulman, J. H., & Colbert, J. A. (Eds). (1988). *The intern teacher casebook.* San Francisco: Far West Laboratory for Educational Research and Development.

Stoddart, T. (1995). The professional development school: Building bridges between cultures. In H. G. Petrie (Ed.), *Professionalization, partnership, and power: Building professional development schools* (pp. 41–76). Albany: State University of New York Press.

Tye, B. B., & Tye, K. A. (1992). *Global education. A study of school change.* Albany: State University of New York Press.

Wilson, A. (1982). Cross-cultural experiential learning for teachers. *Theory Into Practice, 21*(3), 184–192.

Wilson, A. (1983). A case study of two teachers with cross-cultural experience: They know more. *Educational Research Quarterly, 8*(1), 78–85.

CHAPTER 8

Perspectives on Personal Professional Development

Steven L. Miller, Stanley Ray, Tim Dove, and Todd Kenreich

In this chapter, a professor, two field professors, and a former intern write about their experience in the social studies PDS. There are three social studies PDSs with an Ohio State social studies faculty person and group of field professors for each one. They rotate taking responsibility for the two cohorts of MEd students each year giving one PDS a year away from working with students to concentrate on research and writing. The rotation of cohorts provides cycles of different emphasis within the larger social studies PDS Network. These cycles seem to be helpful for interns, teachers, and professors. While there is differentiation in these three PDS groups, there is also a lot of cross-fertilization. In this chapter all three PDSs are represented as they bring their different perspectives to issues of social studies teacher education and reform.

The late Woody Hayes wrote a book that takes its title from a famous quotation of his: *You Win with People.* It seems obvious that educational reform, both in schools and in teacher education programs at universities, can only be won by the people engaged in this challenge. For this reason, in this chapter the authors have chosen to focus on personal professional development as an outcome of the Socials Studies PDS.[1] As mentioned in the introduction, although each PDS enjoys a unique identity, we have some shared goals across PDSs. Among the three social studies PDSs, professional development is one such goal. We contend that PDS has helped us to grow professionally in ways that have improved teaching, both in schools and on the campus, as well as in the professional development of new teachers.

Four of us have written our respective sections to present different voices on professional development in each of our lives. In the first section, Stanley Ray, a high school teacher and field professor,[2] focuses on his teaching with prospective teachers and the mutual benefits to all parties. Tim Dove, a middle school field professor, writes about the impact of a university international collaborative experience on his teaching and PDS participation. The university faculty team member, Steven Miller, describes the influence of PDS on his professional growth. Finally, Todd Kenreich, a graduate of one of the early social studies PDS cohorts and now a doctoral student and teaching assistant, explains the value of PDS to his beginning professional career. He also offers a few suggestions for improving the program.

PERSONAL AND PROFESSIONAL GROWTH

Stanley Ray

In an attempt to solve the ills of our modern educational system, the media has chosen colleges of education as one source of difficulty. It has labeled universities as "ivory towers" where professors are out of touch with current trends and problems in the public schools. It has been suggested that professors of education need to spend more time in the public schools. What is not being reported is that many universities are undergoing a complete overhaul to respond to these very issues.

At The Ohio State University, the College of Education has established PDSs to bring preservice interns into the schools for more meaningful, first-hand experiences. Another way the Social Studies PDS differs from the traditional approach is the participation of middle and high school teachers in the university methods classes. This allows current classroom teachers to bring their expertise to the interns before they begin student teaching.

In fact, it is best to view the methods course in our PDS program as the first of two parts of the student teaching experience, rather than a separate course. The methods course exposes preservice teachers to teaching styles currently being used in the public schools, followed directly by the student teaching experience itself. The methods course includes daily, in-school work with middle and high school classes and a seminar component. Interns spend 15 hours each week with the teachers and classes in which they will student teach, putting into practice the ideas they learn in the methods seminars. During the seminars, field professors are responsible for presenting information and facilitating discussions over a variety of topics.

This provides a symbiotic relationship between the public school teacher (field professor or cooperating teacher) and university professors. Not only does the university benefit from the public school educator's knowledge and experience, but teachers achieve a level of professional development that was not previously available. By teaching others, the field professor is able to reflect on positive elements of teaching methodology. By collaborating with other practicing teachers, they have a variety of current teaching materials at their disposal.

The first meeting with interns is a learning experience for the field professor. It requires that both parties examine their teaching styles. Interns want to know *why* something is done in a classroom. They want to understand the rationale behind the practices of their mentor teacher. When the teacher's practice is scrutinized, he or she may find that the practice is out of date and needs to be changed. Often interns give their field professors new ideas to try. This reciprocity benefits both the university and public school participants.

Extremely valuable for the university and field professors is the communication of ideas from other professionals during the seminars. For example, a discussion may center on classroom management techniques. Teachers listening to a colleague's practices may benefit from hearing about these different approaches. During the course of the discussion, another field professor listening to the presentation may be able to add information to the speaker, benefiting presenter and audience alike.

Several of the seminar sessions feature the field professors in panel discussions that are invaluable to the teachers and students. Some panel discussions focus on classroom management, discipline, testing procedures, student profiles, and other facets of the classroom, some that are mundane, but necessary. In these classes, the field professors are both teachers and students. These panel discussions involve colleagues sharing common problems and solutions. Interns ask questions of the panel that promote reflection and further discussion.

Interns coming through the PDS program are usually older (since this is a postbaccalaureate program), and often have had more life experiences than pre-PDS student teachers. When these interns walk into their assigned schools, they bring with them the resources and knowledge that have been attained in the workplace, such as what skills employers are seeking. This has been especially valuable in the technology program in my school.

Another benefit of PDS for teachers is that the university serves as a source for many innovative teaching materials that can be used by the educational community. While the interns are participating in their methods classes, they are often the first to use these resources. In some cases public school teachers benefit from the PDS relationship by pilot teaching and editing new materials.

In the PDS, interns and mentor teachers are exposed to a multitude of teaching methodologies. They gain experience in cooperative learning techniques, multiple learning styles, simulations and gaming, literature-based education, and alternative assessment procedures. Typically, teachers go to inservice sessions for this kind of training. Through PDS, teachers learn these techniques and save the schools the cost of substitutes and registration fees. Field professors can clarify the techniques and help the interns understand when and how to use them. Both sides benefit.

Another benefit of PDS is enjoyed by the students in the public schools. Not only are they exposed to the latest teaching materials from the universities, they also have the support of more than one teacher in the classroom. At a time where student/teacher ratios approach 30–35 to 1, students can be given more individualized attention when field professors and interns engage in team teaching to improve instruction. There are times when the team teaching scenario allows the class to meet in two groups with adequate supervision to complete more involved lessons such as simulations and cooperative lessons.

The classroom teacher's day is a challenging one. He or she is an administrator, parent, colleague, teacher, and counselor. These multiple roles are difficult to balance without some type of support, but many find a way. Professional development sites provide the assistance that teachers need to engage in a long, rewarding career. It is fulfilling for students in schools, but there is a special benefit to educating future teachers. The knowledge that you are furthering your career by engaging in dialogue with your contemporaries makes the classroom teacher strive to create new experiences for their students, their intern, and themselves.

The universities are not out of touch with the public schools. They are creating an environment where they can share their resources with others and use existing talents to further the effectiveness of both schools and universities.

THE IMPORTANCE OF "N" IN PDSN

Tim Dove

When I became involved in a secondary social studies PDSN (Professional Development School Network), I anticipated being helpful in preparing preservice educators. I had no idea the extent that my own practice would improve, nor the degree to which my own professionalism would expand over the next seven years. As a classroom teacher, I was always interested in pushing the abilities of my middle school students. I agreed to take a public teaching position in a district that wanted team teaching and integration across different disciplines. I knew of no other strategy to better develop collegial relationships and question previous pedagogical strategies. I would work with three to five other teachers and we would plan our curriculum together. I wanted to be able to defend my strategies on a daily basis with these people.

After working with student teachers for 10 years from four different universities, my colleagues and I had many of the typical concerns about preservice education programs. Was the student teacher really ready to teach? And if they were not, what options were there to redirect them into another line of work given that you see them for the first time as seniors ready to graduate after student teaching? To address some of these larger professional concerns, I became involved in PDS. It did not take long to understand that the goals of the PDS program were not limited to better preservice education. Improvement in inservice teaching and sharing action research findings were equally important.

Our PDS network initially had an Ohio State professor and nine teachers representing six different school districts. (It was to grow to a *network* of three PDS groups with nearly 30 field professors and all three university faculty in Social Studies and Global Education.) Our work over the next few years was recognized for its value in preparing preservice educators. My colleagues and I were given the opportunities to write professionally, and give presentations to national, regional, and state audiences. Over time, what used to feel uncomfortable and a bit outside the culture of a public classroom teacher, became very comfortable and even sought after. In the PDS, I received support and encouragement from a network of professors and other teachers to expand my professional horizons.

Poland, Why Poland? This was a question my wife asked when I first mentioned a trip to Poland. The Education for Democratic Citizenship in Poland project provided another professional growth opportunity for me. This project was to review and help create a new social studies curriculum for secondary schools in Poland. Later, I was invited to go to Poland on two different occasions to share some of my expertise in alternative assessment including the development of rubrics. The Poles were also very interested in our PDS structure and the idea of university/public school collaboration.

As with my experiences with team teaching, the opportunities to work with Polish educators created a climate of self-reflection in my practice. To explain to others (especially through a translator), I needed to be very precise in my explanation regarding what I do and why. I was able to work with Polish and American classroom teachers, professors, and government officials and learn many things. In particular, my work with the Poles over the last two years has added to my ability to discuss Central Europe with more understanding.

Another benefit of the work in the PDSN is how it affects my own students. Many 12-year-olds still believe that schooling is complete at the end of high school or college. Through my modeling that I don't know everything (or even enough) about education at the age of 40, students begin to understand learning is a lifelong process.

I believe that none of the above would have been possible without the PDSN. To be able to share insights and work with other colleagues helps to break the isolation and keep us alive as educators. In a global system that changes so quickly, the only hope for education is to be able to serve the needs of our students by creating teacher networks to question and develop the practices in our field.

LEARNING CO-EQUAL COLLABORATION

Steven L. Miller

For some 15 years, I directed the Center for Economic Education at Ohio State, a job that brought me in contact with thousands of teachers in Central Ohio, in hundreds of inservice programs and courses. I consulted on curricula with more than a dozen districts, meeting frequently with groups of teachers to facilitate the process of integrating more economics into their already overcrowded curricula. It was a genuine pleasure to work with teachers in developing and pilot-testing classroom materials. And I was fortunate to have the opportunity to do some "demonstration teaching" in schools a couple of times each year.

All of this activity took me into schools and classrooms fairly regularly. Interacting with students, listening to teachers and administrators, and even walking the halls of the buildings, were all very instructive. In sum, I felt as if I had a good perspective on what was happening with schools, teachers, and students, and that I had developed reasonably good skills in collaborating with K–12 educators. Then along came our new PDS. I was about to learn that I knew a lot less than I thought and that I had some crucial new lessons in collaboration to absorb.

In our PDS, the field professors (FPs) are master teachers who, among other things, cooperatively plan and teach the methods seminar with the university faculty. My first lesson in collaboration was that I had to surrender primary control of this course. This proved to be deceptively difficult, even though I had been forewarned by my colleague, Merry Merryfield. For our PDS to be successful, the FPs' voices had to be coequal with my own in every decision of consequence. This and more was worked out in painstaking detail by a process of repeated meetings and consensus. I organized and chaired the meetings, but I learned to scrupulously avoid pushing too hard for my own ideas or too quickly weighing in on one side when there was a disagreement to resolve. (As an aside, the consensus process required patience on everyone's part, and patience is not my long suit.)

Given my prior experiences, I reflected on why this kind of collaboration was so important, yet difficult, for me. I came to recognize that none of my prior efforts at collaboration with classroom teachers had involved true equality in the power or authority relationships among group members. For example, as an outside curriculum "expert," I had understood that the final authority rested with the teachers and administrators who would have to implement the curriculum we designed, and live with results. In my collaboration to develop curriculum materials, however, I had been the authority, with the controlling power of decision. When teachers had been guest presenters in *my* classes, there was never any question of whose class it really was. In PDS, for the first time, I was ceding control in something that was mine and for which I was responsible.

I also came to recognize that what was underway was the development of mutual trust and respect, and that this could not be realized overnight. Every interaction was part of an ongoing *process*—in relationship building, in redefining our respective roles, and in adjusting our expectations. In the beginning I sensed some doubt that the university professor would really so deeply involve teachers in the professional development of interns. This group of teachers, because they are strong individuals and outstanding educators, grasped the opportunity when they saw it was real. The overture for equal collaboration must be demonstrated in the process, or it isn't genuine.

My own learning about teacher preparation, teaching, schools, and students has been deeply enhanced by the collaborative process, sometimes in obvious ways, at other times more subtly. It was a shock to see topics that I had considered vital to any methods course discarded during the planning process. Cherished lessons that I taught so well, gone! But the discussion about the topics to be included or deleted was revealing. Here were fresh perspectives on the vital essentials for new teachers, thoughtfully articulated by veteran teachers who had guided more than a hundred student teachers over the years. Others might have decided differently, but such judgments represented *our* consensus view of what was most important, given that we couldn't do it all.

And this curricular crunch was itself an ironic lesson for me. All university faculty have some experience in this way, if nothing more than deciding what readings and topics must be kept and which must be discarded. But, the addition of 15 hours per week of clinical experiences in schools to the methods courses, thereby effectively halving the amount of methods classroom time, raised the curriculum crunch to new levels for me. I was being forced to practice what some of us in social studies education had long preached—the value of depth in some topics at the expense of breadth of coverage. It was, of course, nothing new for the FPs.

I learned from them which teaching strategies they favored and why. At least in this area I felt somewhat affirmed. Old, familiar favorites of mine, such as case studies, simulations, and decision trees, were favorites of theirs. I learned that there was not the wide gulf between university prescription and classroom practice that some had suggested, at least not among this group.

Finally, the PDS experience has spurred me to revisit my own teaching practice and professional development. While I have paid scrupulous attention to the comments of students in revising my courses and reading lists, I realized that I had strayed too far from truly reflective practice. For example, I had stopped writing my own course reactions and comments (journaling, if you like). How had I gotten away from doing that?

And I resolved to spend more time teaching in schools (a resolution as yet unfulfilled). I discovered the need to do more than just demonstrate a new lesson idea. I need to get back in touch with teaching in schools on a regular basis. I expect my colleagues will help me with that, as they have with so many other things.

THE PERSPECTIVE OF A GRADUATE

Todd Kenreich

No teacher education program expects to prepare its graduates for every issue they will face during their first year of teaching. A common expectation is that the graduates will not merely survive as new teachers, but will also grow from their professional experiences. Ohio State's secondary social studies PDS equipped me with the knowledge, skills, and confidence to survive and, even more, learn from my first year of teaching. As a graduate of Ohio State's PDS in 1994, I promptly began teaching history at a public high school in Bethesda, Maryland. I would like to share three lessons that I learned from Ohio State's PDS, connect each lesson to my experiences as a first-year teacher, and finally suggest two considerations for improving the PDS.

Ohio State's focus on the importance of including global and multi-cultural perspectives in the classroom helped me to rethink social studies. Like many preservice teachers, my high school social studies courses seldom included multiple perspectives. For example, a "world history" course was actually a Western civilization course in disguise. However, PDS methods, seminars, and readings challenged me to infuse global and multicultural perspectives in teaching and learning. Developing perspective consciousness for each of my students became a crusade.

As a first-year teacher, I was pleased to find that my new colleagues had a wealth of global and multicultural resources. But when would I find time to preview what the school already owned? Between teaching and grading, little time remained for planning three preparations. Fortunately, suggestions from colleagues guided my attempts to preview and incorporate appropriate resources to promote perspective consciousness.

Another lesson learned from Ohio State was the importance of reflective practice. As an intern, I was required to submit a weekly reflective journal that synthesized my field experiences with themes from the methods course. One journal entry, for example, detailed a cooperative learning JIGSAW activity that I implemented to teach students about the Korean War and the role of the press in influencing public opinion. The activity involved students working in groups of four to research and write a correspondent's script for a broadcast news piece about a specific event in the Korean War. In my journal entry, I noted how impressed I was by the students' creativity and enthusiasm for the project. I was troubled, though, that students did not appreciate Korean perspectives of this war. I decided to restructure the activity in the future to include correspondents from news agencies in Korea as well as in the United States. Writing journal entries provided a safe place for me to reflect and to refine my teaching.

Although I did not continue writing weekly reflections as a full-time teacher, I did make a deliberate effort to write down short notes of how I would approach a lesson or event differently in the future. For example, in my first year, I found that students have a difficult time understanding the causes of World War I. Having the students create a time line of key events was a start. With a linear time line, though, the students just did not get it. After I taught the unit on World War I, I made a note to include a greater visual component the following year. The next year I infused more geography at the beginning of the unit. Then, I had the students make a cause and effect web that charted the major causes and effects of World War I. The webs demonstrated that the students had a better sense of what happened but, more important, why events unfolded as they did. Without writing a quick note of how I wanted to change the unit, a year later I might have forgotten how to change it.

In addition to the importance of global and multicultural perspectives and teacher reflection, Ohio State's PDS taught me to use questioning skills to promote critical thinking. Group discussion has been one of my favorite methods. At its best, it provides a safe forum. At its worst, group discussion degenerates. Clearly, the teacher must set the ground rules to promote a healthy discussion. I learned to ask open-ended evaluative questions to promote critical thinking. As an intern, I had trouble knowing when and how to close discussion. I also found wait-time to be awkward at times. With practice, though, I became more comfortable using wait-time and concluding discussions.

In my first year of teaching, class sizes of 33 made group discussions challenging to manage. However, incorporating discussion was one way of sending the message to students that I value their voices. To personalize the class discussion, I would often have students work in pairs or small groups. Then, representatives from each pair would report to the class. I also emphasized the importance of active listening skills to improve discussions. Many students (and adults) are poor listeners. Asking students to paraphrase what another student says can be a useful way of assessing listening skills.

To improve PDS, I offer two areas for consideration: students with special needs, and technology. As a first-year teacher, I was overwhelmed by the number of students with special needs. The official paperwork involved in monitoring students with Individualized Education Plans and 504s steadily flowed in my school mailbox. Legally mandated accommodations such as priority seating, untimed test-taking, peer-notetakers, adjusted test formats, and adjusted homework loads were implemented. Although preservice teachers must take a course in students with special needs, the PDS should include a seminar where field professors illustrate how they make accommodations in social studies courses for students with special needs. As more students arrive in our classrooms with IEPs and 504s, the PDS must position its preservice social studies teachers to be sensitive and proactive about students with special needs.

Another suggestion is that the PDS should rework its technology component to not only demonstrate application of instructional technology but also expose preservice teachers to relevant websites, news groups, and listserves. From my experience, school administrators expect that new teachers know how to use technology in teaching and learning. The PDS should create its own web page, which could help preservice and practicing social studies teachers navigate the World Wide Web for electronic resources. Specifically, though, I envision a significant portion of the page devoted to a "Social Studies Lesson Plan Clearinghouse." Over time, the clearinghouse would maintain multiple lesson plans on various topics within social studies. The PDS web page would emerge as an asset for preservice teacher education and professional development.

I credit my success as a teacher in part to the preparation I received at Ohio State's PDS. Much of the success of the PDS stems from its willingness to incorporate feedback from its field professors, cooperating teachers, and graduates. In the spirit of university and school collaboration, such feedback should continue to inform the evolution of the PDS into the next century.

NOTES

1. There are three Social Studies PDS groups, which among ourselves we refer to as PDS I, II, and III, each organized by a different member of the Ohio State faculty. For example, Ray and Miller are members of PDS II. In this chapter, however, we do not distinguish among the three since authors are relating experiences from all three of the groups. Kenreich was a student in PDS II and Dove, while a member PDS I (the PDS working with Merry Merryfield), had much of his international experience through the efforts of projects generated with Richard Remy and PDS III.

2. In the Social Studies PDSs, master teachers who help plan and teach the methods courses, and manage the clinical experiences of the preservice teachers are called "field professors."

CHAPTER 9

Students Learn Within and Beyond the Walls: A Secondary PDS

Barbara Levak, Anna Soter, and Dan Hoffman

In The Ohio State University PDS initiative, secondary schools were a tough fit. Content domains, isolation, and having few teachers per school befitting appropriate placements for content majors were among the initial challenges. This chapter reveals many more challenges and rewards associated with a secondary PDS. Three different perspectives cast a light leaving no shadows in this picture.

Secondary schools, because they are entrenched in content specific disciplines, rarely explore what could be if their boundaries were flexible. Many high schools are still organized departmentally thus providing few opportunities for cross-disciplinary dialogue. The Reynoldsburg School District faculty and administration decided that it was time to stretch their boundaries using the reform principles of Ted Sizer's Coalition of Essential Schools. In its second year of this reform, the Reynoldsburg High School community initiated a partnership with The Ohio State University in an effort to study and implement their vision of an improved high school. At the same time, College of Education faculty at Ohio State were interested in reforming their teacher preparation programs and sought to connect with a school already engaged in its own reform agenda.

This chapter will present the Reynoldsburg High School PDS story from three different perspectives: school faculty, university faculty, and the building principal respectively. These three voices represent pieces of the story, each seeming to be independent of the other, until we took time to step back, reflect, and see what was really happening school-wide.

ONE TEACHER'S PERSPECTIVE:
INITIAL INTRIGUE, ENTHUSIASM, AND OPTIMISM

Barbara Levak

The concept, even the term, of PDS was foreign to me when I first became involved in 1991. At that time, I, in my twenty-first year of teaching, had transferred to Reynoldsburg High School from the junior high to be part of a sophomore-level interdisciplinary team, a team charged with the implementation of four of the Coalition's Common Principles: personalization, performance assessment, student-as-worker/teacher-as-coach, and backwards building curriculum. I was excited, challenged, and knew, by working directly with Sizer's research, that all eyes would be focused on my teammates and me. To strengthen our work, our team decided to work with a professor from Ohio State . . . actually, we wanted someone to listen to us plan, watch us teach, and observe students learning.

Our team, Debbie Calhoun (Math), Steve Shapiro (Global Studies), Bob Wilson (Biology), and myself (English), soon discovered that we needed constructive feedback and support for our planning on a consistent and frequent basis. Associate Professor Merry Merryfield (Social Studies Education) provided that. For her part, Merry was seeking teachers and a school setting that could serve as a data source for research. Qualitative in nature, Merry's work focused on the curriculum design, teaching strategies, and teacher decisions in Global Studies classrooms. However, because Shapiro's Global Studies classroom was operating in the larger context of a team, Merry's work expanded to include the team. This introduction into the world of PDS excited me. I saw enormous possibilities for changing the culture of both institutions. By reexamining traditional roles, breaking down stereotypical beliefs (e.g., that university faculty live in ivory towers disconnected from the realities of teaching; that high school teachers develop practices unbounded by research or theory), and allowing high school students and teachers to become familiar with university professors and university students, we could learn from each other.

Such a partnership had never existed for me before. My work with universities had been limited to the occasional and cursory visit from university personnel to "check" on their student teachers. Now, teacher and professor were equals, each having knowledge to share with one another in a relationship of true reciprocity.

Our partnership with Merry continued to develop and deepen, largely because, as she met with us regularly during our common planning period for an entire school year, Merry became observer, questioner, research source, confidant, and visionary. She asked questions such as "To what degree is the Connections course a fundamental change from the way you planned and taught last year?"; "What are the easier ideas to implement?"; and, "What influence does the Global Studies focus have on you and your implementation of Sizer's principles?" These questions helped us reflect upon our individual and team growth and decision making, and redirected the team's thinking to a deeper level, all with an eye on the work of our students.

With such an invigorating and helpful first experience with the PDS concept, I eagerly embraced another opportunity to work with the university. This time, the research, conducted by Associate Professor George Newell (English Education) and doctoral candidate Ruth Holt, focused on "Constructing the Literature Curriculum: A Study of Teacher Decision Making" (Newell, 1993). Through extended interviews and classroom observations, I once again was being asked to reflect upon my work, my curricular decisions, my pedagogy. As before, I found this articulation of ideas not only beneficial but revitalizing.

I next found myself drawn to the rethinking and restructuring of the English Education program at Ohio State, especially as led by Associate Professor Anna Soter. As described later in this chapter, the English Education program was now a master's certification program. As a practitioner working with interns, I was affected by and agreed with the needed changes in the program. Specifically, I liked having field experience observers working in cohorts. Working in groups not only provided them support and an opportunity to share their perspectives of my classroom, it provided my students an opportunity to know who might become their student teacher at a later date. With the new program, the prospective interns were already familiar with the school culture, the students, and the mentor. Together the intern and mentor could decide if a match was mutually beneficial. The student teaching process was no longer a mere "placement," but, rather, a pairing of professionals.

Under Anna's leadership, this different approach to the intern experience had natural outgrowths. I did not, nor was I expected to "turn over" my classroom to my university intern: instead, we worked together. We met regularly to discuss the intern's progress and also for seminars with all the English Education mentors, interns, and university supervisors to share, rethink, and challenge one another's thinking. In other words, in true collegial fashion, we pushed the level and quality of work being designed for the high school students. . . . Isn't that a central purpose of PDS work?

Growing Concerns

With these initial, optimistic PDS experiences and with enthusiasm for expanding the work both at Ohio State and Reynoldsburg High School (RHS) in 1994, I broadened my work by becoming the Clinical Educator for RHS. From this vantage point, I now had the opportunity to see the "larger picture" . . . one that revealed that the work, while certainly evocative and deep at some levels, in some quarters, and with some personnel, was not mainstream. Concerns began to surface.

One of the challenges that I daresay will continue is budgetary. Clinical educator positions at RHS have been cut including Bill Gathergood's for the TIE PDS (Technology in Education Professional Development School). His position supported all the PDSs as the cry grows to understand technology use in the classroom. This loss appears to me to be a setback of major proportions. I no longer had release time to attend PDS meetings, or to broaden the understanding of the PDS concept at Reynoldsburg. The result is a growing "burnout" of trying to do all the work in a quality way, of not merely becoming a "gofer" to arrange meetings and find mentors.

Perhaps the most disheartening result of lack of funds has been the inability to finance substitutes for RHS classrooms so PDS teachers can co-teach methods courses at Ohio State. We had done this in the past with encouraging results. After a certain collaborative venture, St. Pierre shared:

> I can't imagine a better way for in-service teachers to help the profession than by sharing their time and expertise with pre-service teachers who are as apprehensive and needy as we all once were. More collaboration of this kind would be enormously beneficial to our profession. Sadly, this collaboration with the English Education program seems to have come to an end unless we can create new structures and budgets to support them.

In addition to budgetary challenges, consistency in the English Education program needs to be addressed. Under the current structure, professors rotate the duties and responsibilities from year to year. While such an approach has merit at the university level, it has become quite challenging, and even frustrating, for us at the high school level. Where once interns observed in cohort pairings, this is no longer true and we were not part of the decision making. Where once regular seminars among interns, mentors, and university supervisors were integral to the quality and depth of the program, these no longer exist. Last year one intern told me that he viewed seminars as just one more "thing" to do and he would not attend. How sad! Now, because of growing numbers of students in English Education and only one professor to oversee the mountains of work, field experience and student teaching has become "business as usual." This is hardly the tenets that the PDS initiative embraces.

The growing number of students in the English Education program has required that schools be used that are not professional development sites. Such a decision begs the questions: How is a PDS school "different than" another school? Are we foregoing joint discussions to try to resolve the concerns and reverting to what had always been done? Does being a PDS still have meaning?

Perhaps one of the most challenging concerns I see now as a clinical educator is that educational reform is occurring only in "pockets" at both RHS and at Ohio State. For many people at both sites, it is "business as usual." Despite numerous joint efforts to explain the purposes of PDS, there are many Reynoldsburg staff members who don't know that we are a professional development school. Others know, but quite frankly, do not wish to rethink their own work, thus creating the chasm between what is taught in the methods courses at Ohio State and what student interns experience at RHS.

Future Challenges and Hopes

Despite these serious concerns, I believe the PDS initiative can thrive. However, for this to occur, we need together to honestly evaluate our work and to set the course for the next years. The tough questions need to be asked: Does Ohio State really want practitioners to be involved in setting the agenda for teacher education or are we to revert to the isolated role of cooperating teacher, seen not as a professional equal but as a placement service? How can Ohio State be assured of having enough teacher mentors to fill their needs if so many practitioners are philosophically opposed to change and they are permitted not to review, research, rethink, and risk? How can this be accomplished while still respecting the integrity of the person and his or her beliefs? How can the work of PDS and the Holmes initiative become a true, recognized part of the entire school culture? How can the work of PDS become a valued, recognized part of the culture of Ohio State?

THE UNIVERSITY PERSPECTIVE

Anna Soter

In March 1991, Dan Hoffman invited me to attend a meeting at Reynoldsburg High School to discuss expanding the participation of

Ohio State faculty at the school, having worked with Professor Merry Merryfield (Global and Social Studies Education) for the preceding two years. Merry had already persuaded me to participate in such a meeting because of the evident success her Social Studies program had had in working with Reynoldsburg Social Studies/History faculty in a new and exciting way (see chapter 7). She particularly believed that Ohio State's involvement in the school would benefit not only our teacher certification programs but also our research interests.

The relationship of the English Education program with RHS up to that time was distantly cordial but we had not been able to place English Education interns for their field component in the district for at least the two preceding years. Informal sources suggested that our interns were not held in high regard by the district. Similarly, we found ourselves in a quandary at the time of the invitation to attend this meeting because we felt that the approaches to teaching reading and writing at RHS did not support the orientation we had in our university program. Briefly, our program had been emphasizing a process-oriented approach to writing instruction and a response-based approach to literature instruction. Additionally, our program supported the use of quality young adult literature even in the high school years whereas RHS appeared to prefer interns who were well versed in canonical authors and texts. Thus, at the time of the meeting, we felt that our interests would not be well-served by placing interns at RHS and similarly, RHS appeared to feel that our interns were not adequately trained to perform well in the high school English classroom. At the same time, we sorely needed good sites for the 25 plus undergraduate certification interns and for a growing number of MA plus certification students who needed student teaching placements.

English Education faculty, as was the case with faculty in every other program, tended to conduct research and consultation services with schools and districts on the basis of personal contact and preferences. Furthermore, RHS, situated as it is on the eastern edge of the city of Columbus, is far enough away from the university to not figure strongly in individual faculty research when other sites could be found nearby. These may not be flattering admissions but all of these factors contributed to our initial disinclination to pursue RHS as a site even for the placement of interns.

The Turn-Around

As with other teacher certification programs in the College of Education, English Education found itself planning a graduate program in English teacher certification. As part of that reform, we also sought more active participation by faculty in schools where students would obtain pre-intern field experience as well as during the intern quarter.

Indeed, we were interested in expanding the internship to cover all three quarters of the academic year. We were also interested in working with English faculty at RHS in planning field experiences and to discuss interns' perceptions of their experiences in the culture of schooling. We were open and eager to have teachers who wished to participate. We believed that our interns would be better able to understand relationships between theory and practice.

Thus, in the initial stages of our renewed involvement with RHS, our concerns were related to a strengthened teacher certification program. At the same time, we were also interested in possibilities for on-site research and for professional development work with the teachers at RHS as part of their reform efforts. The meeting called by Dan proved to be a landmark in our relations with RHS in more ways than one. That story is described in "A Principal's Perspective" later in this chapter.

The Unique Nature of the OSU/RHS Initiative:

I believe the unique characteristic of the PDS at RHS is due to several factors:

1. PDS came to RHS through Dan's reform initiatives at RHS. We were, in effect, invited to participate in whatever way we found we could fit into the RHS reform agenda, which included conducting research into the RHS reform as it progressed (see Hoffman in this paper for further details).

2. Because of Dan's openness, we were free to experiment with our own reform agenda concerning the development of graduate level teacher certification.

3. Dan also invited our involvement in the school's reform initiative in a variety of ways that resulted in our own professional growth.

4. Site-focused field placement in a high school had not been attempted previously (at least on the part of English Education). That is, we had always worked on a wide-net basis, preferring (and with the schools' concurrence) not to place interns at the same site repetitively.

I will address now how we were able to participate in the school's reform initiative and the impact of having our interns work at this site over an extended period of time.

Involvement in the RHS Reform Initiative

Dan asked various Ohio State faculty involved at RHS to consider ways of assisting in the reform agenda at RHS. I cannot speak for other faculty but will focus on ways in which this affected me. I was asked to participate in the Communications Committee's work to consider ways that writing could be better used as a tool for learning. As part of that involvement I developed a summer course on using writing across the disciplines (the integrationist thrust of the RHS reform agenda) during the summer of 1994 (co-taught by Dr. George Newell who was Ohio State liaison with Independence High School) for teachers at RHS and Independence High School. I subsequently began work with Dwayne Blackburn (geometry teacher) to explore the use of writing in his classes both as a way of evaluating what his students knew as well as furthering their learning in that subject. This led to the placement of one of our graduate English certification students as 50% in Dwayne's class (the other 50% being with an English teacher). Jay Eastman, the intern, had expressed an interest in such a dual placement after he had worked with me on an independent study in Dwayne's class the preceding two quarters. He used various forms of writing to help students express geometrical concepts, modeling for Dwayne how to introduce this approach in his classroom. This project also led to working with Ohio State math preservice teachers serving as audiences for the geometry students who wrote them letters about the geometry concepts they were learning. As the geometry students wrote more frequently to an informed and interested readership, they became more specific in their language use and found themselves having to work harder at understanding concepts in order to explain them to others. The project ended with Jay's graduation but had convinced Dwayne of the value of using writing as a tool for learning to the point where he was attempting to involve others in his subject area to work with him.

A further benefit came from working with Bill Gathergood. Bill had already conducted several literature Email projects with students in England, Australia, and Russia. He also taught Shakespeare at RHS and was glad to involve our interns over a two-year period in two of these projects. I found it interesting that approximately half of the interns the first year had not used Email previously but they became regular users of it after this experience. The experience also stretched their understanding of American and other literature as they sought to discuss it with students whose cultural and linguistic backgrounds were different from their own.

The interns and I also participated in the Wednesday morning schoolwide sessions where issues related to the reform agenda were discussed. These discussions included how these movements were being perceived by the faculty as a whole and to the emergence of leaders among the faculty other than the principal and other administrators in the school. The ultimate goal was to have us all see ourselves as integral to the growth of the school community. This may not have been accomplished during my time at RHS but it provided a model for future involvement. University faculty were a part of the school community and responsive to the school environment but not necessarily highly visible. I saw this as a situation where we responded to interest and need as directed by the school faculty rather than the more typical situation where we came in with proposals (to do research or pursue projects) and, then remained isolated from the wider school community.

Growing Pains

Every reform effort has to expect growing pains. We had our share although in retrospect, these are now seen as part of the growth process and are better appreciated in that light.

Site-saturation.   High school teachers, in our experience, do not want to relinquish control of their classes or curricula and often request not to have interns continuously so that they can ensure coverage of their curricula (among other reasons). As a part of the reform initiatives we wanted to pursue in our teacher certification program, we negotiated agreements that interns would initially be at the site for two university quarters, half in autumn and the second half in the winter quarter. They would choose a placement for student teaching in the spring quarter between RHS and Independence and Hilliard (our other sites). Teachers were able to review background material on our interns to find matches in interest and personality. In turn, our interns, in consultation with the teachers and ourselves, made decisions about their placements.

We met as a group four to five times on site during the pre–student teaching quarter to discuss issues related to the field experience, professionalism among teachers, the school culture, the reform initiative at RHS, and teaching from the preservice teachers' perspectives. These meetings were seen as a vital part of community building. We wanted to develop more open discussion of issues and to provide our interns with an inside view of the school's culture.

The benefits of having interns placed in a site for at least two quarters were enormous: they came to know the school well prior to student teaching; teachers and interns got to know each other well; had time to reflect on the school culture and how it might impact their teaching; interns came to know the students they would have in their student teaching quarter; issues that sometimes erupt during student teaching would be dealt with much earlier.

At the same time, we found that site-saturation is still a problem at the high school level. The intern's exposure to various school settings is limited when most of their year is spent at one site. We wanted to work with teachers who wished to work with us in this new way. After two years, the teachers understandably wanted to have a break. What then? This question faces us in any secondary school setting where the size of the subject-specific faculty is typically somewhere between 6–12 teachers. School networks began to appear more and more appealing.

The Question of Leadership under the Banner of Equality

As part of our involvement in the reform effort, we tried to reexamine our roles in teacher education. The perception of the teachers was that decisions involving interns, were the responsibility of the university professor. Yet we were attempting to build a team view of teacher education: co-professionals working together to bring change to the whole profession by reforming the preprofessional program. That view was (and still is) slow to mature.

I recall one incident at a meeting on site, where the preservice teachers were dumping (our term for expressing dissatisfaction). At the time, I was sick and after the long round-trip to meet on site, was less than usually tolerant of negativity. I perceived myself as pushing a democratic agenda. If something was wrong, those who perceived it as such could figure out ways to handle it. Some of the students did not feel they were receiving a sufficiently wide experience by being placed at RHS and one other site (an urban setting). I realized that the PDS process of changing cultures not only involved my culture as an academic, and the school culture of the teachers, but also the preservice teachers' culture—interns pay fees at a large university and expect to be served. They were not interested in taking leadership within the new professional site but were just playing along (because that's what interns do). When they became sufficiently unhappy with what they perceived as an issue, they did not attempt to resolve it but, rather, complained.

With hindsight, I now think that we had not taken into account the perspectives our interns were bringing into the experience. They had just emerged from four years of a baccalaureate degree during which they had learned to perform as expected. Their primary interest was to find out what was required in terms of hours, assignments/projects, and showing up for meetings. Leadership of the kind I was expecting was unrealistic.

It belittles what we were able to accomplish to say that all of the initiatives involving preservice teachers came from the university. Steps toward viewing the teacher education reform as a joint endeavor were small ones. When suggestions came from the teachers at RHS for changes (for example, having interns on site for longer periods of time during the two pre–student teaching quarters), these were often met with restraint because the interns had full-time schedules with course work on campus and many also worked. Furthermore, the teachers rightly wondered how they were benefiting from greater involvement beyond having our interns in their classrooms. We operated on the belief that this was a worthwhile endeavor. This belief works for a while, but not for the long term.

Reiterating History

A minor frustration occurred with the beginning of each new cohort of preservice teachers who did not know the history of the reform both at RHS and with the university involvement. For them, conditions at RHS had not changed nor had the preservice teacher education program in English Education changed. They simply experienced it as it was for *them*. We discussed historical backgrounds at the initial meetings and short articles written during the process of reform but as with anything else, reform must be *lived through* to be understood. It was frustrating to begin at the beginning with each cohort group. I have yet to find a satisfactory resolution to this problem although one obvious solution presents itself now: develop a video consisting of interviews with teachers who lived the reform effort. This might include interviews with previous cohorts and excerpts from group meetings to see the shift in perceptions as we developed a better understanding of our collective goals. The new cohorts hadn't experienced the team teaching between RHS teacher Mike Murray and Ohio State instructor Bettie St. Pierre. They hadn't heard English Education preservice teacher Jay Eastman and RHS Geometry teacher Duane Blackburn talk about using writing as a tool for learning geometry. They hadn't read the student papers that RHS teachers Becky George and Cathy Holley had sent to the composition methods course instructor for authentic feedback from the preservice teachers. They hadn't shared responses on email with high school students in Russia and Australia about *Romeo and Juliet* or *The Great Gatsby* as part of RHS teacher Bill Gathergood's literature email projects. The interns were dealing with their immediate needs and interests and they saw their own role in the preprofessional experience solely as recipients, as one would expect.

What Unresolved Issues Confront Us?

Among these issues (which I see as yet unresolved) are the relationships in the educational community where these are still hierarchical notions of responsibility. Many teachers still see the university as primarily responsible for the education of preservice teachers although we tried hard to share that role. We tried to work democratically but the bottom line in terms of responsibility and initiatives was always site-based (who came from which site). Whether we like it or not, academics, especially when they might teach courses that teachers take, or act as PhD advisors remind us that the lion might talk tame but the mouse isn't fooled.

Another issue we never resolved is the issue of which teachers might be involved in the PDS. The editors' question, "should the PDS only work with teachers who share a particular philosophy," was very relevant in our PDS as well as others. This touches very sensitive ground. I don't believe we ever really dealt with that issue. Do we work only with teachers who are model teachers? Who decides what is a model teacher in a setting where both parties are believed to have equal rights to determine placements? Further, are we not responsible to provide conditions that further the development of teachers who might not be model teachers but who might benefit from involvement in professional development of this kind? It is also problematic when working in sites where subject specialty numbers are not high. But these are not questions to run away from either. Unless we continue to work on them, our relationships with schools will not really change—they will only appear to change.

A PRINCIPAL'S PERSPECTIVE

Dan Hoffman

The difficulty and complexity of school improvement cannot be approached in solitude. As a high school principal who began to realize the need for serious organization and pedagogical shifts in our school, I understood that forging new partnerships and alliances with others would be essential.

The first and most basic of those partnerships is with the leader and the faculty. At Reynoldsburg High School, a trusting relationship with the faculty was created from my earlier positions as a teaching colleague and assistant principal. The trusting relationship allowed for an open dialogue that revealed a collective sense of dissatisfaction with the current status of our school. From that sense of dissatisfaction a new school mission statement was crafted by the faculty and administration. In our earliest undertakings, we had not yet learned the importance of including other important stakeholders in our reform process.

A breakthrough in our thinking on external partnerships came in our measurement and evaluation strategies designed for the North Central Association of Schools and Universities accreditation process. As we embarked on a path of measuring the tenets of our own mission statement, we came to understand that external partners with specific areas of expertise could play both a supportive and critical role in the evalua-tion of our school.

As we began to connect with new adult partners in our school, I began to notice the residual effects of their presence on both teachers and stu-dents. Our new partners began to create an authentic audience that would ratchet up our effectiveness. As I watched teachers interact with members of our community, I saw them work extremely hard at putting their finest ideas into practice. I also noticed that our students were very responsive to other adults and that they wanted their school to be viewed favorably and visiting adults often brought forth their best. Through my experiences with the accreditation process, I began to promote the development of other partnerships with interested parties. In that search, the Holmes Pro-ject brought The Ohio State University faculty to our doorstep.

Advantages for Reynoldsburg High School

From my seat, college faculty working in our building had four advan-tages. The first was simply that more adults would be in the building. This advantage may sound simplistic but I believe it is a basic transition in attitude that many schools have yet to accomplish. In my own princi-palship, I evolved from being one who worried about and guarded against adult visitation in the school to one who literally opened the doors to over 2,000 visitors in my final 4 years.

A second obvious advantage university faculty brought to us was expertise. Many of our teachers were in the midst of challenging their own long-standing pedagogical practices and supportive voices from the ranks of the universities were reassuring.

A third advantage that was openly discussed with teachers was the need for research and documentation of our improvement strategies. This need clearly created a mutual advantage for both our school and a research-oriented university.

A final advantage, that was not immediately recognized, was the intellectual modeling that university faculty provided for public school teachers. Although I have not collected hard data on this issue, my sense is that our interaction with university faculty resulted in increased and improved learning opportunities for the school faculty. Hundreds of graduate hours have been earned by the faculty since our relationship. At least three members of our staff are now enrolled in doctoral study programs at The Ohio State University.

Connections

In the midst and complexity of serious school reform, one of the primary roles of the principal is *sense-making*. To sustain change initiatives while simultaneously allowing new initiatives to emerge requires someone to sense make for the organization. In that sense-making mode, I would like to propose some relationships that I believe exist among the very different PDS projects that emerged in our school. To the naked eye, those initiatives seem piecemeal and isolated. Through a different lens, I would like to sense make about the relationship of the PDS initiatives in our school.

Although connections between Ohio State projects had little inter-action and relevance to one another, each of those projects were directly related to specific facets of our school improvement agenda. Our school improvement plans were heavily influenced by the research of Ted Sizer and the work of the Coalition of Essential Schools. Sizer's research resulted in his call for schools to organize around Nine Common Principles. These ideas guided our school reform. My sense making of the relationship between our school and the university was that the commonsense findings in the Nine Common Principles was the glue. Brief descriptions of PDS-related initiatives will make the case.

Dr. Merry Merryfield's research in Global Education is a prime example of a connection between PDS work and our employment of Sizer's research. Merry was attracted to our instructional delivery plans for World Connections. World Connections was one of our first reform initiatives in which we organized 4 teachers and 90 students into an interdisciplinary learning community empowered with both time and curriculum. Merry and an Ohio State University doctoral student, Bev Cross, became intrigued with the curricular decision-making process that this team of teachers were making as they attempted to identify the essential knowledge, skills, and attitudes that they wanted to promote for each of their disciplines.

Merry was interested with both the interdisciplinary nature of the reform effort and the necessary "less is more" decision making that must accompany such an instructional delivery strategy. Bev's dissertation focused on the decision making and teamwork within this construct.

George Newell became interested in that same decision-making phenomena. George and colleagues studied the differences in curriculum decision making across the English department. He marveled at the empowerment of individual teachers to make curricular decisions under this model. The affirmative research of Merry, George, Bev, and others provided positive, critical feedback to teachers on the limb.

Anna Soter's expertise in writing connected with one of our school improvement strategies that promoted writing across the curriculum. Her philosophy that writing must be taught from all quarters resonates with Sizer's call for high school teachers to become generalists in their teaching.

The school's work with Sizer's research attracted Anna to a third project. She connected with another Reynoldsburg teacher, Bill Gathergood, to develop one of the earliest email projects between preservice English education graduate interns and ninth-grade students in Australia as well as tenth-grade students in Russia as described earlier. The project demonstrated Sizer's teacher-as-coach philosophy that calls for students to be thoughtful, active learners, guiding their own learning through inquiry.

My sense-making of the OSU-RHS relationship is that the activities have not been as piecemeal and disjointed as we first thought. The connecting fiber to our story is a common appreciation for Sizer's research and findings. As Reynoldsburg High School began to:

1. promote generalist thinking,

2. make *less is more* curricular decisions,

3. allow students to demonstrate their knowledge in a variety of ways, and

4. employ student-as-worker, teacher-as-coach strategies,

we also began to connect with Ohio State professors who shared that philosophical lean. My contention across our projects can be traced to the Nine Common Principles of the Coalition of Essential Schools.

Conclusion

From my perspective, our PDS partnership assisted our school in moving forward in an aggressive school reform agenda. In 1992, Reynoldsburg High School received recognition as one of 20 of America's A+ Break The Mold Schools. Reynoldsburg High School had moved from an obscure suburban high school in central Ohio to one that was connected and known nationally. I preface my concluding remarks about the role of the principal in this leap with a loud voice that leadership is not solitary and the credit for any success is diverse and widespread.

Addressing my role in the PDS partnership and the larger school reform agenda solicits several reflections. The observations gather around notions that I valued and my ability to nurture a trusting environment. An inherent faith in the goodwill of teachers is fundamental to my leadership style. A reasonably democratic and participative leadership style allowed me to craft a collective sense of mission and a related evaluation plan.

As my confidence grew in the principalship, the doors of the school opened wider and wider to other adults. Some would say that the walls went completely down as we both encouraged adults into our school while simultaneously allowing our students to begin to learn beyond the walls of Reynoldsburg High School.

Allowing students to learn beyond the walls raises yet another trust issue. Students must sense a tone of trust and decency in their school. Respect begets respect. It seems so simple but so many schools miss this message.

Trust must also exist within the larger school district. Our Board of Education and Superintendent Richard Ross extended and allowed democratic thinking and approaches. Their consistent and logical request was that a clear measurement plan accompany any school improvement innovations.

Beyond the leadership and nurturing trust I believe there are several values that influenced our work. A basic value is hearing all the voices. In any school, the first act of leadership should be listening. I have often been given credit for the ability to have my ideas transformed into the thinking of others to the point that they own the original thought. Certainly this was a leadership strategy that was used, but I contend that the employment of that strategy begins with careful listening. In the words of others, one can often find their own beliefs, values, and ideas.

Another value reflected in our reform efforts is the importance of including all members in the educational community in knowledge about learning. Too often the only discussion about learning centers on the students. Although the development of their intellect is our primary purpose, we must not ignore the adult learning needs in a school community. This value on adult learning created a logical pathway for the university's involvement in our school.

The extent to which this value is reflected in teachers' perceptions and actions was evaluated by the School Communications Committee, charged with "measuring and monitoring" effects of changes to ways in which RHS created opportunities for student growth in the area of communication skills (Communications Committee Report [CCR], October 1997). The committee, established in 1991, sought, among other goals, to learn how far teachers had incorporated writing as a tool for learning throughout the school as an outcome of workshops and consultation with the committee and Anna Soter from 1993 to 1996. The ninth- and twelfth-grade proficiency tests in all areas show a "positive progression in student success in the writing portion of the tests" and a "steady improvement in students' ability to communicate in writing as well as quality writing experiences throughout the various disciplines" (CCR, p. 3). The committee also found that the establishment of a "portfolio collection of written assignments in Art, Math, Science, and Social Studies" was a direct outcome on this focus of writing as a tool for learning (CCR, p. 4). In response to a survey that asked school faculty whether they were doing more writing in their classes than before the above initiatives were undertaken, 54% reported that they were doing more writing, 25% remained the same.

My role as principal in this PDS relationship was one of listening, supporting, sense-making, and match-making. For me, the formula seemed simple: the recognized and realized advantages would make Reynoldsburg High School a better place to teach and learn. Could a principal ask for anything more?

CHAPTER 10

The Growing of a School/University Partnership and the Preparation of Teachers for the Urban Context

Beth Carnate, George Newell, Steven Hoffman, and Rachel Moots

In this chapter, a clinical educator, university professor, high school English teacher, and certification student speak about their experience in a PDS situated in an urban high school in the midst of reform. The authors describe their initiatives related to their participation as a participant in the Coalition of Essential Schools, as well as look closely at a School-to-Work program where the teacher and student are working.

The partnership between The Ohio State University College of Education (OSU) and Independence High School (IHS) began with the acceptance of the IHS application by the Professional Development School Policy Board and the formal designation of Independence High School as a Professional Development School (PDS) in August 1992.

For several years, IHS had been involved in school restructuring. This included intensive staff development and the organization and implementation of a shared decision making cabinet composed of staff, parents, and students, and preparation to implement a trimester block schedule adapted from Dr. Joseph M. Carroll's *Copernican Plan* (1989). As the implementation of the two-hour block schedule approached, the IHS staff had begun the process of rethinking curriculum and instruction for two-hour classes in 60–day trimesters. We believed that the OSU faculty could be of great assistance to us as we moved forward toward changing some of our beliefs, assumptions, and practices.

As part of the PDS application process, IHS had recruited faculty from various departments. After several months of dialogue in this group and networking with other PDS programs and participants, it became apparent that IHS needed to expand its connection to specific program areas within the college. We realized that the faculty we had recruited, though willing to collaborate, did not have direct responsibility for preservice teachers. As a result, no OSU student interns (student observers/student teachers) were in residence during the first year with the exception of one social studies student intern.

Shortly thereafter, IHS was approached by the OSU English education program to serve as a site for observation and student teaching for student interns in the master's of education program. Dr. George Newell and the IHS English department met over the spring of 1993 to develop plans that included an observation quarter, a student teaching quarter for the interns, and seminars for the involved teachers. Our PDS was beginning to emerge.

For several years, PDS activities at IHS continued with English and social studies interns and faculty. During this period, at the request of the IHS Professional Development committee, several OSU courses were planned and conducted on-site for IHS staff. These courses included exploration and development of interdisciplinary curriculum, electronic portfolio development, action research for teachers, focusing on student work, and teachers as peer coaches. Each year we set as a goal to expand the PDS to other departments at IHS and across the various departments in the college. We had not, however, been able to engage faculty in math and science education or other fields such as art, music, family and consumer science, business/vocational or foreign language. As a more global picture of teacher preparation at OSU began to emerge, we realized that several of these teaching areas were not situated in the College of Education. We knew if our PDS was to expand, the PDS team needed to make contact with each individual program area to discuss possibilities for a partnership.

Late in 1995, the Ohio Department of Education announced plans for Goals 2000 Higher Education Partnership Grants. As our PDS team reviewed the grant Request for Proposals (RFP) we recognized its potential to move us toward expanding our partnership. Brainstorming began immediately and a grant proposal was developed that included: an interdisciplinary team of OSU faculty and student interns, IHS teachers, and IHS ninth-graders, a yearlong immersion program for the student interns, and the development and implementation of a ninth-grade

School to Work program (STW). The grant was funded and we rolled up our sleeves.

What followed was an intense 18-month pilot program from which we are all still learning. As part of the proposal, the PDS grant team began recruitment of the STW team. The OSU component included faculty in the areas of English education, math education, science education, family and consumer science education, and technology education. The IHS team included language arts, math, science, family and consumer science, and computer education.

From the start, we encountered problems in the recruitment and scheduling of OSU interns. We had hoped to engage two interns in each subject area as participating team members, but the OSU academic program for students in each area was different. Some interns attended classes in the morning, some in the afternoon, and requirements for observation quarters and student teaching differed as did schedules of university faculty. We were able to recruit two interns in English, one in math, and one in family and consumer science who became yearlong team members. Several preservice science interns rotated on and off the team each quarter.

The STW team met for five months prior to the opening of school in the fall of 1996. The agenda included team building, gaining a knowledge base about School to Work, establishing goals, developing curricular themes, and working through organizational and scheduling issues to support the team and the group of 150 ninth-grade students.

Through our PDS experience of the past seven years, we have come to recognize that:

1. The teacher/mentors at IHS have a deep and extraordinary understanding of minority children that they can pass on to the interns.

2. Interns from White, middle-class America can learn how to teach students who are very different from themselves.

3. Children recognize committed teachers who demonstrate caring and concern.

4. Interns will learn that when they teach students with differing backgrounds the discussions are richer and that there is the possibility of exploring a broader range of experiences.

5. The IHS two-hour blocked schedule enables interns to get to know individual students a great deal better than if they had contact with 135 students for 45-minute periods each day.

6. IHS provides a unique setting in which interns and faculty can explore what it means to teach in the urban setting and how best to prepare future teachers for this opportunity.

We hope that our experiences will provide a "pause to reflect" on several issues that we consider critical. We must become more cognizant of the needs of the students in urban schools and redesign the preparation of teachers to meet these changing needs. We must also work to support and renew practicing professionals in our schools as well as provide opportunities to university faculty to become more involved in the field.

Participants in the OSU/IHS PDS initiative and in the Goals 2000 Higher Education Partnership Grant have contributed to this chapter. OSU Associate Professor Dr. George Newell and IHS English teacher Steve Hoffman have both been involved in PDS work at OSU since 1991 and in the IHS/OSU PDS partnership since 1993. Rachel Moots was one of the English interns on the STW team during the 1996–97 school year and is currently a first-year English teacher at IHS.

A UNIVERSITY PERSPECTIVE

George Newell

As an English education professor I have been and continue to be concerned about the intern teachers' experiences as they attempt to negotiate the "two-worlds pitfall" (Feiman-Nemser & Buchmann, 1985) or the distance between ideas gleaned from a methods class and their implementation in a classroom of 30 high school students. This is important to the development of the "collaborative partnership" between the school and university that Beth described in the previous section. Accordingly, one way to "marry" learning about management issues with concerns for instruction and the realities of teaching is for me to work collaboratively with mentor teachers. Doing so fosters a reflective stance toward teaching and a challenge that seems to have every chance of succeeding given the commitment to teacher preparation I have encountered at Independence High School.

As a profession we know little about how beginning teachers learn to teach children of diverse linguistic and cultural backgrounds. Working in a PDS school on a STW project offered me an opportunity to understand what school-university collaborations might provide the interns. Accordingly, in the spirit of inquiry, I conducted case studies of two of the participating English interns, Doreen Sloan and Rachel Moots. (See Rachel's section of this chapter for her perspective.)

Given that our STW project actually expanded the interns' time in the PDS school setting, I was curious to know how Doreen and Rachel might integrate, if at all, the university teacher education courses into the intensive field work and student teaching experiences that were so central to our STW program. If our PDS collaborations were effectively dealing with the two worlds pitfall, then we should be able to discern developing connections between school and university contributions to teacher preparation. However, I will argue that this is indeed a complex issue in that several factors have to be taken into consideration such as (*a*) the knowledge, beliefs, and central concerns of the student teachers that developed before and during professional preparation, and (*b*) the context of teaching, including the types of students they are assigned to teach and the nature of the mentoring they receive from their cooperating teachers and university supervisors.

Context

For the most part, my PDS work at Independence High School has been with the English department working with English teachers in preparing intern teachers for the classroom. My context, as an English educator, requires me to find ways of making the realities of teaching English explicit to new teachers. I am especially concerned about their becoming effective and reflective about teaching less successful students who often challenge intern teachers' preconceptions of teaching and learning.

Over the five years I have worked with IHS teachers, I have placed intern teachers with mentor teachers at IHS for both fieldwork and student teaching. But our STW program expanded our collaboration considerably and has challenged part of my work at IHS—I have begun to think about my work in teacher preparation in some new ways as a result, especially in terms of supporting beginning teachers to successfully teach all students high literacy.

During the 1996–97 school year, a major part of my responsibilities as an English education professor participating in STW was to support the development of two English interns as they completed field experiences in the autumn and winter quarters and then student teaching in the spring quarter of The Ohio State University's (OSU) master's of education (MEd) program. I have organized this section of the chapter largely around a narrative of their movement through the school year 1996–97 beginning with a summer of curricular planning meetings with the STW team to spring quarter student teaching. Within each major section of the report I have described key events that, in my judgment, contributed to the interns' growth and development during their involvement with the STW program.

The Intern Teachers

Steve Hoffman (English teacher on the STW team) and I selected the two interns for participation in the STW program during OSU's summer term, 1996. Because Doreen and Rachel attended my course titled "Linguistic Materials for Teachers," I had some understanding of their strengths and shortcomings as prospective English teachers. I also wanted Steve's input for intern selection as I realized he would be working collaboratively with our choice for an entire school year. We decided on Doreen and Rachel based on their strong academic records, their performances in my linguistics class, and a commitment to working with less successful students. In retrospect, we were quite fortunate that we selected two dedicated and imaginative interns, but we probably should have been much more systematic in our selection process. For example, in addition to using their MEd applications we might have had applicants write brief position papers about their desire to participate in STW as well as a follow-up interview about their qualifications and intentions relative to STW. However, the timing of the summer planning meetings and the fact that only a handful of English interns began the MEd program in the summer made a more extensive search process difficult at best.

Doreen, a graduate of a major research university's English department, came to STW as a highly recommended student who had worked quite successfully as an instructor for an on-campus summer writing program at that university. She was quite excited about working in the STW program, and she made consistently good contributions at the team meetings from the earliest days of the program. Rachel, who graduated from OSU the spring before she entered the MEd program, came highly recommended as a prospective teacher with a strong academic record. She was a bit older than her peers in the MEd program—she was excited about the possibilities of the STW endeavor, but she was also aware of the challenges ahead.

The MEd program that Doreen and Rachel were enrolled in during the STW program is a 50+ credit hour (quarter system) that leads to a master's degree in education and English language arts certification (grades 7–12) for the state of Ohio. One of the primary goals of the program is to foster the development of reflective teachers who can teach effectively in a range of school contexts with students of diverse ethnic and social-economic backgrounds. The STW program also provided me, as Doreen and Rachel's teacher, advisor and supervisor, with the opportunity to understand what it means to teach in an urban school, an experience that all three of us found valuable.

FROM APPRENTICESHIP OF OBSERVATION TO ENGLISH INTERNSHIP

Doreen's Student Teaching:
Learning about How Students Learn

In reading Doreen's student teaching journal, it became clear to me that by spring quarter her interest in the STW agenda had about faded because she was deeply involved in trying to survive the demands of student teaching. However, as Steve, Doreen, and I often discussed, without Doreen's extended internship at IHS through the STW project she might have had much more difficulty.

> I really am lucky that I spent so much time with Steve out here (IHS) all year. These kids are so different from me and from the way I went to school. I used to love to read and these kids just hate it. Walking in without being prepared for this would have been a shock for me.

Dan Lortie (1975), in his book titled *Schoolteacher*, argues that prospective teachers have a quite limited understanding of teaching and learning. "What students learn about teaching, then, is intuitive and imitative rather than explicit and analytical; it is based on individual personalities rather than pedagogical principles" (p. 62). Lortie calls this limited way of learning about teaching an "apprenticeship of observation." Doreen's remarks about the STW students' approach to school literacy compared to her own are quite interesting in that her time at IHS helped her, to an extent, begin to overcome her apprenticeship of observation.

There were a few key factors with the STW program that enabled her to start this process:

1. Steve, her mentor-teacher, understood this problem and made strong efforts to remind Doreen that she had to understand the students.
2. The fact that she was working with a team of STW teachers enabled her to see that she was not the only teacher struggling, and thus she felt a part of a larger effort.
3. When I worked with Doreen I constantly reminded her that the students she taught saw the world quite differently from the middle-class suburban students she was more comfortable with.
4. Doreen needed a prolonged and intensive involvement with the less successful STW students to see how various groups responded to the same curriculum over time. (Note that the trimester system, which organizes the school year around three 12–week sessions, allows teachers to revise entire courses during the school year.)

Doreen struggled with finding ways to connect with the students, but this was not for lack of trying. She made every effort to consider how the STW students would respond to various activities; the problem was, however, that she did not always know how to respond to their resistance and then move on. Again, if she had not observed Steve dealing with similar issues and lessons across the school year, she might have been more despairing.

One example of how Steve taught Doreen teaching strategies occurred in their efforts to teach writing. The STW students were verbally fluent speakers, but they did not have much skill in formulating coherent written prose. Steve demonstrated to Doreen how, for instance, to take instructions for writing a comparison and contrast essay and break the assignment into series of tasks: listing student-generated ideas on the board for each idea being compared, looking for commonalties and differences, writing a first draft, and so on. Accordingly, Doreen was able to develop a stronger notion of how such instruction was enacted because she had observed Steve in such instruction, then was able to practice doing so during student teaching.

Rachel's Student Teaching: Understanding Instructional Scaffolding for Teaching Writing

When Rachel began student teaching in March 1997, she faced a daunting task. First she had to take the responsibility of teaching STW students without the assistance of an experienced mentor teacher (her first mentor teacher had left IHS for another school), and she had to adjust to a second mentor teacher with whom she had worked for a very limited time during winter quarter. Rachel's challenge was juggling two very different sets of students (STW and "regular" ninth-graders) and mentor teacher expectations. On the one hand, Rachel had complete freedom to make her own instructional decisions when working with a less experienced teacher, and, on the other, she faced more constraints when working with a more experienced teacher. If Doreen's case illustrates the value of yearlong internships, Rachel's case illustrates the problems of moving between mentor teachers.

Accordingly, my role as advisor and supervisor of her student teaching was quite different than they were for Doreen. For example, Rachel wanted to teach persuasive writing, but when she had attempted to do so in her regular ninth-grade class, the students had been confused by the organizational structure she wanted—five paragraphs with the first paragraph to introduce a thesis statement, three middle paragraphs to impact central ideas, and a final paragraph to summarize. When she began to plan to teach such an essay to her STW students, she realized she would have to start in a different way, for her full-year STW internship allowed her to understand the importance of instructional scaffolding or structured support for students as they undertake new and more difficult tasks. "If I learned anything this (school) year it is that STW students need very carefully organized lessons. They are not independent at all, and if they get confused, they won't sit and try to figure things out—they just get frustrated and then quit."

In May 1997, I observed Rachel's lesson with her C Block (12:20–2:30 p.m. class) STW students in which she began with the question, "What does it mean to persuade?" She received helpful responses to the question and then engaged the students for 23 minutes in a discussion of possible topics. As she did so she repeatedly tied the topics (school rules, music, food, etc.) to issues related to the world of work— for instance, "How might learning how to debate and to argue well be valuable if you have to work with people who have differing opinions?" After listing topics for the essay on the board she demonstrated how to develop controversial issues for presentation in a persuasive essay: "You need to have two different sides or points-of-view if you are writing a persuasive essay. Then you need to argue for one side." She then gave her students copies of two essays (she had written these herself) to demonstrate a negative and positive example of such an essay. Throughout the lesson Rachel reminded her students that "you need to learn how to persuade people, especially people who don't know you personally." If Doreen learned how to structure her lessons from her long apprenticeship with Steve, Rachel had to develop much of her structured lessons on her own. She was able to do so due to her prolonged exposure to STW students, her writing methods course, and a natural good sense for teaching. Rachel kept herself motivated using her passionate creed: to foster and inspire her students to be aware of the social issues they will need to face to bring about social change.

Lessons I Learned by Working with Doreen and Rachel

The benefits the interns derived from our School to Work program seemed to be located primarily in long-term internships with mentor teachers. Without her mentor teacher's continuing support with planning, Doreen's student teaching experience would not have been as successful as it was. When a relationship with a mentor teacher was lost, in the case of Rachel, many of the benefits were substantially reduced. Only Rachel's perseverance, intelligence, and passionate creed to serve her students enabled her to be successful. As a result, I understand that as a university professor I must work with mentor teachers to develop bridges between the school and university.

Although Doreen and Rachel sometime wondered how teaching in a suburban high school compared to teaching in their urban PDS school, they took a great deal from a yearlong internship in an urban school that challenged them to clarify their own beliefs and ideas about teaching high literacy to all students. Despite the fact that they did not experience the kind of successes they had expected, they learned a great deal about the social and academic backgrounds of their students and realities and routines of a school whose mission is to educate students living in an urban environment with all of its challenges.

I learned a great deal from my collaborative efforts with Steve. We learned more about the type of intern-teacher we would like to work with in the STW program (self-assured, confident, flexible, imaginative, willing to take on the teacher's many roles, etc.). We also learned that three-way meetings with the interns are invaluable as a way to establish common goals and reflective analysis of teaching.

PREPARING TEACHERS FOR URBAN SCHOOLS: SCHOOL TO WORK AT INDEPENDENCE HIGH SCHOOL

Steven E. Hoffman

In my roles as a teacher in an urban high school, a university instructor in a teacher preparation program, a peer teacher coach and mentor, and a doctoral student, I have often deliberated on the next generation of teachers. My concern is less with those who will take positions in rural or suburban districts. As vast numbers of teachers retire and their replacements are lured to the suburbs, how can our society guarantee that every child, regardless of socioeconomic status, has a qualified professional in their classroom?

For the last five years, I have taught ninth-grade English at Columbus Independence High School in the morning and educational psychology and general teaching methods at The Ohio State University in the afternoon. As a clinical educator, I taught two courses required of all students who were preparing for student teaching in their major subject areas. My typical university classes were constituted of less than 5% minority population. Furthermore, few of my students had any type of urban experience and even fewer had any desire to work in the urban context.

In spring 1996, I was offered the opportunity to work with university faculty and my high school colleagues in the School to Work program. In truth, I was the only member of the English Department who agreed to participate. My own hesitation resulted from my belief that my plate was already overflowing. However, because of my previous efforts on projects with George Newell and Beth Carnate, I looked forward to the new collaboration. Professors from the various teacher preparation disciplines would work with us to develop a program that would provide a career focus for our students and a meaningful field experience for their students. In addition, the university would offer highly qualified incoming MEd students the chance for internships at IHS for the entire school year. These students would follow the high school calendar. The interns would gradually spend increasing time at the high school until they were prepared to take full responsibility for our classes.

On numerous occasions, I had been a cooperating teacher for short- and long-term field experiences, but this was the first time that I would work with a preservice teacher throughout the experience. And with my variety of experiences and longevity, I felt that unqualified success was a certainty.

After a number of future MEd students declined to participate in our pilot program, Doreen Sloan, a 22-year-old graduate of a major university was selected as my English intern. She was available—right away. Not only could she teach in August, but also she could attend the planning meetings during the summer. Despite her small-town background, despite her diminutive stature, despite her youthful appearance (for a long time, hall monitors would stop her and ask for her pass), she felt that she could learn to teach at IHS.

With high hopes, we began the school year. Miss Sloan was in the class from Day 1 and I sought to give her "air time" almost immediately. She observed me teach, wrote reflective journals, helped cooperating groups, tutored individual students, graded some papers, made up a couple of assignments—and concluded that it would be awhile before she could get up in front of the classroom. She felt that the students were much more responsive to me and that when she talked, the students often lost focus and drowned her out with their conversations. (Even her voice was diminutive.)

Truly these School to Work students were a challenge. All were behind in mathematics. Some had passed no courses the previous years; they had received social promotions. A common thread was a lack of motivation, perhaps because of a lack of success. The School to Work students were a challenging group for seasoned veterans let alone a preservice teacher.

Over the year, my attitude toward our MEd students rose and fell with some frequency. Early in the year, I was disappointed with Doreen's inability to make connections with my students. She illustrated conflict with her brother by relating an experience water-skiing on Lake Erie. None of my students had ever been water-skiing and few students had ever been to a lake. Often she complained that the methods she was learning at the university were of no use at IHS because of the students. However, she made little effort to adapt these methods to the abilities of our students.

At times, I agonized over our selection of her for the STW program. What had we been thinking—a White, middle-class, young, inexperienced, naive girl—with an overwhelmingly African American, middle to lower socioeconomic status student body? In many ways, she was less worldly than the students who were eight years younger than her. And such vastly different levels of motivation. She was a Phi Beta Kappa and they were middle school failures. Perhaps the concept of the intern was a good idea, but how could we assume that success was a possibility? Perhaps with a group of highly motivated honor students, she might get and keep their attention. And it just wasn't my MEd student. All the interns were from middle-class, suburban backgrounds. Even the one minority MEd student was from an affluent suburb of Washington, D.C. Were we blind making selections? Who was kidding whom? And yet hadn't I made a similar transition 28 years before? I had known only one African-American person growing up in a suburb of Boston. Is it possible in a matter of days or months to prepare teachers for an urban environment?

Another one of my concerns with the MEd students was their lack of knowledge about child development. Often my student intern was upset with the attitudes of our students. Much of the problem could be traced to the immaturity typical of ninth graders. Can MEd students learn the basics of development strictly through experience?

As a school faculty, we faced a number of problems. Little common planning time had been built into the schedule. Perhaps I was not the best candidate for the project. With my OSU half-day commitment, perhaps my plate was already full. I found that my priority was working with my intern as opposed to planning with my colleagues. My colleagues seemed to be busy also—one making the adjustment to classroom teaching, the other with her numerous time commitments. With another year, might we have had time for more collaboration?

The university offered to administer learning style inventories to our students. The inventories seemed doomed from the beginning. Students didn't seem to take the survey seriously. When the results came back, we had a new set of students, and there never seemed to be enough time to go over the results. A missed opportunity.

Undoubtedly one of the greatest benefits to come from the STW program was the spirit of collaboration between university and public school faculty. Previous field experience supervisors were typically teaching assistants with no urban education experiences. They did not have the time or inclination to explore the culture of the students whom they supervised. With the IHS/OSU STW project, MEd students were supervised by full-time university faculty who spent long hours over the year observing classes and supplying feedback to their students. School faculty accepted university personnel, not as experts, but as colleagues. As the year progressed, the lack of regular meeting time proved to be hurtful to the partnership. Other commitments severely damaged the potential learning community. Instead of meeting as a large group, pairing by subject area became the norm.

Postscripts

My intern, Doreen Sloan graduated in the summer. She has accepted a position in a small Christian school in Columbus. She felt that even after a year at IHS, she wasn't ready to teach in the city. A second intern, Rachel Moots, is now teaching full time at IHS. Like Rachel, hopefully, others who are among the best and the brightest and most idealistic, those who can make a difference, will end up in urban classrooms.

Although the School to Work program is no longer the focus of our collaboration, the school-university partnership continues. Five first-quarter MEd students had their first field experiences at IHS. A group of 28 students in George Newell's methods class presented a lesson to three different English classes. Three IHS teachers have spoken to the methods classes about their approaches to literature. In the spring, three OSU interns chose to do the traditional student-teaching experience at IHS. The most talented of these student interns will begin her teaching career with the Columbus City Schools in the fall.

AN INTERN'S PERSPECTIVE

Rachel Moots

My participation in the School to Work program began with the weeklong planning in early August. I had entered the master's certification program at OSU in June and had just completed my first quarter of coursework. Having missed all the previous STW planning sessions held during the summer and having not yet stepped foot in a high school, I began the program feeling lost and rather overwhelmed. However, I was paired with a wonderful mentor teacher, Janet, who was a tremendous help.

Because of my participation in the STW program, my experience in the MEd was significantly different than those of the other master's candidates (except, of course, for Doreen). I was placed at IHS from the first day of classes; other interns did not begin their internships in high schools until the end of September at the earliest. I was able to spend many more hours at the school than the other interns, for participation in the STW program demanded a more intensive involvement in the school. I was given the opportunity to work with teachers other than my mentor teacher (and in subjects other than English), an opportunity the other interns were not afforded.

Being a graduate student, I was part of the university community. Yet, early on, as a classroom observer, and, later, as a student teacher, I was also part of the Independence High School community. I was part of the STW team, but also, because I was only an intern, I felt I was truly not part of the team. I was an observer of many other teachers and I was being observed by my university advisor when I taught. One of my greatest challenges during the entire year was reconciling all of these dichotomies.

Learning to Teach in an Urban School

Because I had spent most of my career as a student in privileged institutions, being a part of STW during my entire year of teacher training was extremely beneficial for me. Having only attended private and alternative schools, my picture of an urban school was one formed from media sources (movies, newspaper articles) and from discussions with those who had attended urban schools. Although this picture was not entirely incorrect, my biggest misconceptions were those about the challenges of teaching in an urban school. I believed that if I just cared enough, if I was dedicated enough, if I was smart enough, I would be a good teacher no matter what the situation was. What I discovered working with the STW program was that being a good teacher entails more than just care and dedication. What I believe now is that being a good teacher in a classroom like a STW classroom requires knowledge of how to reach students who, for the most part, have not been reached before.

I was told in my university classes right from the beginning that teaching is much more than relating my subject matter to students, and I had no hesitation agreeing with and believing that. However, being in the STW program brought that point home to me early on. I learned that some students need more than a teacher who knows subject matter and a variety of teaching theories and methods. Many students needed a counselor, a mediator, an advocate, an advisor, a champion, and a disciplinarian. These students did not have all the resources I did growing up, nor did they have all the resources many other kids their age had. They brought a great deal of baggage, much of it negative, to the classroom; I learned that this baggage must be dealt with (if only acknowledged) in order for these students to become teachable.

Bridging Theory and Practice

I was continually frustrated with my inability to put into practice the concepts my professors were telling me would work in any situation. At one point, because I took so literally the things I was hearing from professors and the things I was reading in my textbooks, I thought very seriously about a change in career plans. I was convinced that because I could not effectively put into practice the ideas that I was learning in my university classes, I was a failure as a teacher.

However, once I began to talk about these failures with other teachers in the English department, I began to be reassured that maybe my classroom failures were not entirely due to my inexperience as a teacher. I started to listen to teachers who had struggled with this same issue, that of translating theory into practice in an urban setting. What I began to see was that I could not use much of what I was learning in my university classes without a good deal of adaptation. The ideas being offered me at the university were ideas that would have worked, I believe, with much more ease in a suburban setting and with students who were not "lower tracked." Frankly, the students I worked with did not have the educational background to allow for effective implementation of many of the ideas I was learning at the university. I absolutely do not mean to say the STW students were incapable of learning; they simply did not have the tools to learn in many of the ways I was being told to teach them.

As an example, I tried to work with tableaux with the STW students. We had read about and discussed tableaux quite a bit in my methods courses, and I had observed an eighth-grade teacher who worked successfully with tableaux (the first time for both the teacher and her students). However, when I introduced tableaux to my students during student teaching, it was less than an educational experience for them. Their entire educational experiences were basically teacher-centered. They were used to answering very specific questions from the teacher and to traditional forms of responding to literature. When I tried the tableaux, they could not take the activity seriously (I think, because they did not have the sense it was a valid form of response), and they also were unable to have any sort of discussion after the tableaux. Unlike the eighth-graders I observed, these students had not had any experience in discussing a work of literature, let alone creating a meaningful still picture of a work of literature. This activity was so far out of their range of experience that I was unable to help them make any sort of relevant connections to either the text or to their own lives.

Another example of my struggle to reconcile my methods courses with my actual classroom experience was my attempt to use small groups in my classroom during student teaching. I had been told over and over again in my methods classes how effective small groups were in helping students be active participants in the learning process. My professors and textbooks all assumed I would be working with students coming from very different backgrounds than mine did and I was offered very few alternative ways of teaching, ways that could reach the less-motivated, less-able learners with whom I was working. Because my mentor teacher was a first-year teacher (my first mentor teacher had left IHS a few weeks after school started) struggling with the same issues I was, she could not tell me I would have to teach these students how to work effectively in groups. Fortunately, I eventually went to some of the other English teachers and from them I was able to devise a way of helping students be better able to teach each other in small group settings.

Challenges

In addition to the challenge of bridging the gap between theory and practice, there were some other struggles very specific to the STW program. My first mentor teacher left IHS at the end of September to take a contract at another school, leaving her position open. The teacher who filled her position, while a talented and very able teacher, was in no position to be a mentor teacher. She was a first-year teacher, and, in addition to having to deal with the myriad of challenges that that entails, she was being asked to teach me how to teach! Considering the tasks that were before her, I think she did an excellent job, but I am still frustrated that I was made to work with a brand-new teacher.

Another challenge of STW was the entire team and people's fading commitment to the team as the year progressed, particularly as we learned that STW would not continue the following school year. By the time the members of the team were finally set, frustrations with the students in the STW program became overwhelming for many of us. We were working with some of the most difficult students in the school (all put together in one group) and this took a toll on our energy and nerves. Although the STW program faded dramatically by the beginning of spring, I still learned a great deal about how to collaborate with other teachers, both in and outside of my subject area.

CLOSING THOUGHTS

As we close our chapter, the future of our PDS partnership is unclear. These school-university relationships are indeed dynamic enterprises that often require external funding—our partnership is no exception. The project has ended and we are facing the challenge to conceptualize a new direction if we are to continue the interdisciplinary nature of the work.

At the university, PDS funding is now spread across a network of schools directly tied to program areas involved in the preparation of MEd interns rather than collaboration at one school site such as the IHS/OSU PDS. The school system is struggling to serve 63,000 students and though the need is apparent to continue this work, funds are not available to support this intensive PDS collaboration.

However, we continue to work and collaborate whenever possible. Beth continues to lead professional development work at IHS; Steve continues to work with the English MEd program as a mentor of beginning English teachers; George has begun taking the preservice English teachers into the school to work collaboratively with Steve and other mentor teachers to plan and implement writing instruction; the social studies PDS continues (as a network across several high schools in the county); and this school year Rachel will begin her second year as an English teacher at IHS.

It seems likely that yearlong internships, staff and student teaming, experimentation with integrated curriculum, and the close collaboration of professors and mentors will continue to keep alive the shared vision and mission of our PDS. This collaboration strengthens our commitment to the renewal of inservice professionals and to the preparation of prospective teachers to teach all children, especially those in urban schools.

REFERENCES

Feiman-Nemser, S. & Buchmann, M. (1985). Pitfalls of experience in teacher preparation. *Teachers College Record, 87*(1).

Lortie, D.C. (1975). *Schoolteacher: A sociological study*. Chicago: University of Chicago Press.

CHAPTER 11

Project Learn:
Closing the Gap

Barbara Thomson, Eugenie Maxwell, Lizbeth Kelley, and Beth Carnate

In this chapter, participants of the Project Learn PDS describe their focus and activities. This PDS emerged out of a shared interest in learning styles that existed before PDSs were initiated. Their PDS reflects their commitment to the use of learning styles frameworks for learning and teaching. Over time their PDS grows to include a wide variety of educators and schools that are interested in learning styles theories. It is a far-ranging PDS network made up of colleagues in many schools and the interns with whom they work.

There is a continuing discrepancy between student achievement and national student expectations. From *Why Johnny Can't Read* (Flesch, 1955) books of the fifties and sixties to more recent best sellers, such as *The Learning Gap* (Stevenson, 1992), school reform and achievement continue to be hot topics. Closing the gap between actual and expected achievement is a high priority and a national agenda.

In October of 1957 when the Russians launched the first satellite (Sputnik I) into space, politicians, educators, scientists, parents, and concerned citizens criticized schools for lagging academic achievement (Trowbridge & Bybee, 1996). Sputnik became a symbol of the need for educational reform as described by Bruner (1960) and others. An intensive period of curriculum revision and teacher training in science was initiated, but after forty years we are not yet able to ensure academic success for all students. There are currently, however, many new strategies to enhance academic achievement through collaborative, research-based partnerships. The opportunity to develop a PDS allowed us to try out some collaborative reform ideas and strategies.

GERMINATING A PDS PARTNERSHIP

We initiated our PDS issuing a "Call for Teachers" in schools where we had developed previous relationships. We invited teachers to a session to determine several questions: Should we start a PDS Partnership? Who should be involved? Where do we start? What does a partnership mean? How do we germinate this seed?

We decided to initiate a partnership and to explore educational reforms. Some teachers volunteered to recruit others they felt would add strength to the partnership. A university professor, a district teacher liaison administrator, and two classroom teachers formed a management team to keep data, analyze journal reflections, and acquire materials for discussion.

Rather than submit a formal proposal to the College Advisory Board the first year, we met in small groups weekly after school for the entire academic year. A State Department of Education supervisor also joined our group. The university offered three hours of optional graduate seminar credit. Each participant submitted a weekly reflective journal that we used to determine future directions.

The planning team along with the teachers became the Salon of Learning Partnership Core for the pilot year. This group later was referred to simply as "the core group." Journal entries reflected that teachers felt they had a sense of mission and professionalism.

One of the challenges was selecting quality publications for discussion. It became evident to us that many reform initiatives in the literature focused on improving learning outcomes but did not have implementation strategies or much of a research base.

The teachers decided to use personal reflection strategies to examine their past experiences with reform initiatives in order to understand why these reforms did not last. Many teachers wrote in their journals that many of these past reforms were adopted to increase learning, but they did not have the desired outcomes. In discussions they agreed that jumping from one bandwagon to another every few years had taken a toll on their enthusiasm and energy. Professional development with a new initiative year after year had been draining and discouraging. Many of these approaches had no research base and were history before a research agenda could be initiated.

We selected an extensive web of reform literature that we read, discussed, explored, dissected, compared, contrasted, and categorized. Several commonalities rose to the surface: (*a*) we must enhance learning for everyone, (*b*) it takes an extensive community partnership for successful reform, and (*c*) reform recommendations should include strategies to build a strong research base.

It took a year of reading and discussion to reach a consensus that identified the critical questions that would guide our next steps:

1. Which models are really effective for learners?
2. How can we identify how individual students learn?
3. How can we identify how teachers learn and teach?
4. How can we increase learning through instruction?
5. What are similarities and differences among learners?
6. Which learning models have sound research bases?

Enhancing student learning at all levels became the focus for this partnership.

At the end of the first year, the core group wrote a proposal to establish a PDS. The work would focus on learning within a teacher education framework using action-research strategies. We submitted a proposal to the PDS Advisory Board in June 1991 and it was officially approved in August.

Our core group focused on how students might improve their achievement in science, mathematics, and technology across the K–12 curriculum. All OSU students in this PDS regardless of certification would have field experiences in elementary, middle school, and high school settings. National and state standards emphasize the necessity for improving achievement in math, science, and technology throughout the K–12 curriculum and we wanted to explore the learning gap in these subject areas. The TIMSS Report indicates that students in the United States are not as competitive in science and mathematics as students in other countries.

"Project Learn: Closing the Gap" became the title for this PDS. Our shared goal was to increase the learning of all students. When children are not learning the way we teach, then we must teach them the way they learn (Dunn & Dunn, 1992).

ESSENTIAL VARIABLES OF THE PDS

The variables that made our beginning work together successful included enthusiasm, trust, listening, and building a vision.

Enthusiasm

We knew we had to have enthusiasm among the partners in order to function effectively. The excitement and motivation about our work kept our energy levels high. Not everyone was motivated all the time, but keeping everyone involved with important activities was a critical variable.

Trust

A second variable was trust. We started to use each other's strengths to move the core group ahead. Sharing ideas, materials, and mistakes openly with acceptance from everyone helped to build this trust. We used a horizontal management model so there were no top-down, unilateral decisions. Continual communication helped to build trust and a commitment to our PDS.

Building trust among our core group was critical. However, trust from colleagues not involved in PDS both at the university and within the diverse districts created challenges. These groups seemed unable to understand what and why we were doing the various activities and constantly questioned how each PDS could be so different. Having one template for all PDS sites would have been more useful for the uninvolved educators who did not have this vision of diversity and experimentation.

Educators external to the PDS model had difficulty trusting the core to move ahead but they did not want to commit themselves and become involved in this time-consuming partnership. Math and Science administrators often made "top-down" unilateral decisions that caused problems for a horizontal partnership as district partners were left out of the loop. Professors who were not "early adopters" had difficulty allowing the core group to be collaborative and explore learning and teaching questions. Interns were informed that they did not have to follow the PDS model in certain situations. The core group discovered these changes when the interns arrived to work in the school setting. The core group was forced to incorporate changes and eliminate certain key components as interns had been informed that they were not to participate in certain PDS activities. Despite these challenges, the trust among the core group members became stronger with each "top-down surprise."

Listening

A third variable was listening. Teachers like to talk and share; however, listening was difficult. Listening to each other's ideas was a necessary component for a strong partnership. We used the Dunn Productivity Environmental Preference (PEPS) Learning Styles Instruments and the Learning Style Inventory (LSI) (Dunn & Dunn, 1992) to identify individual strengths. The PEPS profiles assisted us in learning about our best modalities. A great deal of humor was a part of knowing about each other's learning modalities. For example, we had a number of low-auditory partners who could remember every word, but only if they took notes. Initially, listening to each other was our most difficult challenge, but it became one of our most powerful tools.

A VISION

As a group, we constructed a vision. We wanted our shared vision to be supported by a strong research base. A powerful research data base functioned as a filter to resolve differences and enhance our knowledge of learning.

Many of the teachers had a particular favorite among the almost 200 learning style models the core group explored. However, few of them had a quality research component. DeBello (1990) and Dunn and Griggs's (1995) analyses of numerous learning models indicated that the Dunn and Dunn model (1992, 1993) had excellent validity and reliability. The PEPS, the K–2 individual LSI, and the grades 3–12 instruments have quality validity and reliability along with many sound research studies including international studies (Milgram, Dunn, & Price, 1993).

EXPANDING THE PROJECT LEARN PARTNERSHIP

During the first official PDS year (1991–92) we started working with K–12 students and preservice teachers as partners in learning. Science education graduate students also joined the partnership to work with the interns. All teachers were given the Dunn (PEPS) Learning Style Inventory. Students took the Learning Style Inventory (LSI) appropriate for their grade level. An individual profile was generated and study prescription were provided with each profile and analysis. Personal implementation strategies were included in the individual student and teacher packets. Teachers used profile data to develop instructional strategies and enhance individual strengths.

Providing innovative preservice and inservice programs for the preparation of teachers created a collaboration challenge. Using only PDS partnership teachers for our field placements, however, created some controversy because:

1. Administrators often wanted to make final placement decisions.

2. Administrators viewed field placements as a way to upgrade district experiences using Ohio State students in classrooms with weak teachers.

3. Teachers who were not PDS partners wanted an Ohio State student without PDS involvement.

4. Ohio State Professors with funded projects in schools, but with no PDS involvement, wanted preservice students to work with their projects.

5. Elementary PDS placements could be clustered in single buildings but secondary math and science had to be placed in many different buildings making supervision and travel more difficult.

6. Some university professors required assignments from their classes to be completed at field sites but PDS teachers did not view these tasks as critical since they were top-down decisions and not an integral part of the Project Learn partnership.

7. Some students wanted placements in certain buildings that were not PDS partnership schools and these requests were approved by administrators.

8. Some professors told students that PDS was a fad and not to take it seriously.

9. Teachers who were not partners were not always happy with the PDS teacher visibility and access to Ohio State technology.

10. Parents from non-PDS classes wondered why their students were not receiving the extra resources and attention to learning.

11. Some educators not involved in PDS were not pleased with the PDS initiative, and did not appreciate the attention given PDS partners.

12. Teacher Education syllabus requirements were negotiated with partners to reflect best practice. Some Ohio State colleagues felt that public school educators should not help professors make content decisions.

These controversial challenges were addressed collaboratively. For many teachers this was the first time they had been asked to help design a program for preservice students. Carol, a kindergarten teacher, said, "This is great but it's much more work and a scary responsibility to be involved in the real preparation of teachers." Linda said, "Working with Ohio State students was so much easier when they were just assisting me. Now that I am responsible to contribute to their professional development, I have to understand what I am doing."

NEW ROLES FOR TEACHERS

Clinical educators are practitioners who teach classes in their district for half the day and work as a teacher educator in collaboration with university coordinators the other half of their time. Supervision, methods, classroom assistance, workshops, conferences, placements, and inquiry were all part of creating collaborative change through the clinical educator and Project Learn partnership. Project Learn also shares two clinical educators with other PDS partners who are in urban schools.

Initially clinical educators met as a group to explore and develop their roles. Field professors were identified in each building. A field professor is a teacher/leader who has been a PDS exemplary partner and requested more involvement. Field professors are full-time teachers, who help with placements in their building, work with the principal, support the interns, find instructional resources, and collaborate with the co-coordinators and clinical educators.

When individual teachers assume new responsibilities, other teachers may be jealous. Jealousy is a definite challenge in PDSs that involve only a few teachers within the school building. Project Learn, fortunately, has had only one school where this kind of jealously was a serious problem. The department chair wanted to be a field professor but had never been involved with the PDS because of responsibilities for coaching and music supplemental contracts. A field professor receives no pay but the role still created a challenge because she had some power the department chair did not control. Consequently, the chair made life difficult for our field professor and talked to non-PDS Ohio State colleagues expressing her dissatisfaction with the program. The principal was aware of the problem but did not want to micromanage a department.

GENIE'S STORY ABOUT BEING A CLINICAL EDUCATOR

"So, what do you do as a clinical educator?" is the question I'm often asked by my teaching colleagues, school administrator, and college faculty. This is not a question that can be answered in a few tossed-off phrases, but when I try to give a brief response it often sounds like a listing of mini-jobs.

During my five-year tenure as a clinical educator, I've combined being a half-time teacher with the position of a half-time clinical educator, but neither of these jobs is truly half-time. For half of my time, I have a regular teaching assignment at Darby High School. The daily challenges of the classroom require preparation of lab activities, addressing the interests and concerns of the students, and maintaining all of the records that are an integral part of any public school teacher's job description. Classroom teaching is important to me. I enjoy the challenges and rewards that are inherent in interacting with young adults. They are usually fun and energizing.

For my clinical educator position, I also work with Barbara Thomson as co-coordinator of our PDS. My duties and responsibilities both at the college and public schools constantly overlap and blend into a unique educational role. The model in which I function is different from that of many other clinical educators, but it provides unique opportunities as I move from the public school arena to the community and then to the "ivory tower" of academia. Frequently this all happens in a single day.

I see my position as one who has "a toehold" in the College of Education and "one foot still firmly planted" in public school teaching. Admittedly this is a balancing act. As clinical educator I am the bridge between the theory of the university and the practice of the public schools. But remember, a "bridge" supports traffic in both directions.

Clinical Educator Activities and Interactions

In *Tomorrow's Teachers* (Holmes Group, 1986) a Career Professional Teacher is described as one who provides staff development opportunities, curriculum improvement, testing and measurement, strengthening home-school relationships, preparing instructional materials, and conducting action research. This describes some of my activities as clinical educator.

When I began the first year as a clinical educator there was initial coolness from some teachers in my school district who also had wanted this opportunity. But I soon found that we were able to continue to work cooperatively as we had for years previously. I am able to smooth out some of the bumps in the bureaucracy of class time schedules, instructor permission signatures, and late registrations, to give insights into specific courses and instructors, suggest specific resources and readings, and help initiate new directions for changes in classroom strategies. My colleagues frequently ask for mentoring support as they begin to question and then refine their teaching practice. My role is seen as a true supporting colleague and not as someone who has deserted the classroom for a "heady" job at the university.

Our PDS has a shared goal to improve the learning of students through identifying and adapting to their particular learning style. As teachers in our PDS schools heard about learning styles through the presentations that Barbara Thomson and I made at faculty meetings and during informal conversations, they requested that their students' learning style strengths be identified as well as their own. They also received information about implementation strategies that could be used in their classrooms to help students learn. We provided seminars and followed these inservice sessions with special evening workshops for parents so they could be an important partner in their child's education. Frequently counselors ask that two of us be present during conferences at which administrators, parents, and the student gather to craft a homework study plan. This is an example of partnering. When suggestions are implemented, it's a joy to see a student happily and successfully working through his/her strengths.

PDS Principles

Professional Development School (PDS) sites were envisioned by the original Holmes Group as bringing practicing teachers together with university faculty in partnerships based on four principles (Holmes Group, 1986). These principles included reciprocity, inquiry, experimentation, and a commitment to the development of teaching strategies for a broad range of children. My co-coordinator and I have facilitated these goals by extending our PDS partnership to many inner-city and suburban schools with diverse student populations. Both teachers and parents want to know new strategies in helping children learn. In particular, teachers learn to give learning-style inventories to their students, interpret style profiles, and experiment with different teaching procedures and homework plans that enable students to work in their strengths with greater success.

While a few teachers have completed research projects, it has been difficult to get more of them to incorporate inquiry into their teaching. They often regard research as an additional chore, and many don't see that examining their own practice is worth the time and energy. Interns, placed with experienced teachers in PDS schools, are required to design and carry out an inquiry project as part of their internship experiences in partnership with teachers. They are learning that research and reflection are key parts of professional development and we hope that the experiences they have will lead them to continue this practice in their profession.

University Clinical Educator Role

In another section of *Tomorrow's Teachers*, members of the Holmes Group address the topic of faculty in teacher education. They suggest that the responsibility for educating teachers includes university and school-based faculty. Practicing teachers from public schools would be considered clinical faculty while college faculty would be referred to as academic faculty. This implies that clinical faculty would have a special status and be reimbursed for their professional contribution. The dean of our college supports my position by providing funds to my school district to hire a substitute teacher for half of my daily classroom responsibilities. She also includes me in the social and academic activities of the college and I feel my efforts are appreciated and my ideas and suggestions are valued. My school district supports my position by agreeing to my partial teaching load while continuing my complete salary and benefits. The district administrators appreciate the opportunities my position brings to our learning community through parent workshops, inservice opportunities for professional development for our teachers, and a pool of talented student interns, all of whom enhance the learning experiences of all our students.

Working With Interns

Before we initiated this PDS, the placement of interns with cooperating teachers in the schools reflected little use of good education principles. Frequently assignments were made to reward teachers for years of service, to give them some time out of the classroom for special projects, or to give "extra help" with a particularly difficult class. No thought was given to teaching style or evidence of exemplary classroom practices. Often student teachers were mismatched with cooperating teachers in subject area or teaching style (Dunn, Dunn & Perrin, 1994). Now my co-coordinator and I take time to know the needs and interests of the interns in order to match them with practicing educators whose styles are compatible and teaching is exceptional. Both interns and experienced teachers benefit from this professional partnership.

Because of this positive interaction, school administrators have come to trust my recommendations regarding hiring new faculty, selecting teachers to be mentors for interns as well as entry-year teachers, and initiating new programs for students and staff. Recently a district administrator told me how pleased he was with how quickly the newly hired entry-level teachers were becoming an integral, contributing part of our teaching community. My recommendations to him regarding the teachers he chose to hire came from my experiences of personally knowing these first-year teachers during their college coursework, observing them while student teaching, and understanding how their teaching philosophy and strategies would complement the learning atmosphere of our district.

It would be a sham to suggest that these five years as a clinical educator have all been trouble free. There have been challenges along the way. For example, a few years ago an exciting program of using learning styles to change the way teachers taught was accepted by a majority of staff members in one of our PDS schools. Teachers embraced this program, participated in a national leadership institute, presented workshops and seminars for their peers, inventoried their students' learning-style strengths, changed the delivery of lessons to recognize and honor these student preferences only to have this thriving initiative thwarted by a lack of administrative support. While the school continues to inventory students' learning strengths, few teachers are actively using this information in their classrooms. Priorities seem to be directed to other areas by the administration and little support is given to the teachers to continue this particular teaching strategy.

In contrast, teachers in another school who piloted this program last year have petitioned the administrator to continue to inventory students' learning styles. Teachers have incorporated this information into the collaborative planning for their team, and counselors have asked that this information be placed in the students' folder for use specifically during parent/staff conferences. The team of teachers involved in the School to Work initiative will include each students' learning style profile in their Career Information Plan (CIP) folder, which students use to build a portfolio for entry to college or the workforce upon graduation. Administrative support is evident. Staff members at a second high school have recently initiated conversations with me to bring our PDS Project Learn to their school.

University challenges are also present. Some academic faculty view clinical educators as cheap help. These faculty make decisions without clinical educator input. Faculty who do not work with a PDS model also have to work with school placements. Faculty who have no commitment to the Holmes agenda should not work with this model unless they are willing to embrace the Holmes goals.

Teaching at the University

Another important goal stated by the Holmes partnership is that of preparation of preservice teachers. Some of my most enjoyable experiences have been when I was presenting seminars and workshops for the undergraduate and graduate students in their methods and theory courses. When we discuss making instructional style adaptation to accommodate learning disabled (LD), severe behavioral handicapped (SBH), and English as a Second Language (ESL) students in an inclusion class, they eagerly make suggestions based on their previous work situation and their college course experiences. Hearing examples from me and other teachers in the field, they realize the importance of including all students in the learning process and the promise of success that using learning-style strengths holds for all students regardless of their talents or challenges.

Usually during the last quarter of college courses we spend one seminar addressing the professional characteristics of a teacher. Following a modified constructivist (Osborne & Freyberg, 1985) approach with an individual survey, large and small group discussion, a bit of encouragement, reflection, and sharing, they are able to construct a composite picture of the characteristics that a professional teacher exhibits. I'm always encouraged by their responses and resolve, and I'm confident in their ability to become contributing members of the teaching profession. PDS makes a difference!

My Own Professional Development

The fifth goal of the Holmes Partnership is to provide high-quality graduate programs for the preparation of a future education professoriate. As a clinical educator I am able to take advantage of fee wavers for tuition to complete the coursework for a PhD in Science Education. When the degree is completed, a part-time clinical adjunct faculty position with a college that follows the criteria of the Holmes Partnership would give me an opportunity to continue teaching in a public school while being directly engaged in pre- and inservice professional development of educators—that bridge between the two educational areas.

While the pressures of time present a huge challenge, these activities and projects have provided such a rich environment for my professional growth that I cherish these past few years and I look forward to new opportunities and challenges in our PDS as my role continues to evolve.

URBAN PLACEMENTS FOR INTERNS

Many of our students have never had urban experiences because they come from rural settings. We believe that it is important for preservice interns and teachers in our partnership to experience diversity and cultural differences. Our interns are provided with rich cultural and diversity experiences as part of Project Learn whether or not they initially would choose this for themselves. For example, Greg, an intern, did not want to teach in an urban setting. After a PDS urban experience, Greg decided that he wanted an urban placement because he found that his strategies and commitment to students made a difference in the lives of urban youth. Although he had never been in an urban setting prior to this assignment, he immediately identified with the equity, diversity, and cultural aspects present in this environment. PDS made a difference in

Greg's goals and he is now committed to making a difference with his urban students.

We still have a few interns and faculty who do not want to work in an urban setting. Nevertheless, we feel that it is critical that we educate teachers at every level, including university educators, about equity and diversity issues and the richness of various cultures. As Project Learn cocoordinators, we no longer have field placement partnership responsibilities so we cannot ensure appropriate diversity and cultural experiences for all students in the Ohio State program. However, in the Project Learn Partnership, in general, we plan for equity, diversity, and cultural experiences for everyone.

COLLABORATIVE INQUIRY

Inquiry has become our most collaborative area with clinical educators, field professors, interns, and inservice teachers working together to learn more about how students process new and difficult information. "Make-it and take-it" intervention materials have been created in mini-workshops. We have conducted "Team Family" workshops so strategies can go home with kids. Has it made a difference? We think it has. Examples from our inquiries will demonstrate our progress.

Teacher Stories

Lizbeth Kelly, as a field professor, coordinates placements of interns in her middle school. Her students in one science section are all Individual Educational Plan (IEP) learners. She worked in a partnership with Project Learn to profile the students and provide them with personal learning power strategies. Even the special education teacher became involved. The students began to understand their own strengths and started making suggestions to teachers in other content areas about ways to accommodate their learning power.

Susie, another field professor, has third-graders whose reading skills range from preprimers to tenth grade. She provides every student with their own individual learning-style profile and works with them on their personal study skills. Teachers noted that many of the students increased their achievement levels. Susie reflected on her own practice and has made some major modifications by matching learning strategies with students' personal learning-style profiles.

Susie personalizes learning for every student based on their LSP, but she must assume all the financial responsibilities for this commitment to learners. She has made numerous petitions to save the district money by not purchasing items that she doesn't use in order to pay for items that would really help learners. These requests have never been approved and yet they consider her one of their outstanding master teachers who makes a huge difference in the achievement of students.

INQUIRY: CHALLENGES AND COLLABORATION

Some of the school principals have been reluctant to allow teachers and preservice students to do inquiry in the classroom. "Research should be done by researchers" was the answer we were given. Both Project Learn goals and the Holmes agenda state that action research should be a part of every classroom and this partnership was willing to work to create the needed change. Currently, most of our administrators have positive attitudes toward inquiry. Teachers conducting research is becoming a regular activity our PDS.

Doing action research, however, is challenging. Jerry tried for weeks to identify an action-research question. Greta, a school librarian, was also trying to settle on a relevant inquiry topic. At a weekly PDS meeting the core group brainstormed possibilities with Jerry and Greta. Both educators had several key concerns but were not able to frame an inquiry question until the PDS group worked as a team. At the end Jerry said, "I have struggled for weeks and now I know exactly how to proceed. It seems so easy when you have a team working with you." Greta has three possibilities and is in the process of making a final decision. Collaboration in a PDS partnership can make inquiry happen.

Action Research

The first summer PDS teachers established an action-research plan and an OSU professor trained the teachers in an action-research model to use during the next year. In the fall, 800 learning-style inventories (LSI) were administered at the request of PDS teachers and parents.

Eighty-two percent of the students in grades 6–12 who were evaluated using the LSI were global simultaneous processors. Sixty-five percent of the students had their most effective processing time in the early afternoon or evening. Practically all (90%) of the students who were considered underachievers were tactual or kinesthetic processors. A number (20%) of the special education students were light disabled and test scores were unusually low. A high percentage (79%) of the students were high-intake processors. Using this information, teachers could help students process new and difficult information more effectively. However, classroom teacher involvement in action research was minimal despite the training and careful personal project plans. Classroom teachers and our core group were stretched in many directions. The action-research plans in most cases were not implemented until student interns became partners.

The core group and interns decided to make students partners in their action research. Students were given the LSI and a personal computerized study skill printout developed by one of our graduate students. Individual conferences were held with each student and these sessions were supervised by graduate students trained in instructional supervision, the Project Learn model, and learning styles by Dr. Thomson. Forty-three action-research studies were completed. A research model to guide these efforts was developed and used successfully for several years.

Restructuring our college led to the restructuring of the PDSs. The sites in Project Learn now had to include students and teachers not schooled in learning styles. Interns were also assigned to non-PDS teachers and buildings because of the increased number of interns in our newly integrated program area. The amount of field hours in schools has been decreased and the numbers of seminars for LSI training has also been reduced. We are struggling with all the changes and trying to educate new faculty to the guidelines of the Holmes Partnership but progress is slow.

SIMULTANEOUS RENEWAL

Teachers who were originally only focused on climbing the salary scale have discovered the importance of PDS professional development. Clinical educators are pursuing additional degrees. Field professors are selecting courses to enhance their capabilities and requesting workshops on how to meet the unique needs of learners. PDS teachers are proposing new courses they want designed for student interns. Professors are being asked to teach courses in new and different ways. This is a different vision for all educators. Project Learn is very busy providing collaborative professional development.

STUDENT RESPONSE TO PDS WORK

In one PDS high school, Project Learn teachers were surprised to discover an article in the school newspaper about PDS and the importance of learning styles. Three students working on the paper wrote about how their LS profiles completed in their science class had made a difference in their academic achievement and in their confidence to learn new material. The seniors described how they had tried for a year to convince other teachers to accommodate to the learning styles of more students to see if it helped their achievement. They had no success encouraging teachers in other disciplines. The students ended the article:

> If this program were open to [the entire] high school, then more peo-
> ple would actually learn something. The fact is, most students don't
> like school. The school cannot cater to everyone's needs, especially
> with the rate at which [this school] is growing. Teachers need to
> develop ways to reach as many students as they can. . . . If this [learn-
> ing] test reached farther than just the science department, then maybe
> teachers could create an atmosphere in which all students can learn.
> (McElheny, 1994)

This full-page editorial was written December 1994 but no policies were ever initiated to respond to the students' pleas for assistance. We thought the editorial might be the catalyst for some changes, but it did nothing but create silence among other teachers. The PDS tried to provide opportunities for additional teachers, but not one teacher stepped forward to embrace this invitation. Project Learn congratulates the students who tried to promote educational change. Once again, Dunn and Dunn (1993) argue, if students are not learning the way we teach them, then we must teach them the way they learn. Helping kids learn is our most important job and we are learning how to help them as well as each other in this complex partnership.

There are many other stories of how Project Learn has influenced students. For example, Jacob is a fun-loving 10-year-old who seems very intelligent and productive but not in school. Jacob's mother is an award-winning teacher who has won many awards for her teaching. Jacob's father is a successful businessman who plans quality time for his family. Jacob's parents have spent a considerable amount of time in the principal's office and with the school psychologist. Teachers' conferences have been numerous and Jacob's parents have consistently followed all the recommendations of the school professionals.

Jacob's mother became a Project Learn partner. After having some professional development training with Project Learn and PDS goals, she asked if Jacob could be profiled using an LSI.

Jacob's LS profile indicated that he is not an auditory learner but rather a global learner. He is an evening learner who needs frequent opportunities for mobility, choices, prefers informal settings, low light, and sound. He is also tactual and kinesthetic. All of these characteristics demonstrated that he was mismatched with the way he was being asked to learn. It became apparent that Jacob needed to use his strengths. It was not possible to transfer to another school or change teachers but Jacob obtained assistance from his parents in helping him with his homework using his learning strengths whenever possible. Research shows that Jacob has a typical profile for an underachieving student.

Jacob made a presentation to our preservice teachers about his experiences. The professional preparation of teachers in our programs should have experiences with the Jacobs in our schools in order to be attentive to the needs of diverse learners. Jacob gives credibility to the importance of teachers knowing student-learning strengths.

CONCLUSION

Contexts, challenges, and consequences are intertwined in our PDS. What is really important about Project Learn "Closing the Gap" is that we are all learning about learning. This PDS provides all of the partnership players with simultaneous renewal and learning strategies matched to learner strengths. It creates a framework for inservice and preservice professional preparation as we begin to unravel the way we process new and difficult information. Project Learn gives us a platform for research as we attempt to acquire new knowledge about learning and learners in diverse settings. Schools exist to help students learn. As educators, our first priority is to help students learn in the most effective way possible. We have the tools and the research to help students learn. We are examining our own practice and the Holmes Partnership has provided us with an opportunity to touch the lives of many learners and teachers as we reach for the vision of excellence for everyone.

REFERENCES

Bruner, J. (1960). *The process of education.* New York: Vintage Press.

DeBello, T. (1990). Comparison of eleven major learning styles models: Variables, appropriate population, validity of instruction, and the research behind them. *Journal of Reading, Writing, and Learning Disabilities International,* 6, 203–222.

Dunn, R., & Dunn, K. (1993) *Teaching secondary students through their individual learning styles.* Boston: Allyn & Bacon.

Dunn, R., & Dunn, K. (1992) *Teaching elementary students through their individual styles: A practical approach.* Boston: Allyn & Bacon.

Dunn, R., Dunn, K., & Perrin, J. (1994). *Teaching young children through their individual learning styles.* Boston: Allyn & Bacon.

Dunn, R., & Griggs, S. (1995). A meta-analytic validation of the Dunn and Dunn model of learning-style preferences. *Journal of Educational Research,* 88(6), 55–64.

Flesch, R. (1955). *Why Johnny can't read.* New York: Harper.

McElheny, M. (1994). Learning styles differ among students. *Hilliard Wildcat,* p. 9.

Milligram, R., Dunn, R., & Price, D. (Eds.). (1993). *Teaching and counseling gifted and talented adolescents: An international learning-styles perspective.* Westport, CT: Greenwood Press.

Osborne, R., and Freyberg, P. (1985). *Learning in science: The implications of children's science*. Auckland: Heinemann Education.

Stevenson, J. (1992). *The learning gap: Why our schools are failing and what we can learn from Japanese and Chinese education*. New York: Summit Books.

The Holmes Group. (1986). *Tomorrow's teachers*. East Lansing, MI: Author

Trowbridge, L., & Bybee, R. (1996). *Teaching secondary schools science*. Englewood Cliffs, NJ: Merrill Publishing.

PART IV

Specialist and Subject Matter PDSs

CHAPTER 12

The Ohio State University Technology in Education Professional Development School

William Gathergood and Keith Hall

This chapter describes a PDS with a special mission. It was established to enable email communication across the PDSs and the college. The goal was to set up equipment and train PDS participants so that they could communicate with each other. Eventually this particular agenda was expanded to include other kinds of courses as well as curriculum and web site development. While financial support for this PDS has been cut, the authors of this chapter and developers of this PDS leave a significant technological legacy as they continue their work within the more traditional confines of their university department and school contexts.

Who are Bill Gathergood and Keith Hall? We were the co-coordinators of the Technology in Education Professional Development School (TIE/PDS) from 1991 to 1997. We are two educators with different academic preparations and perspectives on education and the preparation of teachers. Most importantly within the context of TIE/PDS, we have different venues of practicing our professions. Bill is a secondary classroom educator specializing in English, British literature, speech and drama, and TV production, with 24 years of experience in the Reynoldsburg City Schools. Keith is a professor of education with 34 combined years of teaching and research experience focused on enhancing learning and teaching environments and processes through technology. We share common beliefs and commitments: technology is crucial in the future lives of educators and students of all ages and levels; the professional development of pre- and inservice classroom educators and university teacher education faculty is enhanced through continued collaboration, dialogue, and shared practices; and teaching, professional development, and inquiry are richer if we work collaboratively rather than individually.

For the K–12 educators, both present and future, Bill is credible as a "real teacher" who faces K–12 children in classes every day. His technology projects are models of curricular integration. We discuss those models and their connection to other curricular areas and grade levels. With access to only minimal technology, he has gone beyond the traditional curriculum. His students consider problems and issues of their peers around the world through their authentic engagement with classical literature.

We have used the strengths of each other and contribute where we can; where we can't, we defer to others in our community of collaborators. This documentation of our work reflects a similar collaboration, each of us describes our work from our own perspective. We've written together in the past and find that it works well for us.

A UNIVERSITY PERSPECTIVE

Keith Hall

The Technology in Education PDS (TIE/PDS) was one of the original OSU PDSs. It began as an enabling PDS focused on enabling the other PDSs to do their work through the application of technology—primarily electronic mail (email) to provide communications among the collaborating partners. We began by acquiring and maintaining email accounts and providing training for all participants (nearly 350 during the first year and eventually over 900).

We have shifted from an enabling PDS to a networked PDS—we're not located in a single or even several school sites, but in many school sites and especially in cyberspace where much of our collaboration occurs—with our own agenda: collaboration to learn, create, and share new knowledge about learning and teaching through effective use of technology.

Our agenda is implemented through weekly TIE/PDS Forum meeting (two-and-a-half hours) on Wednesdays after school in a middle school media center of a nearby school district. The location offers the advantages of working on K–12 issues in a K–12, technology-rich environment with easy access and parking, and a tolerance for the consumption of (sometimes) homemade snacks, but always snacks—a socializing element we've found to be crucial to building the community. Although university credit is offered to participants, that is the only element that makes it like a class taught by a professor. We've worked diligently to create a first-name, give-and-take atmosphere where anyone is likely to know the answer to someone else's questions; where the agenda moves (some might say drifts) to meet current needs and issues; and where there are no continuing negative consequences for errors (we're all exploring new ideas and strategies and that exploration is enhanced by false starts and midstream corrections). K–12 teachers and administrators, OSU faculty and faculty from other colleges in the area; university undergraduate, masters, and doctoral level students, and middle and high school students select topics, issues, and projects of special interest to them. Following are brief descriptions and URLs for some of the projects that have been implemented by TIE/PDS participants.

Beth Weingroff, Columbus School for Girls, prepared multimedia lessons about the viola including music scores and recorded musical samples. Her work is available at http://www.coe.ohio-state.edu/khall/tienet/bweingro.

Cathy Hart, Worthington Schools, helped her intermediate students learn to use the World Wide Web as an information source to learn about different countries. The report of her students' work is available at http://www.coe.ohio-state.edu/khall/tienet/chart.

Carmen Rocco, high school senior, created materials to help peers develop calculus skills and calculate the volumes of solid objects. His work is available at http://www.coe.ohio-state.edu/khall/tienet/crocco.

Donald Humphreys, faculty member at a nearby liberal arts college, challenges his colleagues to use technology in teaching composition. Do you teach composition at the college level? Are you thinking about changing from a traditional classroom format to a technological environment? Are you wondering how to get started? Then this is the web page for you. His work is available at http://www.coe.ohio-state.edu/khall/tienet/dhumphreys.

Jennifer Ribar's project engaged seventh-graders in creating a personal intergenerational, interdisciplinary, multimedia timeline using the program HyperStudio. Her documentation of her students' work can be seen at http://www.coe.ohio-state.edu/khall/tienet/jribar.

Tim Dove, a teacher at McCord Middle School in Worthington and field professor for the OSU Social Studies Professional Development School, collaborated with students at McCord and the Worthington Alternative Program High School to create a learning community in which teachers, students, and their parents worked together to create multimedia presentations for school courses. Their work is available at http://www.coe.ohio-state.edu/khall/TIENET/tmdove.

Tom Robbins's fourth-grade students in Worthington used the HyperStudio program to create presentations to share information they were learning about Ohio. Their work is archived at http://www.coe.ohio-state.edu/khall/TIENET/trobbins.

Bill Gathergood continues to create and implement new examples and models of technology-enhanced learning and teaching models. Selected examples are described here, but his ongoing archive of cultural exchange, literary personification, textbooks on floppy diskettes, and others are at http://www.coe.ohio-state.edu/khall/tienet/wgatherg.

The most inspiring decision of the group early in 1996 was to ask a high school student to join us. We were in the midst of learning to write home pages to document our work and Carmen's personal page illustrated clearly that he had skills well beyond those of any current member of the TIE/PDS forum. It is also true that many of us did not understand the humor and cultural nuances in his pages—an experience I've frequently had on the Web that is largely the creative product of a younger generation. Carmen was eagerly accepted and assisted many of the teams with technical assistance in page design and implementation. Carmen gave advice eagerly and professionally—sometimes answering the questions we should have asked rather than the ones we did ask.

Our collective experiences with Carmen during the spring of 1996 led us to add more high school and middle school students as team members working with K–12 educators to create home pages reflecting the works of their school. Much of that work is still under construction and refinement as we all learn more about curriculum and technology integration and as our skills advance.

The participants in the FORUM resemble the flow of hot lava—moving slowly and steadily toward new locations and new vistas. We add some new and leave some old behind, but we continue moving toward new ideas. Dialogue among PDS participants and cyber participants occurs via our listserv TIENET@lists.acs.ohio-state.edu and eventually on our home page where everyone with common interests is invited to participate.

As technology has become more available in the K–12 schools through the Ohio School Net initiative and the demand has increased for collaboration on curriculum integration, the TIE/PDS Forum has adopted a three-quarter strategy for collaborative development, implementation, data gathering, and reporting. This enables participants to join the group at the beginning of any quarter and continue until their interests have been satisfied. In the first quarter, participants design and create a curricular-integrated technology project for their classroom. Collaborative dialogue within the group identifies potential problems areas, strategies for coping with them, and timetables for implementation. During the second quarter, participants implement the projects in their classrooms, make progress reports, and provide support and assistance. The third quarter they document and publish the findings from their project. The heart of this successful process comes from capturing the surprises, the excitement from unexpected discoveries and insights, and the challenges met and overcome by both the youth and adult participants.

The problems and the issues are the typical problems and issues experienced in all of education—not enough time, not enough resources (especially technology), many other demands, the false belief that we need "permission" from colleagues, administrators, or supervisors to proceed with our creative ideas. We don't. We need only to give ourselves permission to proceed. The problem is not a lack of creative ideas or creative educators. The conflicts occur at the intersection of differing perspectives, experiences, and differing solutions. These are all resolvable through commitment to common goals with shared respect and time for dialogue, debate, and collaboration. At the time of this writing there are approximately 125 educators in central Ohio who identify TIE/PDS as their professional development connection with The Ohio State University.

A K–12 PERSPECTIVE

Bill Gathergood

As a PDS clinical educator and co-coordinator of TIE/PDS, I have had the opportunity to work with K–12 teachers throughout central Ohio as well as university faculty members and administrators. I have had the opportunity to travel, to speak at national and international conferences. In addition, access to the Internet has enabled me to keep abreast with what is being done throughout the international educational community, as well as to publish my own findings in my clinical research projects.

My role as Clinical Educator means that I teach half-day in my home school, Reynoldsburg High School, and then work for the university. Of course, my duties for the university do not fit neatly into the second half of the school day. Part of my role is to serve as administrator of email accounts for K–12 teachers in central Ohio. The first year, this meant many trips to the various PDS schools to inform teachers about the availability of email accounts, in many cases having to explain what email is. After the initial year, I set up support people in each building who could help acclimate their teachers once I acquired the accounts. My duties also included conducting international projects with my own classes to attempt to model the classroom of the future.

As the projects developed, I began speaking in one of Keith's university classes, sharing examples of how technology can affect the classroom. This eventually led to my involvement in developing TIENET, an ongoing seminar made up of teachers who are making similar technological advances with their students.

The PDS program at Ohio State was designed as a five-year experiment that has brought many opportunities for me personally, collaborating with a university professor and many other clinical educators. The following projects are examples of the work my students and others around the world have been able to do, thanks to the PDS program.

Electronic Mail Projects in the Classroom

It may help to look at some general issues inherent in the medium. Many technological media require large investments of money to provide hardware, software and account access for students. But email projects require a minimum investment and take advantage of technology that is probably already in place. All that is required is a computer lab with word processing capability and one teacher's email account. Students are linked with partners in other locations anywhere in the world. Students write their responses that are merged together by their teacher and sent back. These are downloaded in the same way for distribution. The feeling is the same as old fashioned pen-pal letters, but they are instantaneous, cutting mail time down from several weeks to a few seconds. Students can send a letter on Monday and get a response back the next day.

A teacher's first reaction to this concept might be, "That's too much work for me to do!" But it is important to understand that uploading and downloading files is only complicated until it has been done a few times. Once familiar with the process, a teacher with twenty-five students, writing to five locations, can save, upload and send all the letters in 10 minutes.

There is another important point to be made about letters flowing through the teacher account and that is that it creates an assessment bottleneck that is very important. Schools that provide email accounts for all students often encourage direct links between students and their partners. While this is a good way to teach students the power of the system, it also takes a critical element out of the loop—the teacher. I raise this issue, not as an aspect of censorship, but out of a genuine need to keep the teacher involved as a guiding element. If left alone, two students from opposite sides of the globe will carry on pen-pal type correspondences. But that has been done for years without high-tech equipment. If we are to take advantage of instantaneous transfer of information on a personal level, then the conversations must delve into deeper issues. It takes a teacher's guidance to encourage students to dig deeper; to consider, not only what is written in the letters, but what is not written in the letters. It requires a teacher's guidance to help students read what is between the lines of their letters, both the letters going out and those being received.

In one of my earliest 1992 projects, I linked Shakespeare seminar students in Ohio with literature students in Moscow. One of my students, who was assigned the task of writing about *Taming of the Shrew*, wrote instead: "I don't know why I should bother talking to you there in Russia. We have all the bombs."

Because my students' letters flow through my account, I have the opportunity to read them all—not extra work—English teachers have to read their students' work anyway. I resisted the urge to censor the letter and sent it to Moscow with the rest. But I also wrote a letter to the teacher, explaining that I was sure we all have students who are crass and less than serious. I asked her to give his letter to one of her better students. She did and my student received a letter back that became one of those extreme teachable moments.

Often letters from Eastern bloc countries require some interpretation, even though they are written in English. A teacher can make the difference between a student's confusion and understanding of symbolic references from another culture.

So it is very important that the teacher remains in the loop, especially with international projects. But I would strongly discourage the use of this involvement to represent any form of censorship. The free exchange of information has served this country well for over 200 years. Often the greatest learning takes place when the student moves himself from an expressed negative attitude to one of discovery and wonder. He becomes like the Phoenix, rising from the ashes of despair and destruction to new heights, new beginnings. (Now if a student came upon a reference like "the Phoenix," it might help to have a teacher in the loop to help interpret its meaning for students unfamiliar with that reference.)

The best way to examine how students are directly affected by increased use of technology in the classroom is to look at specific projects that have been used over the last few years. I intend to discuss just a few here in the areas of literature and social studies because these are the areas in which I work. I break down projects into cultural studies and literary personification. Cultural studies include interdisciplinary approaches to daily life and the history of a people.

The Geography Project

Each student is linked with a partner on the other side of the globe. So, for example, Mary, a junior in central Ohio, is linked with Titania, a fifteen-year-old in Cheliabinsk, Russia. They begin by exchanging a simple pen-pal letter. Each student then answers a series of 30 questions that are designed to dig deeper into the daily life of each student. Because everyone uses the same questionnaire, each student merely sends a letter with the numbered answers. The questionnaire was designed by a team of teachers from five countries around the globe to ensure that cultural biases were minimized in the questions themselves.

After Mary and Titania receive each other's questionnaire answers, they each use traditional means—maps, encyclopedias, atlases, books, music, or art—to understand what the daily life of their partner must be like. Mary then writes a paper entitled "A Day in the Life of Titania." In it, she describes what she perceives as Titania's day from the time she gets up in the morning until the time she goes to bed at night. She gives as many details as her research and her imagination can muster. Of course, Titania is writing "A Day in the Life of Mary."

These papers are sent to the partners and the project is completed sending a critique of the paper back to the author. Mary might explain that Titania is not aware that most American teens have part-time jobs and that three hours of Mary's day is spent flipping burgers at the local fast-food restaurant. Titania might point out that she does not have to stand in a line to buy bread, or that her favorite pastime is listening to rock music on her CD player.

The project encourages students to look at maps in a new way as they analyze the lives of the people who live there. One 12-year-old American, whose Russian partner mentioned skiing as a pastime, decided that he must cross-country ski because the closest mountains on the map were 150 miles away with no major highways connecting to his city. His decision was correct. The Russian boy said they cross-country ski because they have no mountains. Using maps to make decisions about daily lives of people is a new and exciting concept for students, but it is something professional geographers have always known. Often much of our lives can be revealed through a study of our environment.

The Beowulf Project

This project was an attempt to study the culture behind a work of literature. The students were already familiar with the story of Beowulf, so it was time to get the feel of Beowulf's society. We began this locally by turning our classroom into a Mead Hall. First, the students had to stand up, not yet having earned a bench in our Mead Hall. They earned this as Beowulf did, by telling wielding stories about their ancestors, bragging accounts about the deeds of family members who had come before them. Each wrote a true story about their ancestor who had overcome barriers to achieve greatness. As they read their stories to the class, they earned a bench, or desk in the Mead Hall. They also brought symbols of those heroes—trappings to hang on the walls of the hall. These were displayed in the classroom.

We also took part in competition locally, stealing a Mead Bench from a neighboring classroom that was also studying Beowulf in a more traditional manner. After stealing the bench, (desk) our students sent a tribute of coins to the neighbor, honoring their rightful ownership of the bench, but our strength and cunning in the theft of it. We still have the bench.

But Beowulf was not content to stay in his homeland. He wanted to earn a bench in a foreign land. So we too had to earn a place in a foreign Mead Hall by sending our wielding stories to another Mead Hall. Students exchanged stories with students in Moscow. Both Russian and American students were surprised to read of the accomplishments of the ancestors. Each student was formally accepted into the other school's Mead Hall. Symbols and gifts were also sent to each other to display in the hall.

Rather than merely reading the story again, the students felt what it was like to live in Beowulf's time. This process I call "living a culture."

Literary Personification

Literary Personification projects are the brainchild of Dr. Brent Robinson of Cambridge University. Dr. Robinson hired a professional writer to play a character in a novel. He then invited an eighth-grade class to read the book and write to the character in the book with questions and comments. All communications were done through email. Being able to talk to the character enabled the students to more easily visualize the action of the novel as having a reality of its own. Discussions of the readings develop at a higher level when the students can communicate with an author representation or a character. I would like to cite three examples, linking students with Harper Lee and William Shakespeare.

The process of literary personification can be an important tool for the teacher playing the role as well. In 1995, a group of students in Moscow read Harper Lee's *To Kill a Mockingbird* and wrote letters to the author. These letters were handed off to preservice teachers from The Ohio State University. One of those preservice teachers (Alan), who happened to be an African American male, born and raised in the North, found himself having to take on the role of a Caucasian female child from the South. Alan chose to play Harper Lee as the young child represented by the narrator of the story. Through a series of letters to one girl in Moscow, Alan's Harper Lee explained the history of racial conflict and the strides made by the Civil Rights movement from 1950 to the present. In these exchanges Alan had the opportunity to immerse himself into the character of the author and, therefore, learn much more about the author's interpretation of what has happened since. The relationship between the student and the preservice teacher would have been much different if the student had known the background of the teacher. Instead, she had a sense of who she was speaking to because she had read Harper Lee's story. They became fast friends with a trust that permitted Alan to take the lesson to a much higher plane than would be possible in a traditional classroom. Also, the use of literary personification permits the introduction of ethical questions to the classroom without placing the teacher in the role of moralist. The teacher can lead discussions as a third party, observing conversations between the students and the authors/characters.

But the greatest progress has been in the use of this method to teach Shakespeare to modern teenagers around the world. Shakespeare's work is so complex that the author and several characters are sometimes necessary to handle the discussions. I have played the bard and often invite students to take on a play, explaining a few of the basic themes to look for as they read. Playing the role has forced me to stay on my toes as there are so many unusual interpretations of Shakespeare's work.

"Hamlet" is an offshoot of the last project. I have pulled together, in cyberspace, several teachers with strong backgrounds in Shakespearean literature. Each plays a character from *Hamlet*. When students in our classes read Hamlet, they are invited to write to any character. Letters are forwarded to each teacher who has agreed to reply to each letter within 48 hours. The quick turnaround of letters and the mystery of not knowing where the letters are coming from enables the students to suspend their disbelief and think of the communiqués as coming from the characters. The students then use quotes from the characters when they answer essay questions on the *Hamlet* test. The main advantage of this process is that the characters are very good at linking the events in the story with modern life. So Ophelia talks of her relationship with her father in such a way that modern teenage girls relate to a father's lack of trust. Claudius paints himself as a modern-day pacifist who eliminated his warrior brother on the eve of a destructive battle that he was able to avoid through negotiation. His excuses for his actions lead to discussions of such complex issues as negotiating with terrorists and buying off enemies to avoid war. A character that is traditionally seen as the clear villain of the piece steps in and demonstrates to students the complexities of international politics.

During one overlap of spring breaks, it became necessary for me to fill in and answer Ophelia's letters because she was away from her computer. I was amazed at how differently I viewed the events in *Hamlet* when I saw them through the eyes of Ophelia. My attitude about every event changed. I believe every teacher should go through the exercise of viewing the literature as different characters. It might help to understand why some students see different things when they read the same literature.

With that thought in mind, I wanted my own high school students to experience literary personification from the writer's perspective. So I invited students in Florida to read *Much Ado About Nothing* and write to the four main characters. I then passed out the letters to my students after they had read the play. Their goal was to answer a letter in character so that the reader would think they were that person, but they also had the responsibility to link the events of the play with modern problems teenagers face so that the reader would have a better understanding of how Shakespeare's play speaks to modern cultures. The work they produced was very interesting. Understanding intellectually that the source of all this discussion is a 400-year-old play then gives the students a sense that their own problems are not insurmountable because people have been dealing with them for many generations.

Getting involved in literary personification projects is very easy. Most English teachers have a strong background in at least one area of literature. It is simply a matter of advertising a project idea in news groups and listservs to find partners who want to work together. Whether a teacher plays the role of an author or links students with an author representation somewhere else, the potential for studying literature in a whole new way is immediately evident with the first letters.

Cultural studies and literary personification are just two concepts for email projects. Others are as numerous as there are people to try them. But they all represent a new way of looking at education in America; a tearing down of walls, a blurring of teacher/student roles and a genuine understanding that knowledge is there to be discovered around every corner.

Final Thoughts

It has been the work of the PDS, and for me specifically the TIE/PDS, that has enabled school and university participants to stimulate each other intellectually and constantly ask two very important questions: "Why do we do the things we do?" and "Is there a better way to do them?"

As we began our collaboration four years ago, it was easy to ask these questions. Few of us in public schools had asked them before. But the real strength of the collaboration is now that we have made great strides with new technologies and new programs, we have the fortitude and the wisdom to continue to ask the questions.

Shakespeare, in *As You Like It*, created three negative images that might have been seen as the major players in educational institutions of old:

"Full of wise saws and modern instances" (the professor)

"[S]eeking the bubble reputation even in the cannon's mouth" (the K–12 teacher)

"With satchel and shining morning face, creeping like snail unwillingly to school" (the student)

The university professor, K–12 teacher, and student no longer fit these images. We have seen the student leading both the professor and teachers in the development of Web pages. We have seen all three collaborate on critical curriculum development issues. "Wise saws" come from all directions, "bubble reputations" fall by the wayside, and, in the excitement of it all, no one creeps "unwillingly to school." Every day is a new adventure for all as we help to set this "worldly stage" for the next millennial act to come.

EPILOGUE

Education is what remains after everything that was taught has been forgotten. When viewed from the perspective of a legislator, a district superintendent, a business leader, or a university administrator, the state of professional practices in K–12 schools and teacher education is slow to change and measurable changes in performance may be difficult to detect. When viewed by students, classroom educators, and university faculty who have worked together through collaboration and dialogue, the changes are clearly evident and significant. And when those "production line" workers are empowered to chart their own courses of action, truly great moments of learning occur—leaving positive images in the minds of all who were engaged. Such changes don't occur as the result of a professional development event but rather through the sustained, long-term professional development experiences that empower the self—the teacher, the professor, and the student.

Traditionally institutions demonstrate an attention span of about five years—a plan is envisioned, funded, and implemented with appropriate evaluations along the way. By the end of five years, other problems or visions of new solutions come into vogue or new drum majors with a need to demonstrate their leadership acumen assume the baton. And without regard for the knowledge, insights, and perceptions of the "production line," hands-on workers, a new "solution" is implemented—generally demonstrating once again that our problems are caused by solutions. Our perception and acknowledgment of this cyclical problem is the first step in breaking the cycle; and the break is worth making because we have discovered a style of learning and teaching (engagement); and a method (collaboration); and a means (technology) that cannot be squandered in the cyclical shuffle.

The words of Alfred Lord Tennyson in "Ulysses" speak to our current status and the resolve of the production-line educators and students who have embraced and are committed to engagement, collaboration, and technology: "Tho' much is taken, much abides . . . that which we are, we are. . . . One equal temper of heroic hearts, made weak by time and fate, but strong in will. To strive, to seek, to find, and not to yield."

CHAPTER 13

A PDS Network of Teachers:
The Case of Art

Michael Parsons

*This chapter describes a PDS that networks K–12 art educa-
tors from four very different school districts. The focus is Discipline-Based Art Education (DBAE), an approach to art education that extends the focus of art lessons from expressive
activities to a study of historical and interpretive aspects of art
and argues for the importance of art in the school curriculum.
The PDS also overlaps with a large national grant that
intends to integrate art into the wider school curriculum and
life of the school. Because the Art Education Department is in
the College of Fine Arts rather than Education, it presents an
interesting case of collaboration both across colleges at the
university and with the schools.*

In all education projects, context matters. Certainly, the context has
greatly influenced the development of our PDS for art teachers, code-
named ART (Art Research and Teaching). For one thing, at OSU the
Department of Art Education, which has responsibility for preservice
and inservice programs for art teachers, is not in the College of Education. It is in the College of the Arts. This situation is not uncommon and
it has advantages and disadvantages. It allies us more with our subject-
matter colleagues and it distances us a little from our education colleagues. In this respect, it exaggerates the typical situation of art teachers in the public schools, where they tend to feel somewhat distant from
other teachers. They often feel that they teach a subject that others don't
understand well, that cultivates qualities and abilities in students that are
not appreciated sufficiently by other teachers, and that has an insecure

place in the curriculum. In addition, there is only one art teacher in most schools, except large high schools, and at the elementary level in Ohio many art teachers have to teach in more than one school. Consequently there may be a sense of isolation within the school. In these circumstances, professional connections with other art teachers often become more important to them than connections with other teachers at their own school. No doubt all teachers experience the pull of these two kinds of affiliations: subject-matter ones and within-school ones. Art teachers (of course there are exceptions) tend to experience the first as more important than the second.

For these kinds of reasons, it seemed to us from the beginning that art required a PDS that is structured as a network of art teachers rather than a single site. Logistics alone pointed that way. When ART was first planned (ART was one of the first PDSs at OSU to be planned), the Art Education Department at OSU graduated an average of about 30 art teachers each year (the number has since declined a bit with the move of the program to the graduate level). Certification to teach art in Ohio is K–12 and so we needed an average of 30 elementary and 30 secondary placements each year for student teachers. That meant that we needed at least 60 cooperating art teachers actively engaged each year in the PDS, which in turn meant almost 60 different schools. At the beginning, there was considerable discussion about the logic of the network idea. It was not the standard model of PDSs in the literature and we could find little precedent. But it seemed inevitable. And we could quote the university's graduate school as a similar use of the word "school" to mean more than "site." Also, it was clear that other subject-matter specialists were in the same position. Those in physical education were particularly active at OSU at the time and we took comfort from them.

Two of the department's faculty were normally assigned to work with the field experience aspects of the certification program and one of these (Marjorie Schiller), together with the then chairperson (Michael Parsons), held a series of meetings with local teachers. The idea was, they argued, to establish a more collaborative arrangement between the teachers and the department. The purposes of the collaboration were to be three: preservice education, inservice learning, research. There was to be frequent communication, group decision-making, experimental attitudes, sharing of power and responsibilities. We had little difficulty recruiting teachers. Art teachers are typically dedicated professionals, they look for professional connections, and the department has long had good relations with many local teachers.

But from the beginning we noticed the tension inherent in the network-of-individual-teachers idea, the tension between viewing the teacher as an independent subject-matter specialist and as a school faculty member. Thought of the first way, the art teacher was an independent professional individually contracting to join the PDS. Certainly, that is how we talked about it. At the same time, for a variety of reasons, they needed support from within their school (or schools), from other teachers and especially from the principal. The most obvious of these reasons was the need to free up some teacher time to attend meetings for a variety of ART-related purposes. The principal was the one who could make this happen, together with the district's policies that lay behind the principal. So in practice, the network was also a network of schools and districts, although we did not like to dwell on this. We adopted two kinds of criteria for selecting teachers who wanted to join ART. One set applied to individuals, the other to the school and the school district in which they worked. The individual ones included the following:

- Successful experience in teaching art in public schools.
- Educational philosophy congruent with that of the department.
- Desire to work collaboratively with colleagues and the university.
- Willingness to work with student teachers.
- Flexible attitudes regarding curriculum and instructional issues.

The institutional ones were:

- Teaches in a school where the principal is supportive of art in the curriculum.
- Teaches in a district that is willing to spend resources on the professional development of art teachers.

There are close to 20 school districts in Franklin County but the department had particularly good relations with four of them, two of them urban and two suburban. So we organized ART with teachers from only those four districts. Each district signed an agreement with the department establishing the PDS and agreeing to provide appropriate resources for teachers.

We created an advisory committee for ART that consisted of representatives of the four school districts (and of the department) and we used the districts as a structure for organizing a variety of activities. For example, we rotated student teachers to a different district each quarter and had meetings about supervision issues with the art teachers from that district each quarter. This proved popular with teachers because it gave them a voice about supervision issues and it also served as an opportunity for them to discuss districtwide issues affecting art education.

So we organized a network of individual art teachers who volunteered to work together for common purposes, within a structure that included school districts and gave them representation on an advisory committee. Moreover, we actively solicited the support of school principals and invited them to professional development activities. This duality has continued to manifest itself throughout the history of ART. And as suggested above, there is a parallel at the university. We thought of ourselves as acting independently of our colleagues in the College of Education and much of the time we did so. But we also gained considerable support from them, both intellectually and organizationally. We were, after all, part of the university's PDS initiative, sparked by the Holmes Group and its publications. There was an administrative policy-making structure that supervised all of the PDSs, to which we reported. And the College of Education gave us a regular petty cash fund, which paid for things like teacher lunches and coffees at meetings.

INITIAL STEPS

One of our early steps was to hire a clinical educator, as the other PDSs did. The clinical educator was to be an experienced art teacher, released half-time from one of the schools. The primary duty was to share the work of communication and problem-solving with Marjorie Schiller.

We advertised this position in the school districts and the ART advisory board chose Elizabeth Katz, an experienced art teacher in a middle school in the Whitehall City School District. She turned out to be an excellent choice for the position, able to work effectively with local teachers, with students and with university faculty.

Another early step was to reorganize some of the arrangements for student teaching. We held meetings with art teachers, sometimes within districts and sometimes across districts, to discuss items such as student placements, expectations of student teachers, evaluations of student teaching, schedule of supervisory visits, the weekly seminar meetings. Wherever possible, decisions were made jointly. For example, specific criteria for evaluating student teachers were arrived at jointly at the beginning of each quarter with the teachers from each district, and so was the allocation of responsibility for this evaluation between the cooperating teacher, the supervising university person (who was usually a graduate student), and the university faculty member. The evaluation of student teachers had in the past sometimes been a subject of misunderstandings between school and university people, in spite of efforts to put the department's expectations in writing, and the topic had occasionally led to inefficiencies. Our experience was that joint decision-making about how evaluation was to be done and which criteria were to be used did much to make the evaluation of student teaching run more smoothly. The same thing could be said about student placements and the schedule of supervisory visits. These were decided in a collaborative way, as a result of group discussions, and the level of mutual understanding was greatly enhanced. There were fewer problems in the system, and problem-solving, as for example when a student's placement might need to be changed, became much easier.

We also reorganized the weekly seminar that traditionally accompanied student teaching. This had been run on lines very like a regular class at the university, by the faculty member responsible for student teaching. We experimented with designing the seminar at the beginning of the quarter with the art teachers of the district in which student teaching was going to occur. We reached common agreement on the important topics for the students to discuss and the seminar became almost a group responsibility. A number of teachers volunteered each to lead the seminar one evening and to host it at their school. In this way, it rotated between schools. This provided an additional motivation for some teachers to attend, for they would be able to see colleagues' classrooms. The arrangement also allowed students to visit a number of different schools. The curriculum dealt with a number of topics, such as classroom discipline or curriculum, but teachers also treated it as an opportunity to explain their own situation and approach.

CURRICULUM CHANGE

Another contextual factor that influenced ART was the presence within the department of a long-term effort to change the art curriculum in schools throughout Ohio. This effort was funded in part by an annual grant from the Getty Institute for Art Education and was channeled through an organization called the Ohio Partnership for the Visual Arts (OPVA), also a collaborative enterprise between school districts in Ohio and the department. The traditional curriculum in art in the United States has been oriented toward the creative expression of children, through having them make art. The purpose of the OPVA was to help teachers move from an expressive curriculum to one oriented toward understanding and interpreting artworks, including adult works, both contemporary and traditional, as well as the children's own works. The department has long been identified nationally as a champion of the view that the purpose of art education is understanding rather than expression and it has held many curriculum inservice institutes and workshops for teachers across Ohio. The Getty Institute called the curriculum movement Discipline-Based Art Education. The Ohio State Department of Education has now embodied it in its guidelines under the title Comprehensive Art Education.

It was natural, given the importance of this curriculum issue, that it should affect the Art PDS from the beginning. One way in which this happened was mentioned above: it meant that the teacher should be in favor of Comprehensive Art Education. We felt that because our teacher preparation program prepared students to teach such a curriculum, we wanted them to do their student teaching in a classroom where it could be found.

Another way in which the OPVA affected ART was through the inservice workshops on curriculum issues that it regularly offered for teachers across Ohio, including in Franklin County. Many of these workshops were funded by the Getty Institute. In Franklin County, the teachers who volunteered to join ART also tended to participate in these inservice activities. This made it easy for us to tailor some of these opportunities to the particular needs identified by the ART teachers. For example, many of them wanted more knowledge of the art of contemporary minority and women artists. Others wanted discussion of methods of teaching art criticism to children. And so we organized several one-day workshops on these topics primarily for, but not limited to, the teachers in ART. We also required our student teachers to attend some of these inservice activities.

In short, the presence of OPVA in the department meant that ART had an unusually strong orientation toward curriculum development and probably included more professional development activities than would otherwise have been the case. At times, indeed, with respect to professional development, their activities overlapped almost completely. There were important differences, however. ART was also concerned with instructional and supervisory issues and in that way it stretched beyond the official concerns of OPVA. OPVA in turn was involved with schools across the entire state and in that way included much more than the teachers in Franklin County. It was not uncommon for teachers to be unclear which activities belonged to which.

ART AND THE REST OF THE CURRICULUM

Part of the goal of the DBAE movement was to mainstream art within the school. It did this in part by making it clear that art was a subject comparable to others in the curriculum, equally demanding and equally worthwhile. For these reasons, it was argued that art should stand as an equal beside other school subjects and have equal curriculum space and resources. A somewhat different argument was that art connected unusually well with other school subjects. Understanding an artwork requires understanding its subject matter in the context of the culture of its production. For example, if an artist makes an artwork about ecological concerns (an important contemporary theme), understanding it will require some sense of the ecological issues that the artist addressed. This may mean an understanding of biological, chemical, economic, political, historical, issues (to the degree that they affect the artwork) and consequently the potential overlap with the rest of the school curriculum is extensive. The point is quite general: art is related to and encapsulates culture. So understanding it requires not only the language arts—talking, reading, writing, about artworks—but also, potentially, the study of any school subject.

Note that on the traditional view there was very little such overlap, because teachers aimed mostly at promoting children's expressive abilities through making art. On that view, art required quite different skills or qualities—expressive, creative, visual—from those required by the rest of the curriculum—linear, logical, verbal. It was this view that created the sense that art was different in school.

Because of the overlap argument, we had been trying for some time to involve all kinds of teachers and other school personnel in our professional development activities about comprehensive art curriculum. The idea was that if one wanted children to learn to study artworks, to read and write about them and understand their social reference, then the art program needed support from the whole school. Children could write about an artwork as part of language arts and study its social references in social studies classes. Groups of teachers could get together and plan to work with their students on particular works, artists, themes. For these reasons we had encouraged teams of teachers to attend our workshops along with the art teacher.

We had had sporadic success with this. There were schools, especially at the elementary level, where a group of teachers planned together to teach art through the curriculum. Sometimes the effect was very visible in the corridors and throughout the school building. This was almost always where the principal was a strong supporter of the arts. The most notable case was probably Gables Elementary, where the principal (Don Cramer) was very supportive, the art teacher (Brigid Moriarty) was very strong, and many of the teachers had attended our workshops.

An interesting feature of Gables was that it also participated in one of the other PDS structures, the ECC, which was a group of elementary schools working together. This situation provided a rich set of possibilities that we never quite took advantage of. For example, we placed an art student teacher every year with the art teacher in Gables but we never assigned one with a regular classroom teacher. At a slightly more systematic level, the fact that Gables was a part of two PDSs suggested greater collaboration between the PDSs, with respect to both student teaching and to professional development activities. We had good informal relations with the ECC PDS and had conversations along these lines. But nothing formal came of this. Shortage of time and the formal structures of both the university and the school proved too much to overcome.

FOUR YEARS LATER

This discussion takes us four years into ART. It took two years of discussions and planning to initiate it and for two years it has operated with some success. Its principal successes have been with student teaching and with professional development activities. With student teaching, it has improved communications, engaged teachers more fully in the process, and relieved many of the problems that arose at times in the previous system. It did not succeed in changing other aspects of the teacher preparation program, though with more time that might still occur. The context of change at the university, and its traditional reward system for faculty, have been such that it has been hard so far to pay serious attention to suggestions from the field for further changes to the certification program.

With respect to professional development, ART has been quite successful in organizing curriculum-oriented activities collaboratively, both short ones during the year and longer ones during the summer. It has also brought art teachers together, especially within districts, in ways that promoted mutual support and understanding. Through the student teacher seminar, it also raised instructional issues among teachers, though the discussions were more limited than we would have hoped.

Like the other PDSs, we announced that collaborative research was a goal of ART. Changes in the certification program itself required that the student teachers engage in action research. But so far, the imperatives of program needs and the shortage of time have meant that this goal has had low priority and there has been little research planned and accomplished within ART. It is of course possible that this is still to come, since ART is only two years into full operation.

This brings the story up to the point of writing. And here again the particularities of context play a hand in the story. It happens that several key personnel changes are occurring all at the same time. The clinical educator is changing at the end of a two-year cycle, as was planned.

The department chairperson is stepping out of the chair and going on a sabbatical leave. And Marjorie Schiller, who has had primary responsibility for student teaching and is the one who knows all of the relevant people, is leaving the university for another position.

The structure of ART is still in place and we hope it will grow and prosper. But the structure of ART does not penetrate deep within either the department or the schools. Within the schools, it is primarily dependent on the good will and energies of individual teachers and principals, with few claims on the hard resources of teacher time and funds. Within the department, it is a primarily a way to organize student teaching, which is an aspect of teacher preparation, which is one of the department's programs. It is not clear that the university's reward system supports the structure of ART or that it has been sufficiently connected to research activities to attract widespread support from faculty.

In short we are optimistic for the future of ART but aware of the fragility of collaborative enterprises that cross institutional boundaries without changing them. In this respect, ART is no different from other PDSs and it will be the extraneous features of the context that will decide the future.

CHAPTER 14

Weaving a Web of Relationships

Sandra Stroot, Mary O'Sullivan, and Deborah Tannehill

This PDS of physical education educators was the first net-work PDS. The faculty in physical education teacher educa-tion gathered together K–12 physical educators across nine urban and suburban school districts. This network PDS has provided support for physical educators, who often feel iso-lated in their school buildings. The network structure, how-ever, makes communication, coordination, and collaboration difficult. This chapter describes how this collaborative group addresses some of these challenges and the consequent rewards.

For seven years, Franklin County Academy of Physical Educators (FCAPE) has sought to play a role in school reform by advocating for better physical education in schools and for quality professional prepa-ration for preservice teachers. In particular, our goal is to provide prospective physical education teachers with skills, knowledge, and a commitment to a socially responsible physical education. We want to challenge and engage students in meaningful and exciting experiences with sport and physical activity.

A BRIEF OVERVIEW: CREATING A PDS NETWORK

Over many years, teachers, faculty, and doctoral students in the Physi-cal Education Teacher Education program were engaged in program-matic supervision research, and over two dozen doctoral dissertations were completed with assistance from cooperating teachers in the schools

(Dodds, 1975; Eldar, 1987; O'Sullivan, 1983). Extensive field experiences in this teacher education program and the quality work of cooperating teachers in supervising their novice teachers served as a model professional preparation program nationwide (Taggart, 1988). This collaborative effort was established and maintained almost exclusively with individual teachers. There was little systematic effort by university faculty to engage the cohort of teachers, or as a group of professional educators to discuss professional preparation or issues facing the physical education profession (except on occasion to take a graduate course on campus).

For the most part, physical education teachers lived professional lives isolated from other physical educators without opportunities to engage in professional discussion and inquiry. The physical education staff had their offices in or by the gymnasium, isolated physically from the rest of the school. Afterschool coaching or lunchtime intramurals kept most of them from engaging in faculty meetings or sustained decision making at their schools.

Few of the school-reform documents address the role of physical education in the education of children. Some significant documents even discourage the inclusion of physical education in the school's main curricular efforts (Sizer, 1992). Staff development opportunities rarely address the concerns and pressures of teaching physical education. While all educators are under pressure from the public, parents, and the media to improve schooling, the role of physical education is rarely understood and less often discussed.

The unique characteristics of our field require a different framework from the usual model of a school site as the PDS (Holmes Group, 1990). In many school buildings there is only one physical education teacher, which restricts collegial interaction for the teacher and limits access as a professional development site for preservice teachers. With this in mind, our PDS includes multiple schools rather than one school site.

The scope of our network PDS presented several benefits and challenges that differed from the other types of PDSs at Ohio State. Due to many years of involvement in programmatic supervision research and an extensive supervisory training program in physical education, we had a well-developed relationship with teachers in the various school districts before the PDS. This previous work placed university faculty, graduate students, and teachers in a position to work together toward common goals in the training of preservice teachers.

An FCAPE advisory board was developed to represent all teachers in the academy. One physical educator from each school district and one from Ohio State was elected. One teacher from the elementary level and one from the secondary level co-chaired the board. The purpose of the advisory board was to devise meeting agendas, disseminate equipment received from grant funds, and administer new funds received by the PDS. Board members were also responsible for disseminating information to PDS members and other interested teachers in their districts.

The major problem with the advisory board format was a lack of commitment by some representatives, resulting in poor attendance at meetings and later a complete breakdown in the dissemination network within school districts. Those attending FCAPE meetings and other events tended to be the same group of highly motivated teachers and faculty.

We moved away from district representation on the board to six members (two elementary, two middle school, and two high school), chosen at large from across all school districts. Board responsibilities were redefined and clarified. While commitment from this smaller group was higher, it appeared that dissemination of information was not increased dramatically, and the same group of dedicated teachers chose to attend FCAPE sponsored events.

At the beginning of the 1996–97 academic year, 20 teachers who have consistently attended and collaborated as FCAPE participants were invited to a planning meeting. This self-selected group of teachers and three Ohio State faculty designed and delivered a series of workshops throughout the year on selected topics of interest to meet our professional needs. The workshops were delivered either by the teachers themselves or by guests selected for their expertise. Each workshop was a success and well attended, and while the invitation to attend was distributed through a written brochure to an additional 100 teachers and Ohio State graduate students (MEd, MA, and PhD), few outside the "active" group chose to join us. Our current goal is to serve the professional development needs and concerns of FCAPE members interested and willing to play an active role in achieving the goals of the academy.

Getting Started

Over 25 teachers joined the PDS the first year. Most of the teachers were female and most were elementary physical educators with a few from middle and high school settings. These initial meetings were difficult for several reasons. First, it was a large group of professionals who did not know each other and who had no history of meeting and talking about physical education issues. Second, the university faculty tended to be viewed as the "leaders," and teachers waited for them to provide direction. Third, the level of interest and commitment varied among teachers as to how much they could or would do beyond the release days. These days were agreed to by the school district administrators as a condition of joining the PDS initiative.

Teachers attending these early meetings represented all grade levels, providing an opportunity to impact the scope of physical education experiences for children across K–12. The flip side of this heterogeneous group was that the teachers had little in common beyond the sharing of a subject matter. One of the early decisions was to break the group into smaller, grade-level teams with each team deciding on a project of mutual interest within the mission of the PDS.

The group applied for and received a grant to purchase eight laptop computers and modems to establish and maintain a consistent communication link with each other through email. Some of the release time was diverted to small group meetings for completion of their projects. These included developing an integration project, planning for the annual conference for physical education teachers, creating teacher resource materials on fitness activities, and planning international activities for use in the gymnasium.

Challenges

Four challenges emerged in the early days of FCAPE, and they persist today: time, communication, wearing different hats, and differential commitment levels.

Time.   All teachers are busy people and physical educators are no exception. The coaching schedules of teachers, especially at the secondary level, make it frustrating to arrange nonschool times for meetings. Getting started in the fall meant many middle and high school teachers did not come to meetings after school. This is still an issue, but some teachers have rearranged their schedules or chosen different priorities to allow them to engage in PDS work. We scheduled a weekly meeting last winter to move forward on several goals, and arranged for teachers to receive university credit. As a result, the PDS was more successful in gathering teachers and faculty to discuss a topic of mutual interest for a sustained period of time. The topic was the preparation of physical education teachers for the 21st century, and the forum debated goals, scope, and sequence of the postgraduate teacher certification (MEd) that was collaboratively designed and then implemented through FCAPE.

Communication.   The second challenge has been communicating consistently and effectively with 25–30 professionals scattered across several school districts. Without constant communication, teachers and faculty began to feel separated from the conversations and their enthusiasm waned. Initial distribution of laptops, specific training on use of the Internet, and access to email have been critical factors for successful communication among some teachers.

Teachers have also connected with their peers, discussed the supervision of student teachers, and shared teaching ideas. They have been an effective support system for those facing individual challenges at their school sites. The College PDS newsletter "Building Bridges," edited by FCAPE members for four years, was another means of communication and served as a public relations vehicle with administrators and school districts.

Multiple hats.   A third challenge has been school and university-based participants coping with the demands of "wearing multiple hats." University faculty serve as advisors and instructors to some of the FCAPE teachers in their graduate programs. It was not easy to break the "hierarchy" of faculty-teacher and faculty-student. After four years of patient effort, we have developed a mutual respect for what each of us brings to the collaborative process, and an increased willingness to challenge each other's ideas about teacher preparation and improving physical education in schools.

The PDS teachers also wear multiple hats. They are teachers of children and youth but also are colleagues to university faculty, helping them better understand the realities of school life. They are also teacher educators, mentors, authors, and presenters of collaborative scholarly inquiry on school physical education. Those who have assumed the role of clinical educator have become instructional designers, teachers in the MEd program, and mentors for both interns and peers.

Differential commitment.   With a large organization, and we consider this group large, there are some members who were committed and devoted much time and effort to the goals of the group. After five years these "pioneers" are tired and have some resentment toward those who have taken advantage of the system (attended the release day meetings but did little or nothing during the rest of the year). In addition, newer members need to be socialized into the group and find their way to contribute, so they can maintain the high standards set by those before them. Perhaps the professional growth and development of these pioneers is the greatest accomplishment of the PDS to date. Their stories are evidence of the power of collective professional involvement in providing opportunities for thoughtful, creative professional leaders to emerge.

Anne M's story (pseudonym) provides an example. Anne worked in a very difficult urban high school setting without any support or opportunities to talk about physical education or her life as a teacher. In the four years since her involvement in FCAPE, Anne has completed her master's degree in physical education, has worked with another clinical educator to co-teach methods classes for MEd preservice teachers, has taken substantive leadership in the design and implementation of a new physical education curriculum for high school students, and has been a leader in organizing the annual COTA Day conference. By her own admission, Anne has grown professionally in substantive ways, especially from her role as a clinical educator, and will begin doctoral studies shortly.

A similar story was told by Karen, an elementary specialist who has worked as a cooperating teacher for many years. She is one of the original FCAPE members, and recently took on the role of a clinical educator. Karen valued the opportunity to communicate with other physical educators, as she was the only physical education specialist in her school building. She has been one of the core members, and has contributed a great deal to the group. Her most recent venture, that of a clinical educator, has put her in a different role. Karen said she was able to expand her ideas. In particular, she verified that her curricular and pedagogical choices were appropriate, and discovered that she and the university faculty member that she was teaming with were more alike than different. She felt that getting involved with research and course materials was beneficial to her. Karen is completing her master's program. Her thesis addresses conflict management, a focus at her school.

There was a cost involved as well. Karen also maintained her position as a physical education specialist in her school setting. She was fortunate to have a substitute teacher who came each day she was released for her work as a clinical educator, but Karen continued planning to assure consistency for her students, and maintained her professional involvement in her school building through her involvement on committees, schoolwide projects, and staff meetings. It was a challenge for Karen to pursue a new clinical educator role while maintaining her current professional commitments in her own school setting.

Perhaps the most important contribution of FCAPE has been the professional development of its members, both university and school personnel, in terms of our theoretical and practical understandings of each others' lives and the development of theories of action (Goodson & Fliesser, 1997; Goodson, 1997). Less important but still useful, we have developed materials such as resource materials for physical education and new units of instruction.

The continued commitment of a smaller group of school and university participants has resulted in several important outcomes. Teachers in the cooperating teacher support group (Tannehill, LaMaster, & Berkowitz, 1994) use electronic mail to assist each other in their role as cooperating teachers. They have become more effective mentors of novice teachers and developed professional friendships. They have come to respect each other's work, and share ideas on teaching, planning, and programming. They have also learned to view themselves as having expertise to share with others, and to seek help with program improvement. The development of computer literacy allowed many to achieve specific goals in their programs. Many subsequently have purchased their own computers and modems.

SCHOOL AND UNIVERSITY PARTICIPANT RELATIONSHIPS

The decision to engage with local teachers in a professional development school for physical education was a decision made by our cohort of faculty in the teacher education program for physical education. This group of faculty had a strong programmatic focus and broad consensus about the goals, the scope and sequence of the program, and the delivery process. There was a great deal of pride in the quality of our graduates, which was reinforced by external agencies and high employment rates of graduates in local schools.

Restructuring efforts in the College of Education resulted in a collegewide movement to integrate teacher preparation and collaboration between school and university personnel. As an outcome of this new focus, university faculty were the initiators of FCAPE. However, they worked hard to ensure that teachers had the opportunity to take on leadership roles in establishing a professional development focus for the group.

The collaborative seminar to develop the MEd in Physical Education was attended by 10 teachers, the Physical Education Teacher Education (PETE) faculty cohort, and PETE doctoral students. This seminar was offered in winter 1995 to begin planning specific course materials for the MEd program that would begin the following autumn. The planning seminar represented a major step forward for faculty, as teachers had their ideas woven into the content, goals, and assessment of the program. The discussions grounded faculty in the realities of school as they worked with teachers to design optimum coursework, field experiences, and internship sites for the initial cohort of MEd students.

As a result of this seminar, the PDS began the 1996–97 school year as a partner in the development and delivery of the new physical education MEd. An integral part of our PDS is the effort of the practicing teachers, who function both as classroom teachers and as clinical educators with the university. These clinical educators play a key role in the preparation of teachers who will positively impact students in our schools. They have assisted us in moving the preparation of teachers off-campus and into the schools where they have the chance to experience all aspects of a teacher's life under the guidance of both school and university PDS participants.

Each year, an invitation goes out to teachers to apply for an elementary and secondary clinical educator position. An FCAPE committee reviews the applications and makes a recommendation to the faculty on which teachers are most qualified to fill this role. Faculty then formalize the appointment of the clinical educators by negotiating with building principals and linking the teachers to the college of education. Our goal in working with a clinical educator is to incorporate a teacher's perspective into the process of teacher education, and to more closely bridge the "gap" between the university and school setting. We solicited feedback from all parties involved during the initial 1996–97 school year of the program. One of our major strengths is the systematic nature of our program, as we work closely together as a collaborative group to assure the connectedness of our respective courses. As an outcome of our efforts to connect program areas, we successfully infused the general and adapted physical education content through team-teaching efforts, and the melding of both content areas in our MEd course work. We also responded to suggested changes for the second year. We view the collaborative involvement as a dynamic process, and will continue to modify according to the changing needs of our students as they matriculate through our program

Clinical educators serve in a special role within the PDS. They have access to the resources and benefits available to all FCAPE teachers as well as additional opportunities for professional development as teacher educators, such as:

1. Playing a significant role in the preparation of new physical education teachers by sharing teaching strategies, and influencing the way physical education is delivered in the school.
2. Enrolling in courses and workshops at the university.
3. Working as a team with graduate students, faculty, and preservice teachers to deliver physical education to children and youth in their own school programs.

The clinical educators agree that the position, nevertheless, has several significant downfalls that might prevent them from repeating the experience. These problems include:

1. The ambiguity of the role.
2. Being away from their school setting resulting in loss of time with students.
3. Adjusting to different cultures (structured school timetable to an unstructured one).
4. Being split between two cultures.

We continue to work with our clinical educators to minimize the downfalls and build on successes, but this is a slow and arduous process.

It is critical to highlight how our work impacts the children and youth we teach in our schools, the school programs themselves, the districts as a whole, and the university teacher preparation program. Students in our collaborating public schools enjoy unique advantages working with FCAPE. These include:

1. Current innovations in our field are brought to their programs.
2. Innovative instruction is designed to challenge and promote learning.
3. Instruction is delivered from a team of educators including clinical educators, graduate teaching associates, and university faculty.
4. New technologies designed for physical education and sport are introduced.
5. New curricular ideas and strategies are designed to meet specific needs and interests.

Practicing teachers who take part in FCAPE have access to various professional development opportunities that can impact the programs they deliver to children and youth. These include:

1. MEd projects developed and left with the programs in which the graduate student interned. These projects include new curriculum packages, alternative assessments, and instructional strategies.
2. Professional development delivered through FCAPE workshops: annual and monthly workshops focused on educational issues, curriculum, and activities.
3. Inquiry into their own teaching and students' learning through action research projects with Ohio State graduate students or faculty.
4. Reviewing and implementing new instructional strategies to deliver physical education content to children and youth while receiving support from other physical education professionals.
5. Increased communication with physical education colleagues to reduce the isolation experienced in the gymnasium.

The Physical Education Teacher Education Program enjoys several benefits from this collaborative work with physical education teachers and their quality programs. These include:

1. Opportunity to place preservice teachers in quality programs with innovative teachers who want to improve the teaching of physical education to children and youth.
2. Opportunity for university faculty to work with clinical educators, practicing teachers, graduate students, and preservice teachers to deliver physical education in the public schools.
3. Opportunity to develop long-term professional relationships with practicing teachers and clinical educators committed to the physical education of children and youth.

This collaborative effort is still unfolding. This past year we have worked collaboratively to share supervision, courses, and assessment of the program. The effort has been equitable, worthwhile, and professionally challenging for teachers and university faculty alike. Two part-time clinical educators worked with university faculty to design, teach, and evaluate the preservice teacher preparation program. They were leaders of several inservice initiatives for FCAPE members that included authentic assessment, a grant-writing workshop, and a discussion on the 1996 Surgeon General's Report on Physical Activity and Health and its implications for our programs and communities. They also organized an upcoming two-day conference on teaching about self and social responsibility in physical education.

IT TAKES TIME

Hindsight is always 20/20 vision. In our efforts to be inclusive and engage as many physical educators in professional development as possible, we spread the work of the group too thin. We have struggled until quite recently to maintain cohesion and a genuine collective vision for FCAPE. However context is a critical factor, and our awareness of the isolated nature of physical education teachers in many schools prompted us to provide professional opportunities for all, given the paucity of such opportunities in the past.

We were determined that our PDS initiative would be a collaborative effort. We knew it would take time, and both teachers and university faculty worked hard to establish a peer relationship. In our desire for teacher leadership to develop, faculty held back, tried to listen more than talk, and shared more than directed. This process of trust building was slow and painful. Teachers and faculty alike walked on egg shells as we tried to ensure that all were able to speak. Our meetings were endless hours of unfocused discussion with little continuity. We didn't know how to lead each other. In time, we began to question and challenge each other's ideas, focus on a project, and just do it.

We began to notice that not all teachers and faculty were equally involved and committed and decided that we needed to focus on those willing to actively participate. The main projects and goals of FCAPE are now directed by three faculty and about ten teachers. We decided on selective membership (those actively involved in FCAPE) as distinct from egalitarianism (anyone can join) in order to achieve a collaborative and effective teacher preparation program and sustained inquiry. The broader professional development goal for physical education teachers at large is accommodated with invitations to courses, workshops, and an annual physical education conference sponsored by FCAPE. The wisdom of moving to a more selective, some might say elitist, group of committed teachers and faculty is still being tested.

THE PROCESS OF CHANGE: BENEFITS AND CHALLENGES

A benefit of the initial large group of teachers from multiple sites was that we could share common concerns about our subject matter. As the content of physical education is often marginalized in the schools, it was beneficial to address issues and concerns with a group of professionals who valued and were committed to a similar focus. We were able to select a topic, share concerns from various contextual settings (i.e., urban, suburban, elementary, secondary schools) and discuss possible solutions and survival strategies. Through these formal and informal conversations, the problems did not disappear, but the knowledge that others had the same experiences was cathartic. We could share strategies and move forward because we knew that other teachers understood and supported us.

Elementary specialists in FCAPE have been working for three years on a project that integrates math, science, language arts, and other subjects into local physical education curricula, and provides activities for classroom teachers to integrate movement into the classroom. As classroom teachers expressed an interest in the project, they were invited to contribute to the Integration Activity packet with ideas to integrate movement and other school subjects into the classroom or gymnasium. This project has resulted in the compilation of a resource booklet and the implementation of an integrated curriculum with several classroom teachers in the same building collaborating with the physical education specialists.

Another faculty member, graduate student, and three high school teachers developed an instructional unit in the high school physical education curriculum to encourage students to examine sport from various perspectives. They implemented this project, studied the perceptions of teachers to the curricular initiative (a Sport Studies Unit), and assessed the factors that inhibit or enhance such change efforts in high schools. A second study has examined the perceptions of students toward this innovation.

CHANGE IS HARD AND SLOW

Although some improvements to local physical education programs have occurred, it has not been without struggles. We began by being polite to one another. When we encountered resistance, we backed down and compromised or changed the topic. Our efforts to collaborate have only recently moved beyond the polite stage. We are beginning to challenge one another to improve physical education and better prepare teachers to achieve that goal. We have made small incremental steps in this direction.

As university faculty, we have come to recognize the expertise of the teachers in the school setting and their contribution to the educational experience of preservice teachers. University faculty have begun to relinquish control of some of the program decisions, and act as advisors and coordinators in instances where teachers take on a more assertive role. The major role change here is that of the clinical educator, yet as MEd interns are spending more time in school settings, the cooperating teacher role is changing as well. Teachers are talking more, and university faculty are listening. Although the change is slow, it is happening.

PHYSICAL EDUCATION—BENIGN NEGLECT

Many schools in our vicinity were undergoing changes as a result of local school reform efforts. Efforts to include physical educators in the reform movements were negligible. It seemed again, that physical education was to be marginalized, as those directing the reform efforts in the various school districts bypassed its potential contribution. If reformers are attempting to educate the whole child, why are physical educators once again on the periphery of the discussion? When there was change it was insufficient. For example, changes at the secondary level were often limited to varying the amount of class time from 55–minute classes to two–hour blocks of time in some schools. Some acceptance of the integrated curriculum was found at the elementary level, but it was only accepted by small pockets of teachers within school settings, rather than by the educational community.

Most of the changes we were seeing occurred through individual efforts of physical education specialists in particular school buildings. The impact and contribution of physical education in the overall education of children and youth did not seem to be a major goal. Physical education is so marginalized that it is not even included in the discussion, and becomes a victim of "benign neglect."

We must strive to impact and improve physical education at the university and in the schools, and to help other educators value the contribution of physical education in the educational process. It is imperative that we speak to other physical educators, teachers, and administrators about our professional goals, ideas, and needs. If we continue to be polite, we will continue to be benign. Our PDS has helped to create a place where a different kind of conversation and change can take place.

REFERENCES

Dodds, P. (1975). A behavioral, competency-based peer assessment model for student teacher supervision in elementary physical education. *Dissertation Abstracts International, 36*(6), 3486A. (University Microfilms No. AA17526570)

Eldar, E. (1987). The effects of a self-management program on interns' behavior during a field experience in physical education. *Dissertation Abstracts International, 48*(9), 2273A. (University Microfilms No. AA18726625)

Goodson, I. (1997). Representing teachers. *Teaching and Teacher Education, 13*, 111–117.

Goodson, I., & Fliesser, C. (1997). *Exchanging gifts: Collaborative research and theories of context*. Unpublished paper, University of Western Ontario.

Holmes Group. (1990). *Tomorrow's schools*. East Lansing, MI: Author.

O'Sullivan, M. M. (1983). The effects of inservice education on the teaching effectiveness of experienced physical educators. *Dissertation Abstracts International, 44*(6), 1724A. (University Microfilms No. AA18318413)

Sizer, T. (1992). *Horace's school: Redesigning the American high school*. Boston: Houghton Mifflin.

Taggart. A. C. (1988). The systematic development of teaching skills: A sequence of planned pedagogical experiences. *Journal of Teaching in Physical Education, 8*(1), 73–86.

Tannehill, D., LaMaster, K., & Berkowitz, B. (1994). Communication within FCAPE. *What is different? What has changed? Professional Development School Publication Series*. Columbus, OH: The Ohio State University.

CHAPTER 15

Inaugurating a Professional Development Network for Foreign and Second Language Educators: Flying the Plane and Repairing It at the Same Time

Deborah Wilburn Robinson

This chapter describes the beginning stages of a new PDS for educators in foreign and second language. Planning details and organizational arrangements are carefully described, as are the challenges of these beginning stages of development. The planning committee surveys potential participants and uses this information to shape the PDS including ways to screen mentor teachers and establish goals.

On paper, establishing a Professional Development Network (PDN) for foreign and second language teachers seemed easy. We followed the same guidelines for conceiving a Holmes Partnership that other OSU PDSs have employed. Our vision appeared to capture a spirit of collaboration between schools and the university. In practice, however, there remains a tension as we seek to make our vision a reality.

BACKGROUND

Educators from fields other than foreign language education might benefit from reading about some of the unique challenges of our content area in terms of both pre- and inservice teacher development. In Ohio, prospective foreign language teachers are granted a specialist pre-K–12 license. This necessitates that interns have a variety of experiences both programmatically (immersion, foreign language experience, foreign language in the elementary school, middle school, traditional high school, and proficiency-oriented programs); socioculturally (rural, suburban, urban); and linguistically (the Ohio State Foreign and Second Language Program certifies teachers in 10 languages). Therefore, as with other network PDSs described in this book, it was unreasonable for us to designate a single site or school for a PDS. A network more adequately provides us with a critical mass of diverse teaching contexts.

In terms of inservice teacher development, it is essential to understand that typically the teacher is the only person in a beginning-level language classroom with any knowledge of the discipline. The content of instruction is also the medium of instruction. In other words, the teacher talks about the structures, vocabulary, morphology, and culture speaking in the language to be learned. Very often, this teacher is also the only one in the building that teaches his/her language. The idea of a PDN for these individuals is critical to ongoing growth in both linguistic and cultural knowledge as well as pedagogical techniques for teaching that particular language.

The case for English as a Second Language (ESL) teachers' participation in a network is equally strong. In the state of Ohio, an individual cannot be certified to teach ESL. Rather, ESL validation or endorsement is added to an existing license. Not considered part of the core program, these educators are often called aides or tutors rather than teachers. With the strength of the English Only Movement in this country, these teachers often feel more marginalized.

As with many fields, the lack of qualified substitute teachers has had a particular impact in conceiving our PDN. It is next to impossible to find stand-ins for a clinical educator role to be released from their teaching responsibilities. Rather, we chose to hire field educators who remain in their classes during the school day and address school-university partnership issues after school hours.

HISTORY OF OUR PDN

The Foreign and Second Language PDN had been in existence for a short 14 weeks at the time this chapter was written. Prior to the arrival of our first MEd cohort in September 1997, area teachers, administrators, and university faculty and graduate teaching assistants began to build this network based on the six strategic goals of Holmes Partnership Schools.

In reviewing the literature on existing partnerships and in speaking with colleagues involved in other college PDSs, it became clear that communication was a key issue in the success of these endeavors. In May 1997, we were committed to "start where the potential participants were" in terms of the feasibility of a network. Three-hundred-and-fifty surveys were sent out to Franklin County public and Catholic school Foreign and Second Language teachers and to 66 administrators to ascertain attitudes about and willingness to participate in partnership programs.

We received responses from 90 teachers and nine administrators. We collected demographic data about years of experience, languages, number of classes taught per day, and the nature of administrative positions held. Further we obtained information on the nature of continued professional development activities, what teachers and administrators would be willing to provide to mentor preservice teachers, areas of interest in classroom-based inquiry, and areas where help was needed to work with preservice teachers and to continue their own professional development. Assumptions and conditions for collaboration were also gleaned from the survey.

Results from the survey established that educators from the various levels must believe that collaboration between university and school participants has the potential to better all programs. Educators who take the initiative to become involved in a PDN must believe that all participants in the equation have something to offer, that this something is valid, and that, through collaboration, good things will happen. Many respondents also addressed the fact that, if the network were a success, it would solve the much-documented problem of interns' perceptions that the methods and techniques that they learn at the university are too lofty for practice in the field. (For complete survey results, see Robinson, 1998.) The results of this survey, combined with themes from the literature, informed how our PDN has been conceptualized to date.

UNIFYING DIVERSE EXPERTISE

In June 1997, area teachers and administrators as well as university professors from Foreign Language Departments, and College of Education faculty, administrators, and graduate teaching assistants participated in a daylong planning retreat. During this initial meeting, which attracted 32 area educators in K–16 foreign and second language programs, participants listened to colleagues from both the university and area schools who had participated in PDSs. A former principal, Don Cramer, now the coordinator of PDSs for the university, presented the goals of Holmes Partnerships and explained how pleased he was that the voices from the field were finally being heard. He also addressed how hard it is to actually institutionalize PDSs but challenged us to do so. Next, our associate dean of programs, Susan Sears, who has worked closely with PDS initiatives, told the group about the State Department of Education's new licensure standards. She explained how our PDN might tie into these requirements for both preservice and veteran teachers. Next, a social studies field educator, Keith Bossard, shared his experiences as a practicing teacher involved in a PDS. Once again, we heard stories of how his work in the collaborative had launched a renewed interest in all aspects of teaching. Too, he lauded the model for having forced him to engage in inquiry. Having chapters published in the literature on PDSs has given his students renewed respect for him and his own view of himself as an educator has grown. On a final note, he too warned of the time commitment involved but said the effort was well worth the sacrifice.

After these tales, I explained what the literature had to offer on PDSs. We did not skirt the hard issues of mutual respect, collaboration, the various systems of reward, or the perceptions of prestige that often accompany the term "professor" but not "teacher" (Contemporary Education, 1996; Dickens, 1993; Garfinkel & Sosa, 1996; Goodlad & Sirotnik, 1988; Rosean & Hoekwater, 1990). The themes of collaboration, professional development, and inquiry from the Holmes literature were also fully explained, though no recipes were given for how these themes might play out in our new venture (Holmes Group, 1986, 1990, 1995). Next, I explained the successes of another school-university partnership, the Collaborative Articulation and Assessment Project (CAAP) focused specifically on issues of high school–to–college articulation and assessment in French, Spanish, and German programs in the state. We proposed to build upon CAAP and expand the network by bringing in ESL, Latin, less commonly taught languages, and K–8 teachers.

After these presentations and discussions, the participants broke up into three, smaller working groups. One group focused on preservice teacher development. To frame the discussion, the group was given the following questions:

In what kinds of activities are student teachers engaged?

What kind(s) of feedback do they need?

What role(s) can teachers in the field play in developing prospective teachers?

What roles should field educators have?

The second working group focused on inservice teacher development and worked with the following guiding questions:

What kinds of workshops/courses would you like to see offered?

Who should organize them?

Should it always be the university's responsibility?

The third group's task was to discuss how the inquiry component of the PDN might function. Again, questions were provided to start the discussion:

In what kinds of projects might we wish to engage?

What kind(s) of help do inservice teachers need to engage in inquiry?

These first two initiatives, the survey and retreat, were funded by a grant from the Central States Conference on the Teaching of Foreign Languages and by the Associate Dean of Programs of the College of Education.

In August 1997, four graduate teaching assistants and I reviewed the applications we had received for our six field educator positions. Using a rating scale focused on years of experience, evidence of continued professional development, letters of support from other teachers and administrators, and service to the profession, we made our decisions. These six teachers represent a range of elementary and secondary program models and languages. Along with the interns' mentor teachers, field educators have been instrumental in revising methods syllabi, readings, and university- and field-based tasks.

FLYING AND REPAIRING THE PLANE AT THE SAME TIME

When our first group of MEd students began in mid-September, the syllabi were revised to reflect the input of practicing teachers. Methods-class visits to local classrooms were included in the syllabi. Field educators each chose a week to co-facilitate the evening seminar with the GTA assigned to the course. These practicing teachers addressed a variety of topics such as classroom management, using technology in the classroom, multiple intelligences, and incorporating culture in the classroom with the interns. Furthermore, field educators were able to share fresh successes and challenges related to all aspects of teaching and learning with the prospective teachers. One of our field educators, Al Corn, himself a mentor teacher writes of his experience:

My association this year with my field experience student [intern] was excellent. The more focused assignments and more clearly defined requirements were a tremendous asset in making sure that the field experience was worthwhile for both student and teacher. Having the student spend a full ten days of concentrated observation, as well as the weekly observations, was a very good idea. This should be maintained and continued as part of the program. . . . We shared many educational and personal experiences. This development of rapport before the actual student teaching is an excellent idea.

Similar reactions were gleaned from interns. Three excerpts from journals follow. (Note: Students were not asked in advance to write something for this piece. What follows are candid remarks from the reflection journals they have been keeping since the beginning of the program in which they document their evolving teacher selves.)

HEIDI RUSSO. I would like to start this journal out by saying that it is a wonderful idea to put us into the schools so early in this program. So many times, schools only allow the students to student teach in the spring and it makes it even harder for the developing teacher. . . . I feel like I have established a relationship with the students I will have in the spring. They know that I will be returning and I think that they look forward to that—I know I do. (I cannot wait to get into the classroom again!) I know that this school-based participation has helped me as a developing teacher because I was able to try out the things that we learned about in class and through the readings.

JOY BERLIN. Throughout the quarter, we have been discussing the newest theories and methods in the field of foreign language. Although I know I have acquired so much information, this past week in the schools really put things in perspective. The five hours a week [spent in the field each week] provided me with a good foundation of what to expect when I'm there. . . . [T]eaching there every day has given me a more genuine feeling of the classroom dynamics and the students' learning styles.

RYAN WERTZ. Writing this journal entry coincides with a time when everything we've been studying and talking about in class, on our field trips, and in our cooperating teachers' classrooms is falling into place. All of the interrelationships and interdependencies are becoming clearer and clearer, and it's no longer easy to talk about just one isolated aspect of teaching without mentioning its connections to several others as well. I have truly enjoyed this [methods] class and know I will look back on it as a cornerstone in my professional development as a foreign language teacher. . . . This class also provided me with a safe environment for trying out what I learned.

Early in the fall we established a steering committee that includes the state foreign language consultant, several school administrators, an assistant professor from the Russian program, a handful of mentor teachers, and all the field educators. During our monthly meetings, our team redesigned the traditional four-hour written masters exam into an MEd capstone exam. Following good curriculum development, "begin with the end in mind," we recently have completed the co-development of this alternative assessment. It is interesting to note that, in comparing what we generated with our section guidelines for alternative exams, we came up with comparable tasks. This process served once again to validate both aspects of the program, giving credence to the fact that teachers in the field do have experiential knowledge about what future teachers must know and be able to do.

Perhaps one of our field educators, Elvina Palma says it best when documenting her own personal and professional growth as a member of the partnership:

> My participation in partnering with Ohio State preservice teacher development has impacted me both professionally and personally. On a professional basis I have become more aware of what good teaching is. I have found it difficult at times to express what good teaching is because I am convinced that it is the result of a combination of characteristics of individual teachers. . . . By partnering with Ohio State, I can get feedback from professionals in the field as well as excellent theory about the teaching profession. . . . I appreciate having the opportunity to hear new and fresh perspectives about the field of teaching, and I enjoy trying to incorporate them into my own teaching. I also enjoy sharing these views with my colleagues. I have learned through the years that not everyone wants to hear new ideas and use new perspectives. I feel the need to listen and the need to have people listen. Being part of this partnering gives me the opportunity to do both.

In order to monitor and advise the work of the partnership, the steering committee also considers and rules on all matters of policy. Moreover, the group decided that, based on the survey data, we would also work on screening mentor teachers; ensuring that interns are prepared for student teaching; communicating clear expectations on roles, duties, and responsibilities; and establishing better means of communication. Although screening potential mentor teachers is a dicey subject, results of our initial survey support the concept. Overwhelmingly, 80 of the 90 respondents advocate a review process for mentor teachers (five replied "no"; five had no response) that includes one or more of the following: interviews, vitae, survey, classroom observations, attitude measures, self-evaluation, and compatibility screenings.

By far, the most recommended criteria for potential mentors are the desire to work and the past history of working with preservice teachers.

Respondents recognize that although one might be a master teacher him/herself, it takes a unique individual to be able to deconstruct the teaching act, look at practice objectively, and allow novices to grow into good teachers through practice and feedback. Survey participants also described the personal characteristics that a good role model might exhibit. Participants suggested that mentors be nominated, either by administrators or by their teaching peers. Other criteria focused on classroom management and rapport with students. A record of continued professional development and service to the profession coupled with belief in the philosophy of the network were also desired characteristics for a possible mentor. Finally, understanding university expectations for preservice teacher development was cited as a necessary element to being a successful model teacher.

We will need at least a full year to develop this network. But the rewards have been encouraging. One of the mentor teachers, in conjunction with her technology educator, is fashioning a web project for the interns. A field educator, in his own right a successful grant writer, is working with me to secure funding for PDN endeavors. The Spanish Department, responding to the need for courses to increase language proficiency, offered a late afternoon course on pronoun usage. A lone faculty member could not possibly manage all of these disparate elements of collaborative pre- and inservice professional development, especially where responsibilities include other program activities.

CHALLENGES

While our efforts feel promising, we are finding challenges as well. In particular, supervision and communication have been formidable tasks in our PDN.

Supervision

While syllabi and tasks for university and field components have been successfully co-developed, the parameters for supervision remain unclear. Both the May survey and the June meeting highlighted this deficiency in university/school collaboration in foreign language teacher education. Teachers have expressed frustration with the lack of guidance from the university on this topic in the past. University GTAs and faculty have also been reluctant to intrude too much into the mentor teacher-intern dyad and their means of communicating. Past student teachers complained about the need for clearer expectations and more focused feedback during their final student teaching quarter. Clearly supervision has been the weak link in our program.

Our frustrations are substantiated in the literature. Woodward (1991) delineates several factors that must be accounted for in good supervision. These include, but are not limited to, the opportunity for change; personality and experience of participants; time and space, constraints; materials; and styles of learning, teaching, and training (p. 209). Given the differences in university and school cultures in terms of these factors, it is no wonder that partnership participants currently have more questions than answers.

Hall and Davis (1995) report that when university and school personnel came together prior to the student teaching practicum to clarify expectations and means of communication, everyone felt more ownership in preservice teacher development and understood their roles better. Moreover, these researchers documented that the relationship between a student teacher and his or her mentor is more successful if it is reciprocal rather than complementary. Where the relationship that develops is instead complementary, where one teaches and the other learns, one supervises and the other is supervised, one facilitates and the other is facilitated (p. 38), the relationship is less successful.

The issue of supervision becomes even murkier with the advent of the reflective teaching movement (Nunan & Lamb, 1996). Coupled with this emphasis on teacher reflection is the fact that each teaching situation necessitates different solutions for reaching and teaching students. "Most educators have come to realize that social constructivist pedagogy in classrooms and constructivist-oriented administrative practices are not well served by professional development models that rely on top-down, transmission-oriented activities and materials" (Rueda, 1997, p. 2).

To address these challenges, our network is seeking funding to (re)unite mentor teachers, field educators, interns, administrators, and university teaching assistants and faculty in a two-day workshop on supervision. The major goals for this gathering are: (1) to discuss the purposes of supervision, (2) to establish common processes of supervision, and (3) to determine which observation instruments (e.g., Praxis, COLT) we will employ to support reflection yet provide guidance for interns.

Communication

Most of the field educators are comfortable in the knowledge that they will not be "abandoning their posts" during school hours to work on the agenda of bettering preservice teacher education and reflecting on their own practice. But, finding the time for frequent collaborative discussions and decision making after hours when we are all tired is problematic. Kristin Scott, a field educator and mentor teacher, laments:

> I would also like to see our PDN be released half a day [each week] from school for the whole school year to work closely with the Ohio State students and coordinate the PDN. This could really alleviate some work for you, Debbie! Too, I wish there were more time to interact with the students. Perhaps in future years, the PDN should meet twice a month—once with and once without Ohio State students. I still feel a gap between "their" world and mine, yet, I feel privileged to be a part of this PDN. My colleagues continue to amaze me with their dedication and I often leave questioning whether I deserve to be part of such an elite group!

Not only would increased interaction between field educators and interns be desirable, but also attracting more foreign and second language teachers in general would be helpful. Yet, as a result of the May survey, we know that some have a "wait and see" attitude. They want to be kept abreast of our activities but have made no commitment to join. Unfortunately, attendance at meetings by mentors who are not field educators is spotty as well. Incentives beyond participation in a worthy endeavor need to be established.

I, too, feel the need for greater communication among partnership members and potential members. Even though I know it would be more expeditious, I continue to resist the temptation to make lone decisions because it would be counter to the spirit of our PDN. Yet, as an untenured faculty member, I am always aware of the need to create time to do what is typically rewarded at the university—research, publishing, and grant writing. My responsibilities with the PDN, however, are more administrative than scholarly in nature. There is a general lack of understanding about the time-consuming nature of partnerships on the part of many university faculty who are not involved. Coordination of a PDN should be equivalent to teaching a course each quarter, including summer so that time can be allocated to completing tenure-track expectations.

One final challenge related to communication remains. We must find a way to document the development of our PDN so that if current parties leave, the next participants are not starting from scratch. The roles of mentor teacher, field educator, and professor-coordinator are planned for rotation. To institutionalize the concept of a PDN, other individuals should be able to step in without having to begin the dialogue all over again. Yet it is the human element that makes a network function, and humans need time to develop trust and come to understand each other's worlds. This raises the question of whether collaborative efforts like PDNs can survive the norms of institutionalized programs that are built on the assumption of interchangeable parts and people?

CONCLUSION

The Foreign and Second Language Professional Development Network is in its inaugural year. We give the Holmes Partnership goals a distinct flavor based on the needs in our content area. The data from the survey and from our initial retreat allow more than intuitions to inform our PDN. We know the wealth of human potential we have to work with as well as the challenges. We are convinced, however, that by continuing to fly the plane and repairing it at the same time, we will succeed in making a difference in the professional development of us all.

REFERENCES

Birckbichler, D., Robison, R., & Robinson, D. W. (1995). A collaborative approach to articulation and assessment. In G. Crouse (Ed.), *Broadening the frontiers of foreign language education.* Report of the Central States Conference on the Teaching of Foreign Languages (pp. 107–123). Lincolnwood, IL: National Textbook Co.

Contemporary Education. (1996, Summer), 67(4).

Corl, K., Harlow, L., Macián, J., & Saunders, D. (1996). Collaborative partnerships for articulation: Asking the right questions. *Foreign Language Annals, 29*(2), 111–124.

Dickens, C. (1993). Too valuable to be rejected, too different to be embraced: A critical look at school-university collaboration (Forum, Paper No. 1). Professional Development School Publication Series, Columbus, OH: The Ohio State University.

Garfinkel, A., & Sosa, C. (1996). Foreign language teacher education in a professional development school. In Z. Moore (Ed.), *Foreign language teacher education: Multiple perspectives* (pp. 97–121). Lanham, MD: University Press of America.

Goodlad, J., & Sirotnik, K. (1988). The future of school-university partnerships. In K. Sirotnik & J. Goodlad (Eds.), *School-university partnerships in action: Concepts, cases, and concerns* (pp. 205–225). New York: Teachers College Press.

Hall, J. K., & Davis, J. (1995). What we know about relationships that develop between cooperating and student teachers. *Foreign Language Annals, 28*(1), 32–48.

Holmes Group. (1986). *Tomorrow's teachers.* East Lansing, MI: Author.

Holmes Group. (1990). *Tomorrow's schools.* East Lansing, MI: Author.

Holmes Group. (1995). *Tomorrow's schools of education.* East Lansing, MI: Holmes Group.

Nunan, D., & Lamb, C. (1996). *The self-directed teacher.* New York: Cambridge University Press.

Robinson, D. W. (1998). Creating a Professional Development Network for Foreign and Second Language Educators: Unifying Diverse Expertise. In A. Moeller

(Ed.), *Celebrating diversity in the language classroom.* Report of the Central States Conference on the Teaching of Foreign Languages. Lincolnwood, IL: National Textbook Co.

Rosaen, C., & Hoekwater, A. (1990). Collaboration: Empowering educators to take charge. *Contemporary Education, 61*(3), 144–151.

Rueda, R. (1997). CREDE Program showcase: Professional development. *CREDE Talking Leaves* 2(1), 4.

Woodward, T. (1991). *Models and metaphors in language teacher training.* New York: Cambridge University Press.

CHAPTER 16

The Special Education Professional Development School

Gwendolyn Cartledge, John O. Cooper, Ralph Gardner III, Timothy E. Heron, William L. Heward, Richard D. Howell, and Diane M. Sainato

The chapter of the newest OSU PDS comes last. The PDS works with preservice special education MEd students. The faculty in this program area work collaboratively with one elementary school and other teachers in special education settings. The program has a coherent focus of Direct Instruction and chooses field placements to support this instructional orientation. Since we are just beginning our PDS work, this chapter lays out our goals and the structure we have set up for our PDS and the interns with whom we will work.

This chapter describes a Professional Development School (PDS) under development by the Special Education Section (SPED) within the School of Physical Activity and Educational Services. This SPED-PDS will provide each MEd intern with two different, but complementary, quarter-long internship experiences in: (1) a special education setting (e.g., a resource room or self-contained classroom) working under the guidance and supervision of a *special* education mentor teacher, and (2) an urban school where they will learn how to use the Direct Instruction (DI) curricula from a *general* education mentor teacher.

This PDS initiative is the first time that we have collectively supervised two internships combining special and general educators within and across schools. As an outgrowth of changes in the teacher education climate, the timing is right. New teacher licensure standards to go into effect will require performance-based, teacher education outcomes, and this program lends itself to achieving those outcomes. Our faculty has reached a "critical mass" in terms of numbers whereby efforts to sustain a PDS can be managed simultaneously with continuing efforts to conduct viable on-campus and branch-campus programs.

GOALS FOR THE SPED-PDS

We have seven goals for our PDS:

1. Teach MEd interns to develop, implement, and evaluate Individualized Education Programs for students with disabilities.
2. Instruct cohort groups of SPED's MEd interns in the effective use of the Direct Instruction curricula and instructional methods.
3. Prepare preservice special education interns to teach a variety of diverse student populations across levels.
4. Prepare SPED's MEd interns to collaborate with professionals in special and general education classrooms.
5. Contribute to empirically supported instructional practices in the SPED-PDS schools/classrooms.
6. Conduct collaborative inquiry on effective instructional practices.
7. Disseminate SPED-PDS research on teacher preparation and instructional practices.

DIRECT INSTRUCTION

There are several reasons to embrace the DI model within the context of our PDS. These include the programmatic features of DI, its research base, and the growing movement to include students with disabilities in general education classrooms.

Programmatic Features

The Direct Instruction model is derived from research by Siegfried Engelmann and Wesley Becker and their colleagues at the University of Oregon. Two major principles underscore Direct Instruction (DI): "Teach more in less time," and "Control the details of the curriculum." Teaching "more in less time" recognizes that even if students with disabilities are taught by an effective program that enables them to progress at the same rate as their nondisabled peers, they will always remain behind. Only by teaching at a faster rate can their achievement gap be reduced. Designing and controlling the details of the curriculum—the selection and sequencing of instructional examples—are at the heart of the Direct Instruction model.

DI lessons control background knowledge carefully so that *all* students can "build hierarchies of understanding." More important, mechanistic skills evolve into flexible strategies, concepts combine into schemata, and success in highly structured situations develops into enhanced performance in naturalistic, unpredictable, complex environments (Johnson & Layng, 1994). DI also involves specific teaching procedures. Scripted lessons prescribe what the teacher says and does for each task presented in a lesson. Scripted lessons ensure consistent, quality instruction. DI is typically conducted with small groups of children (5 to 10), and allows more teacher attention, feedback, and individualization than large-group instruction. High rates of active student response are generated by having students chorally respond in unison to a rapidly paced series of teacher-presented items (Carnine, 1976; Heward, Courson, & Narayan, 1989). To help the pacing and the simultaneous participation by all students, the teacher uses hand signals to cue the student when to respond. Correct responses are praised, and corrective feedback is provided for incorrect responses.

Research Base

An evaluation of the Direct Instruction model conducted by the nationwide Follow Through Project and involving more than 8,000 children in 20 communities showed that students made significant gains in academic achievement (Gersten, Carnine, & White, 1984; Watkins, 1988). These children caught or surpassed students according to the national norms on several arithmetic, reading, and language skills as measured by the *Wide Range Achievement Test* (Jastak & Wilkinson, 1984) and the *Metropolitan Achievement Tests* (Prescott, Balow, Hogan, & Farr, 1985). With spelling, the DI students finished slightly below average, but still showed significant gains over other methods. None of the other educational approaches evaluated by the Follow Through Project was as effective as DI.

Inclusion Movement

Students with disabilities are assigned increasingly to general education classrooms (Heward, 1996; Kauffman & Hallahan, 1995). This situation changes the special educators' role from working with students in isolated "pull out" programs to working alongside general education classroom teachers in least restrictive, inclusive settings (Graden, Zins, & Curtis, 1989).

The Direct Instruction model (Carnine, Silbert, & Kameenui, 1997; Stein, Silbert, & Carnine, 1997) offers an effective method for sequencing and presenting instruction and feedback across multiple curricula areas to all students (Kameenui, 1993). Classroom research has shown repeatedly the measurable effectiveness of Direct Instruction, especially where instructional settings include students with special needs and where many students do not perform at grade level (Gardner et al., 1994; Kameenui, 1993).

THE INTERNSHIP PROGRAMS

The Interns

A total of 23 special education MEd interns participated during the inaugural year of our PDS. The interns were divided into two groups. Internship placements for the two groups was switched during the subsequent quarter. Under the co-direction and supervision of clinical educators, mentor teachers, and Ohio State faculty, MEd interns gradually assumed all the assessment, instruction, and classroom management responsibilities of a classroom teacher. Each intern completed 20 clock hours per week for 10 weeks for each internship. This 400–hour internship practicum constituted their student teaching experience.

Further, our expectation was that our interns participate in larger school functions (e.g., faculty meetings, parent conferences, curriculum meetings, coaching experiences, art/music projects) so as to gain a fuller understanding and appreciation for the complexities and challenges of an inner-city school. It was essential for interns to become part of the school fabric if larger PDS goals were to be achieved.

Individual Special Education Placement Component

Students with disabilities receive instruction in a variety of educational environments, and an increasing number receive all of their instruction in inclusive settings. Still, many students with disabilities receive at least part of their instruction in a resource room or self-contained classroom. The MEd interns completed their second 200–hour internship with a "master" special educator in one of these settings.

Arlington Park Elementary School

Arlington Park Elementary School enrolls approximately 400 students in kindergarten through grade five; 94% of the student body is African

American and many come from low-income homes. There are seven children with severe behavior disabilities enrolled in the school. The students are included in general education classrooms for most of the day, and the special education teacher works collaboratively with the general education teachers to ensure that each student receives needed academic and behavioral support.

In 1994, the faculty at Arlington Park, under the leadership of the principal, implemented the Direct Instruction model in reading and math with the kindergarten and first grades. Direct Instruction is used as the primary curriculum by teachers at Arlington Park. Student scores on district-administered achievement and competency tests have improved substantially since DI's introduction.

Mentor Teachers

Each MEd intern was placed with a mentor teacher at Arlington Park. The mentor teacher (1) modeled the appropriate usage of DI within the classroom, (2) supervised MEd interns in their classrooms, (3) provided day-to-day verbal and written feedback to the interns, and (4) collaborated with Ohio State faculty to develop the interns' professional skills. Also, Ohio State faculty and mentor teachers collaborated on intern projects.

FACULTY ROLE

Three Ohio State faculty per quarter supervised MEd interns at Arlington Park, and collaborated with them and their teachers on a range of intern projects. In the future, faculty and doctoral students will conduct inservice courses and workshops with Arlington Park faculty, and Arlington Park teachers will provide on-site inservice programs to our faculty and our graduate interns.

Likewise, when interns were enrolled in the resource room internship, faculty conducted visitations at least once per week. Oral discussion of the lesson also occurred. Coupled with cooperating teacher feedback, and a weekly faculty-led debriefing seminar, interns received a supervised opportunity to improve their teaching methodology.

INQUIRY THEMES

The MEd project focuses on a social or academic behavior-change intervention for students with special needs in a school setting. MEd interns work with their faculty advisers and mentor teachers to develop, implement, and evaluate the project in the internship setting. Interns collect data daily to determine the effectiveness of their instruction. Each student writes a final report detailing instructional procedures, analyzing student data, and discussing student accomplishments. The MEd project is completed by the end of the intern's program. Examination of their project occurs following the rules established by Ohio State's Graduate School and the Graduate Studies Committee in the School of Physical Activity and Educational Service.

Inquiry themes for the faculty extend to broader areas and include questions such as:

1. Did this dual format to educate master's-level interns work? Did the interns learn to teach using DI procedures? What effect did the program have on doctoral-level students who participated as supervisors?

2. Did the elementary general and special education students learn academic, social, or behavioral skills as a function of our instruction?

3. Did the DI skills learned at Arlington Park generalize to other instructional areas or settings?

4. Did the faculty, interns, parents, or administrators view the program as effective, positive, or socially valid?

FUTURE CHALLENGES

The most significant challenge affecting our PDS has been the recent reassignment of the school principal. Not only was the former principal an advocate for Direct Instruction within and outside of the school system, but she was also a trained DI master teacher herself. Fortunately, her successor is also a trained DI teacher. It is our expectation that we will be able to continue the liaison and communication link between Ohio State faculty and Arlington Park teachers.

Programmatically, a second challenge will be to generate cost-benefit ratio data that demonstrate that the student outcomes produced by DI were reasonable. That is, that the ratio of positive student gains produced per unit of instruction exceeded the effort expended to produce these outcomes, and that these outcomes outpaced gains that would have accrued had another instructional methodology been in place.

Third, our faculty is interested in working with Arlington Park teachers, administrators, and parents to help design, implement, and evaluate a *home-based education* initiative that would extend the Direct Instruction program to the home setting. This initiative places staffing, scheduling, and logistical challenges on the Ohio State faculty who have unresolved staff and schedule concerns.

Finally, given the 12–month nature of our doctoral training program, our faculty, in collaboration with Arlington Park staff and community leaders, would like to help to design, implement, and evaluate a Direct Instruction *summer school program* for children attending Arlington Park. Since many of our current faculty, and all of the Arlington Park teachers, have summer as an "off-duty" quarter, collectively we face the challenge of realigning our staff to cover programs that might be offered during this period.

A FINAL NOTE

We believe that our PDS offers a "win-win" situation for children, interns, and the respective faculties. Ohio State's special education faculty have prepared for this initiative by redesigning our curriculum and practica experiences, communicating with the principal and teachers on joint benefits to be gained by this initiative, and by attending the Midwest Direct Instruction Conference during the summer, 1997.

Further, during a recent orientation for our special education interns, faculty, and alumni, Dr. Cathy Watkins, a teacher educator at California State University, Stanislaus and an internationally recognized expert on DI, served as our keynote speaker. In the months ahead, we will be working diligently on the following tasks.

1. Supervising the next class of master's-level interns at Arlington Park and our other sites.

2. Working with teachers, administrators, and parents to help design, implement, and evaluate *home-based education* initiatives that would extend the Direct Instruction program to the home setting.

3. Conducting and participating in inservice training with Arlington Park teachers, aides, or related-service personnel.

4. Discussing a *summer school program* for children attending Arlington Park.

5. Exploring the fuller range of collaborative research opportunities to evaluate the positive student achievement outcomes that have come to Arlington Park students as a function of the Direct Instruction program.

In the end, we believe that our interns will be better educated, Arlington Park teachers and Ohio State faculty will have a closer working relationship, and, of course, student learning will be enhanced. Our respective future plans will be changed by this program. What we learn will help to inform our curriculum. What the teachers learn will help to develop enrichment, parent education, and summer programs. What our interns learn will fortify their instructional repertoires. What the pupils learn will improve their performance. In accomplishing these goals, the SPED-PDS will serve as a model for future special and general education endeavors.

REFERENCES

Carnine, D. W. (1976). Effects of two teachers' presentation rates on off-task behavior, answering correctly, and participation. *Journal of Applied Behavior Analysis, 9,* 199–206.

Carnine, D. W., Silbert, J., & Kameenui, E. J. (1997). *Direct instruction reading* (3rd ed.). Upper Saddle River, NJ: Prentice Hall.

Gardner, R., III., Sainato, D., Cooper, J. O., Heron, T. E., Heward, W. L., Eshleman, J., & Grossi, T. (Eds.). (1994). *Behavior analysis in education: Focus on measurably superior instruction.* Pacific Grove, CA: Brooks/Cole.

Gersten, R., Carnine, D., & White, W. A. T. (1984). The pursuit of clarity: Direct instruction and applied behavior analysis. In W. L. Heward, T. E. Heron, D. S. Hill, & J. Trap-Porter (Eds.), *Focus on behavior analysis in education* (pp. 38–57). Columbus, OH: Merrill.

Graden, J. L., Zins, J. E., & Curtis, M. J. (1989). *Alternative educational delivery systems: Enhancing instructional options for all students.* Washington, DC: National Association of School Psychologists.

Heward, W. L. (1996). *Exceptional children: An introductory survey of special education* (5th ed.). Upper Saddle River, NJ: Prentice Hall.

Heward, W. L., Courson, J. H., & Narayan, J. S. (1989). Using choral responding to increase active student response during group instruction. *Teaching Exceptional Children, 21*(3), 72–75.

Jastak, S., & Wilkinson, G. S. (1984). *Wide range achievement test-revised.* Wilmington, DE: Jastak Associates.

Johnson, K. R., & Layng, T. V. J. (1994). The Morningside model of generative instruction. In R. Gardner III, D. M. Sainato, J. O. Cooper, T. E. Heron, W. L. Heward, J. Eshleman, & T. A. Grossi (Eds.), *Behavior analysis in education: Focus on measurably superior instruction* (pp. 173–197). Monterey, CA: Brooks/Cole.

Kameenui, E. (1993). Diverse learners and the tyranny of time: Don't fix the blame; fix the leaky roof. *The Reading Teacher, 46*(5), 376–383.

Kauffman, J. M., & Hallahan, D. P. (1995). *The illusion of full inclusion: A comprehensive critique of a current special education bandwagon.* Austin, TX: PRO-ED.

Prescott, G. A., Balow, I. H., Hogan, T. P., & Farr, R. C. (1985). *Metropolitan Achievement Tests* (6th ed.). San Antonio, TX: Psychological Corporation.

Stein, M., Silbert, J., & Carnine, D. (1997). *Designing effective mathematics instruction: A direct instruction approach*. Upper Saddle River, NJ: Prentice Hall.

Watkins, C. L. (1988). Project Follow Through: A story of the identification and neglect of effective instruction. *Youth Policy, 10*, 7–11.

CONCLUSION

We end the book by looking retrospectively at what it was like before PDS and what it is like now. As editors we do this individually and then we look collectively at some lingering issues. Individually, each of us feels that our lives as professionals have been significantly influenced by our involvement in PDS reforms. Our narratives situate us as editors as well as draw together the themes of change that you have encountered throughout the book.

A TEACHER'S PERSPECTIVE:
MIGRATION FROM ISOLATION TO COLLABORATION

Tim Dove

Picture this . . .

You are hired and given your first teaching assignment. For most of us, this meant you received a teacher's handbook, went to some type of orientation, were shown to your classroom, and then given a master schedule, a graded course of study, and a stack of textbooks. The principal, department chair, or grade-level leader said good luck and then you sat at your desk, excited but a little overwhelmed. For many classroom teachers across the country, this was the beginning of isolation. An occasional department meeting, staff meeting, and district inservice opportunity was scattered among day after day after day in your classroom with your students. Things went well (or not) for some time. If things went well, you were left alone to do your job. If things didn't go well, supervisors came to evaluate and maybe not provide assistance. After a few years, a supervisor of some level asks if you are interested in working with a student teacher.

Many say yes. Here is an opportunity to give to the profession. Two weeks later you are introduced to an undergraduate, given a university handbook, and a schedule of the quarter. The university supervisor, who is very busy with his or her own studies and many other interns, sets up a time to come back and review progress. Midpoint progress is documented and a final assessment of student teaching is made through conversation and some type of written account.

This was the experience common to many of us before PDS. There were many problems with this system in training our future colleagues. What if the intern had no sense of how to work in the classroom and didn't take direction very well to shift practice? What if the cooperating teacher was more interested in the money, fee waivers from the university for graduate work, or "time off" than being a mentor? What if the cooperating teacher was of good intentions and a decent teacher but only valued the "tried and true" for their classroom with little interest in more effective methodologies? What if the intern was not being either a student or a teacher? What is done with someone who fails student teaching? How can an intern learn from the experience of more than one veteran teacher? Do all effective teachers teach the same way? Isolation has been a contributing factor in our inability to solve these problems. In isolation, the success of training preservice teachers is hit and miss at best.

Membership in a PDS and the subsequent network of individual teachers, prevents isolation and expands the perspectives of the group. In our PDS, a combination of classroom teachers from urban and suburban settings was critical in expanding our own perspectives and those of our interns. The group discovered a new energy.

By developing and team teaching a methods course together, we became more reflexive about what we value as educators and how to enable our interns to benefit from our years of experience. The insights we got from each other were also shared with colleagues at our own schools. The discussions broke down many of the barriers of teacher isolation.

We productively used our multiple perspectives to develop an initial rubric to evaluate the field performance of our interns. We identified six goals for assessment and descriptions of targeted outcomes for each goal.

Goal 1—Preteaching Interaction and Behaviors. The intern interacts well with students (shows interest, engagement, involvement, and motivation in getting to know the students), demonstrates a positive and professional attitude with students and faculty, models teacher behaviors (as opposed to student behaviors), and demonstrates a commitment to becoming a professional teacher. The intern questions conventional practice, internalizes reasons, researches alternatives, works to overcome biases, and continually looks for ways to improve.

Goal 2—Instructional Planning. The intern has an internal drive to find available resources. This includes media centers, local libraries, on-line sources, departmental resources, and university sources. The preservice teacher quickly identifies who the client is and what special needs he or she has (such as learning disabilities, English as second language, severe behavior disability, reading abilities, range of IQ, etc.) and focuses on meeting student needs. Instruments to screen for learning styles and multiple intelligences are used during planning in an attempt to reach as many individual students as possible. The intern recognizes his or her own values and biases and how they affect the delivery of curricula.

Goal 3—Instructional Methods. The intern uses a variety of instructional methods that encourage active learning, meet the different learning styles of students, and are congruent with content and educational goals. This includes teaching strategies that have students actively find, process, use information, examine global/multiple perspectives, lead a class discussion to get students to think about, articulate, evaluate, and act on what they are learning.

Goal 4—Student-Centered Focus. The intern demonstrates awareness and support of their students as individuals and as learners. This includes building rapport with and respect from every student, and making a concerted effort to help each student grow at least one year in knowledge and ability.

Goal 5—Questioning Skills. The intern uses questioning techniques that build higher-level thinking skills and awareness of the limits associated with personal bias. This includes asking students motivating and divergent questions that require them to go beyond recall of knowledge and comprehension to the application, analysis, synthesis, and evaluation of content.

Goal 6—Becoming a Professional. The intern continues the process of personal reflection to improve his or her teaching and learning as a professional educator. This includes a positive attitude toward more training, reflecting upon and improving one's own instruction, being able to articulate one's own teaching style and how it affects students, and developing as a professional through local, state, and national organizations.

How can interns become aware of the importance of the above issues during a career? The art of teaching cannot be done effectively in isolation. Part of our responsibility is to model for our preservice teachers and our classroom students the value of lifelong learning. The intern's experience is not theory versus practice or the university versus the local schools. The intern needs to have knowledge and confidence from experiencing both. Our new colleagues need to experience a network of support so that they can help break out of the old system of isolation and maintain an ongoing professional dialogue.

(IR)RECONCILABLE DIFFERENCES:
A CELEBRATION OF (UN)LIKE MINDS

Patti Brosnan

Before PDS, school/university relationships were not built on trust, principles, or on mutual concerns. In fact, relationships were not built, they just existed. Interns and mentor teachers were just assigned to each other, faceless and businesslike. The don't-ask-don't-tell rule was firmly in place. The intern was sent on a mission. Go and do well. Get the job done. Put in your time and don't be late. Dress appropriately.

After PDS, we would not consider working with an unknown mentor; we need to know whether we share important philosophical positions. To be a part of our PDS, you have to be student-centered and willing to change roles and relinquish control. You have to be the type of teacher who questions your own practice and shares decision making with students. You need to allow students to think for themselves and to become whom they want to be.

With these shared commitments there is room for differences. However, we make a distinction between reconcilable/welcomed differences and irreconcilable/intolerable differences. Using welcomed differences among people as a valued commodity is a phenomenon that became a sustenance of our school/university partnership. When building a relationship, we begin with trust. This trust is nurtured by conversation and experience. Where there is shared vision, shared mission, shared passions, and shared beliefs and practices, there is ground worth the cost of nurturing. The cost will be great, so the foundation must be built with strength and integrity.

Before PDS, we thought about, rather than discussed, our positions on educational issues. Where there were (ir)reconcilable differences, each party would shake his or her head or roll his or her eyes rather than confront the conflicts and work toward resolution. When we tried to further develop relationships between school and university faculties, there were problems with hierarchies, hidden agendas, sugar-coated politeness, and empty promises. Time and scheduling conflicts were used as excuses to (dis)continue the (non)development of the superficial relationships.

After PDS, our conversations grew from petty disagreements and identifying barriers to literature-based middle school approaches to the relationship between teaching and learning, an open-ended curriculum, and relinquishing authority in the classroom. In our middle school PDS, we began by listening to each other before we worked together. Through these discussions we developed common values, common passions, and common missions in our professional lives. While we pride ourselves on the shared philosophy that brought us together, we celebrate the diversity that keeps us together. It was through our individual diversities in such areas as content backgrounds, cultures, experiences, and points of view that our relationships deepened.

When our philosophies of education were similar, having differences in other areas presented either reconcilable problems to be solved or welcome new dimensions to our group. Reconcilable problems included things such as coming from different content backgrounds, scheduling concerns, or teaching styles.

When working with people, one must decide which battles to fight. The decision is usually based on fundamental philosophies. For example, if my irreconcilable difference with a colleague is my philosophy of teaching, then I could choose to accept his or her perspective if the students were still treated with respect and permitted to explore their own thinking. However, if the opposing philosophy disallowed students to use their own thinking and showed disrespect, then I had two options. I could choose to fight the battle openly, or I could fight the battle subversively. Either way, I chose to fight; if not, I would have sacrificed part of my self. This is demeaning—this is irreconcilable.

To build lasting working relationships, it is essential to begin with people of like minds and common philosophies. The fundamental philosophies must be mutual enough so that even if we differ, we can respect each other's work and have faith that our underlying principles will not be compromised.

A PRINCIPAL'S PERSPECTIVE: TRADITIONAL STUDENT TEACHING PLACEMENTS VERSUS MED INTERNSHIPS

Don Cramer

As a career principal in the Columbus Public Schools, I regularly had student teachers from Ohio State placed in my school. Students were put with teachers who were experienced, who wanted students that particular quarter, and who were cooperative with university faculty. Schools were given preference if they could accommodate large numbers of students and were conveniently close to the campus.

Prior to the move to the MEd and PDS certification programs, it was common to have 300 to 500 students placed for student teaching during a school year. Because of these numbers, it was not feasible to spend large amounts of time determining individual placements. The university contacted school district personnel and they in turn set up placements in the schools. The school districts were anxious to place students in their schools because teachers and administrators were rewarded with fee waivers to the university. Fee waivers were determined by the number of students placed each quarter. Teachers frequently received advanced degree and continuing education relying totally on fee waivers.

I have had the opportunity to serve as a principal prior to PDSs and then as a principal in a PDS school. With this perspective in mind, I am convinced that the PDS approach is a superior way to clinically prepare preservice students to teach. In addition, I have also had the opportunity to be administratively involved as a co-chair of the PDS Partnership Board, and more recently as a retired principal. In these multiple roles, I have been involved in developing and institutionalizing the PDS and MEd program at Ohio State. From this perspective, I have observed the ways that each MEd program area has placed students on their own, according to program area requirements and their respective PDS sites. The flexibility in the clinical aspect of the program is one of the strengths of the PDS initiative.

As a PDS principal, it was interesting to observe the interns as they worked in my school and with our mentor teachers. Working with university faculty and the interns themselves, my staff and I helped to make decisions about where interns would be placed. After their placements, they quickly began to observe and understand the culture of our school. They learned this from actually becoming school community members, taking part in committee meetings, home visits, parent conferences, and school planning initiatives. This was far different from the traditional student teaching placements where the school staff hardly got to know the student teachers in their 10–week placement. With PDS yearlong internships, cooperating teachers and interns become colleagues and participate together in the life of the school community.

From the principal's view, the pay-backs to the school and the school system from these PDS placements and collaboration are enormous in terms of professional development. Not only does the PDS learning community provide an "on-site" academic community, but it adds additional resources that are so important to the day-to-day operations of an urban school.

One commonality across the PDSs at Ohio State is that they have developed new supervision models to guide the interns' clinical experience. By purpose, these models are different in order that they can more accurately evaluate students based on the uniqueness of each program area. Teachers and principals are now deeply involved with the supervision of OUR interns. No only are they in our schools for longer and more intense periods of time, but they are immersed in our yearly program and its planning. This provides me, as the principal (recruiter) with a wonderful opportunity to observe and hire our own interns as future teachers in our PDS sites. In my school currently, three of our teachers are former interns.

Another commonality among our PDSs is that inquiry is now an integral part of our expectations for MEd interns as well as all other PDS participants. Interns are asked to keep reflective journals and these can be used as data for action research projects. We encourage interns to be reflective and to engage in professional conversations with their mentors, particularly in the area of teaching practice. Defending their practice is an important part of this reflective process. Inquiry projects done in PDSs provide a mirror on the school and its challenges and help the staffs to shape future reform and professional development agendas. I was always anxious to learn about the interns' inquiry projects in our school for these important reasons.

No longer are efficiency, convenience, and rewarding large numbers of placements (for fee credit) the guiding principles. Now we are building professional communities in which students learn to be reflective, collegial professionals as we promote our own professional development.

In retrospect, having been a principal of a PDS school has significantly changed my professional life and that of the teachers, interns, parents, and students in our school. I think that we now view our school as a professional laboratory and community where new and innovative practices take place. We are more intellectually open about our teaching practice and the implications of our work. The students and parents have benefited from the wealth of rich instructional and academic resources that the university has brought to our community. I feel strongly that the teaching professional has benefited from helping to develop a quality product called our future teachers.

A PROFESSOR'S PERSPECTIVE:
PRE- AND POST-PDS TEACHING A METHODS COURSE

Marilyn Johnston

I used to teach my social studies methods course in a solid, but traditionally structured, teacher education program. I had no idea what the students were doing in their other methods courses, and I had even less information about what happened when they were out in the schools. They wrote lesson plans for course assignments and they were expected to teach them in their field placement classrooms. They frequently reported that the classroom teacher didn't have time for them to teach their lessons. If they did get to teach and it went poorly (which it often did), the classroom teachers often said that what they were doing just wasn't workable in the "real world." What I believed was important in teaching social studies, my students seldom saw happening in the schools. I often felt like I was beating my head against the wall.

The contrast between this pre-PDS teaching and my work within the PDS is like night and day. My PDS has 45 or so teachers and I see them at our PDS meetings every Thursday after school. I also have been in many of their classrooms. We have been working together for nine years and most of us know each other well. Each year our 30 plus MEd students are the benefactors of our continuing reform efforts to create more collaborative and cohesive teacher education program.

In the PDS, I teach my social studies methods course with one or more classroom teachers and often a graduate student as well. We plan, deliver, and evaluate the course together. We plan the students' assignments with the other methods course instructors so that our assignments are integrated across subject areas. We also meet with the other PDS teachers in order to coordinate curriculum in their classrooms with the students' assignments. Our primary goal is to better integrate theory and practice. Initially we saw our roles as distinct and tied to the theory and practice distinctions defined by the stereotypes of university professors and classroom teachers. We have come to understand that these are arbitrary distinctions that get in the way of making explicit the relations between thinking and doing, between beliefs and practice.

We haven't overcome all our differences. The kinds of differences that made pre-PDS work in schools difficult for students are still there, but now our differences are part of our discussions within and outside our methods course. Students see us respecting our differences and learning from each other in ways that create a strong collegial dialogue. It makes them more willing to struggle and define their own beliefs rather than try to please their mentor teacher or supervisor. Their method course teachers no longer speak with a common ideology or oversimplify teaching because it is removed from the complexity of classroom problems and concerns. We are taking risks to try things together in our shared classroom, that is, the methods courses, just as we are encouraging them to take risks as they are learning to teach. They see the co-teachers trying things in their classrooms and evaluating the pros and cons of their efforts. Things don't always go perfectly. From this they seem more willing to assess themselves in productive ways because they don't expect everything to work perfectly for them either.

Collaboration in teaching new teachers how to teach has benefited both students and those of us who teach these courses. As we struggle together to prepare future teachers, we are examining our own beliefs and practices. As we work across the differences that have long separated schools and universities, we struggle to justify what we have constructed together. We hold each other accountable in ways that were not possible when we worked with students in isolation. We must walk the talk. We must practice what we preach.

This is reform born out of dialogue and collaboration. The risk and self-exposure should not be underestimated, nor the difficulties that result from our situatedness in different institutional orientations and expectations. As a result, however, our students are better prepared, have a wider professional outlook, and understand the complexities of professional work in ways we never accomplished working separately.

CONCLUDING REMARKS

We are acutely aware that the changes resulting from PDS efforts are fragile. Our successes have been significant, but progress brings its own problems. Each PDS has become tightly coupled with a certification program. In the beginning stages of experimentation some PDSs worked only with selected certification students or sometimes focused primarily on school reform or urban education. As PDSs have become institutionalized, they also have become more regularized. And so we have a different worry. As they become institutionalized, will our PDSs lose their innovative vigor? As more faculty and new teachers become involved, can collaboration and reform be sustained?

Most college certification programs now have a PDS. More faculty are involved, some because they have been pressured by administrators, others because they realize it's the only game in town. Their interests in collaborative forms of governance or teacher education reform, however, are not always as strong as with those who initiated PDSs. The associate dean now has full responsibility for the PDSs and is strongly supportive, but she has many other college and community items on her plate. Decisions about PDSs and MEd students are situated more centrally in the schools where these programs reside. This means that the previous Partnership Board rarely needs to meet. Many PDSs no longer have co-coordinators because decision making for the PDS gets done in the college program areas where teachers' voices are often not included. We seldom meet as a group to talk across our PDSs, because there is less need for such meetings. The newsletter and publication series that provided a college-supported avenue and incentive to write are no longer operating.

The funding for PDSs has been moved from the college level into the School budgets. This moves the money closer to the actual operational level of PDSs, but what will be the influence of faculty who are not involved in PDSs making funding decisions? Monies for clinical educators are spent in varied ways. Some PDSs pay teachers for afterschool work and for teaching in the MEd courses. Some pay substitutes so that many teachers can be released to do a variety of PDS things, including supervision. Some clinical educators are paid primarily to supervise interns but are not involved in wider PDS coordination, development, or decision making. This diversity is nothing new, but there is little conversation across the diversity. There are no ongoing discussions of what PDSs should be, or need to be, to build shared goals and expectations.

On the one hand, more faculty are involved in routine discussions of PDS matters; on the other hand, this results in less opportunity for input from the schools. Maybe the changes will make the PDSs more manageable. Their ownership will clearly sit with the program areas and the faculty who ought to care about reform. There may be less of a load on individual faculty and more shared university participation within programs. There may be more equitable support for those involved in PDS work because there will be more general policies and funding tied to those decisions. Nevertheless, we worry whether we are moving toward less collaborative relations with the schools, or are we just simplifying the organizational structures to make them easier to maintain? Or is it both? Are PDSs becoming more inclusive and central to certification programs in the college, or are they being diluted by the involvement of those who prefer less collaborative, more "efficient" modes? A faculty person who is new to PDS work said recently after a few visits to a PDS school, "They don't seem to like me much out there." He seemed to have little sense that PDS work requires building relationships and a willingness to examine how he is teaching his courses at the university.

This set of issues and moves toward institutionalization speaks only to the organizational structure at the university. In our other institutional arena, the schools, our PDS collaboration has had little impact within school districts. Many changes have occurred with individual teachers and administrators and many schools look different because of PDS involvement. There is yet, however, no institutionalized space for PDSs in the school districts. We worry that PDS goals and initiatives will not be able to survive the rapid turnover that is occurring in many school districts and schools. Columbus Public Schools just hired its fourth superintendent since our PDS initiative began, each of whom knew nothing about PDSs at the beginning. Some PDS schools have had as many principals in the same period of time. Budget cuts and tight resources have meant that the few perks initially offered by school districts have mostly evaporated. While PDS initiatives have general support in most of the school districts, would we have this without the lure of fee waivers? Can PDSs survive with so little institutionalization into the organizational structures of school districts?

We are obliged to wonder about the long-term effects of our PDS work. What is left for individuals or schools as the collaborative work of a PDS ends? Will the changes initiated in these schools be sustained without ongoing nurturing? Will teachers who found collaborative dialogue supportive of their growth and development feel abandoned when PDS work ends in their schools? Will they create other collegial and collaborative situations to sustain them, or will it be back to business as usual?

The long-term effects of change initiative are usually thought to be important indicators of the project's success. Although we worry about continuity and cannot forecast the future, we can revel in our accomplishments. There have been significant changes. For one, we are convinced that our interns are better prepared as professionals and better understand what a professional stance entails. They are aware of the institutional barriers to change and the challenges of culturally relevant teaching. They acknowledge their responsibility to be reflective practitioners who are involved in the lives of their students and their school community, and they are generally convinced that teaching is a lifelong learning endeavor. Many of us, teachers and professors, feel a great sense of accomplishment and personal growth. Collaborative reform has born fruits, even as its fragile future continues for us as an improbable dream.

PDS Publications

Listed below are publications authored by participants in our PDSs. The lists vary in length because some PDSs have been working since 1991 and others are very new. Some PDSs have had consistent membership while others have had changing leadership and participants. These things, of course, influence publications. In addition to these publications, PDS participants have made more than 75 presentations at state, national, and international conferences.

In addition to the publications listed below, the College of Education supported a publication series that ran for three years before budget cuts resulted in its demise. The editorial board included teachers, graduate students, and university faculty. We published a series of papers called the Forum Papers, a quarterly newsletter called *Building Bridges,* and two theme issues with writings from participants across the PDSs. The first theme issue, *What Is Different? What Has Changed?* was published in 1994 (122 pp.) and the second issue *Mission, Motivation and Persistence* came out in 1996 (75 pp.).

CHAPTER 4: URBAN PROFESSIONAL
PARTNERSHIP SCHOOL (UPPS/PDS)

Blosser, Carrie. (1997). *Educating tomorrow's teachers: RE-searching literacy education in diverse settings.* Unpublished dissertation, The Ohio State University.

McLean, M. M. (1994). The role of a boundary spanner in school-university collaboration. In *What is different, What has changed?* First annual theme issue of the Professional Development School Publications Series. Columbus, OH: The Ohio State University College of Education.

Trautmann, P. (1994, Spring/Summer). Writing about math: Using process portfolios to support the conceptual thinking among urban middle school students. *Ohio Journal of English/Language Arts, 35*(1).

CHAPTER 5: EDUCATORS FOR
COLLABORATION CHANGE (ECC/PDS)

Adams, T. (1993). A collaborative adventure. *Literacy Matters, 5*(2), 5–9.

Bricher, R., Hawk, M., & Tingley, J. (1990). Cross-age tutoring for at-risk students. *Teaching and Change, 1*(1), 91–97.

Christenson, M., Eldredge, F., Ibom, K., Johnston, M., & Thomas, M. (1996). Collaboration in support of change. *Theory Into Practice*, 35(3), 187–195.

Christenson, M., & Serrao, S. (1994, Winter). Cooperative learning in a hostile environment. *Teaching and Change*, 4(2), 137–156.

Hohenbrink, J. (1993). *The influence of collaboratively teaching a social studies methods course: University and school.* Unpublished dissertation, The Ohio State University, Columbus.

Johnston, M., with PDS colleagues. (1997). *Contradictions in collaboration*: New thinking on school/university partnerships. New York: Teachers College Press.

Johnston, M., & Kirschner, B. (Eds.). (1996). The challenges of school/university collaboration (vol. 35). *Theory Into Practice*. Columbus, OH: College of Education, The Ohio State University.

Johnston, M., & Kerper, R. M. (1996). Positioning ourselves: Parity and power in collaborative work. *Curriculum Inquiry*, 26(1), 5–24.

Johnston, M. (1994, Summer/Fall). Postmodern consideration of school/university collaboration. *Teaching Education*, 6(2), 99–106.

Johnston, M., & Thomas, M. (1994). School and university collaboration: Can we reframe our differences? (Forum Paper No. 4). Columbus, OH: Professional Development School Publication Series, The Ohio State University.

Johnston, M., & Kerper, R. (Eds.). (1993). *School/university collaboration: Collaboration, collegiality, and change* (vol. 5). Columbus, OH: Martha L King Language and Literacy Center at The Ohio State University.

Johnston, M., & Thomas, M., with PDS participants, (1997). *Evaluation Report: Elementary and Middle School MEd Program and the Educators for Collaborative Change (ECC) Professional Development School (PDS), 1991–97,* 72 pages.

Nalle, K. (1993). Democratic processing of children's classroom concerns. *Teaching and Change*, 1(1), 25–54.

Nalle, K. (1994, Fall). A democracy of third graders. *Teaching Tolerance*, 3(2), 54–57.

Saleem, D. (1995). *Service learning in PDSs: Personal experience and cultural traditions in African American culture* (Forum Paper No. 5). Columbus, OH: Professional Development School Publication Series, The Ohio State University.

Westhoven, L. (1993). Swimmy: A role model. *Literacy Matters*, 5(2), 2–5.

CHAPTER 6: THE MIDDLE SCHOOL PDS

Beane, J. A. (1993). A middle school curriculum: From rhetoric to reality. Columbus, OH: National Middle School Association.

Brosnan, P. A., and FitzSimmons, J. A. (1993, May). Mathematics portfolio assessment from teacher and student perspectives. *Ohio Journal of School Mathematics*, 26, 26–31.

Brosnan, P., Erickson, D., and Edwards, E. (1996). An exploration of change in teachers' beliefs and practices during implementation of mathematics standards. *Focus on Learning Problems in Mathematics*, 18(4), 35–53.

Erickson, D. (1995). *An exploration of change in teachers' beliefs and practices during implementation of mathematics standards*. Unpublished doctoral dissertation, The Ohio State University, Columbus, OH.

Martin, K. (1994). *The process of integrating the curriculum in a sixth grade class.* Unpublished doctoral dissertation, The Ohio State University, Columbus.

Thornton. (1996). *Students voices in the process of middle school reform.* Unpublished doctoral dissertation, The Ohio State University, Columbus.

CHAPTER 7: NETWORK IN SOCIAL STUDIES AND GLOBAL EDUCATION

Chase, K. S. & Merryfield, M. M. (1998). Bridging the gap between campus and school. *From the Inside Perspectives in PDS Work, 1*(1), 17–19.

Chase, K. S., & Merryfield, M. M. (1998). How do secondary teachers benefit from PDS networks? Factors teachers associate with the effectiveness of building a learning community in social studies and global education. *The Clearing House, 71*(4), 251–254.

Dove, T., Norris, J., & Shinew, D. (1997). Teachers' perspectives on school/university collaboration in global education. In M. M. Merryfield, E. Jarchow, & S. Pickert (Eds.), *Preparing teachers to teach global perspectives: A handbook for teacher educators*. Thousand Oaks, CA: Corwin Press.

Levak, B., Merryfield, M., & Wilson, R. (1993). Global connections. *Educational Leadership, 51*(1), 73–75.

Merryfield, M. M. (1995a). Institutionalizing cross-cultural experiences and international expertise in teacher education: The development and potential of a global education PDS network. *The Journal of Teacher Education, 46*(1), 19–27.

Merryfield, M. M. (1995b). *Teacher education in global and international education.* Washington DC: ERIC Clearinghouse on Teaching and Teacher Education, *ERIC Digest* (EDO-SP 943).

Merryfield, M. M., & White, C. (1996). Issues-centered global education. In R. Evans & D.W. Saxe (Eds.), *Handbook on teaching social issues*. Washington DC: The National Council for the Social Studies.

Shapiro, S., & Merryfield, M. M. (1995). A case study of unit planning in the context of school reform. In M. M. Merryfield & R. C. Remy (Eds.), *Teaching about international conflict and peace*. Albany: State University of New York Press.

Wainer, B. (1995). Developing preservice teachers' thinking in multiple perspectives and a global world view. Unpublished paper.

CHAPTER 11: PROJECT LEARN

Brunner, C., Given, B., & Thomson, B. S. (1997). The international learning-styles network: Who, when, what, where, why—and why not? *National Forum of Applied Educational Research Journal, 11*, 24–27.

Thomson, B. S., & Maxwell, E. W. (1998). Learning styles: the STW connection. In S. Pritz & M. Casto (Eds.), *Steps of change: Walking the walk teachers resource manual* (pp. 47–49). Columbus, OH: Ohio School to Work Office.

CHAPTER 14: FRANKLIN COUNTY ACADEMY OF PHYSICAL EDUCATORS (FCAPE)

Knop, N., LaMaster, K., Norris, M., Raudensky, J., & Tannehill, D. (1997, Winter). What we have learned through collaboration: A summary report of the NASPE Teacher Education Conference. *The Physical Educator, 54*(4), 170–180.

Tannehill, D., Berkowitz, R., & LaMaster, K. (1996). Teacher networking through electronic mail. *Journal of Technology in Teacher Education 4*(3), 76–89.

Tannehill, D., & LaMaster, K. (1996). Mentoring in teacher education through electronic mail. In B. Robbin, J. D. Price, J. Willis, & D. A. Willis (Eds.). *Technology and teacher education annual.* Greenville, NC: Association for the Advancement of Computing in Education.

CHAPTER 15: FOREIGN AND SECOND LANGUAGE PDS

Wilburn Robinson, D. (1998). Creating a professional development network for foreign and second language educators: Unifying diverse expertise. In A. Moeller (Ed.), *The Central States Conference Report on the Teaching of Foreign Languages.* Lincolnwood, IL: National Textbook Co.

GLOSSARY OF
TERMS AND ACRONYMS

ART—Art Research and Teaching PDS focused on integrating art across the curriculum (chapter 13).

Clinical Educator (CE)—professional working half time in school as a teacher, half time as a university liaison, and taking the lead in PDS research.

Cooperating/Mentor Teacher—the veteran teacher responsible for ongoing assessment during the student teaching experience of an OSU student.

ECC—Educators for Collaborative Change, an elementary and middle school PDS focusing on collaboration (chapter 5).

EPIC—Educational Programs for Informal Classrooms, a program with a 25-year history that was combined with the Urban PDS resulting in the new LEADS PDS (chapter 4).

FCAPE—Franklin County Academy for Physical Education, a K–12 PDS organized as a network across numerous school districts (chapter 14).

Field Professor—is a classroom teacher who plays a role in the development and teaching of the methods course, shares responsibility for the research component of the PDS, and is an on-site liaison for the university (chapters 7, 8, 11).

LEADS—Literacy Education in Diverse Settings, an elementary and middle school PDS focusing on issues of urban and diverse settings (chapter 4).

MEd—Master's in Education. As a Holmes partner, certification programs at Ohio State have moved from undergraduate to graduate-level programs.

Middle School Network—PDS group specializing in the needs of middle school–aged students (chapter 6).

PDS—Professional Development Site (or School), comes from the Holmes idea of saturating one site for professional development through university and school collaboration.

PDSN—(or PDN) Professional Development School Network. Some secondary schools created a network of different school sites from different districts. (chapters 7, 8, 11, 13 through 15).

PDSC—Professional Development School Community (chapter 4).

Project LEARN: Closing the Gap—A K–12 PDS group with a learning-styles focus (chapter 11).

SPED—Special Education PDS focused on Direct Instruction (chapter 16).

Student teacher/intern—These two terms were used somewhat interchangeably as OSU moved from undergraduate to graduate-level certification. After PDS, student teachers are referred to as interns.

TIE—Technology in Education was an enabling PDS that supported the technological needs of the PDSs (chapter 12).

University Supervisor—A graduate assistant position, most often a doctoral student, responsible for the supervision of student teachers in coordination with the cooperating teacher.

UPPS—Urban Professional Partnership School, a PDS that merged with EPIC to become the LEADS PDS (chapter 4).

CONTRIBUTORS

Patti Brosnan is an Associate Professor of Mathematics Education at OSU, School of Teaching and Learning. Her area of research is the relationship between teaching and learning mathematics K–13. She teaches graduate courses on campus and many inservice courses in the city schools. Email address is Brosnan.1@osu.edu.

Beth Carnate has multiple roles at Independence High School, Columbus, Ohio. She is a half-time Clinical Educator who is shared with English, Social Studies, and Science PDS activities. For the other half of her full-time position in the school she coordinates Innovative Projects in her building. Beth teams with Barbara Thomson every quarter in an on-site PDS graduate course to explore strategies to review and improve teaching practices. Her interaction with Coalition for Essential Schools and PDS initiatives have been a catalyst for change among PDS participants and within the school.

Gwendolyn Cartledge is an Associate Professor at OSU, School of Physical Activity and Educational Services, special education programs. She teaches courses that focus on the academic and social development of children with mild disabilities. Her research emphasis is on teaching social skills to children and youth, particularly those with serious emotional disturbances (SED/SBH). Email address is cartledge.1@osu.edu.

Sue Chase teaches advanced placement government and social psychology at Hilliard Davidson High School. She is a field professor, for social studies education at OSU. Her education/research interests include improving teacher education, student motivation as it relates to teacher behavior and student activism versus student apathy. Email address is suechase@juno.com.

John O. Cooper is a Professor of Special Education at OSU. His current research and teaching interests include precision teaching and the behavior analysis of academic and social behaviors. Specifically, his interests focus on precision teaching in teacher education, inner behavior, academic fluency, and verbal behavior.

Don Cramer is presently Director of the Office of Professional Practices at OSU, Prior to this appointment, he served as a public School principal in the Columbus Public Schools where he also co-chaired the College of Education PDS program. His interests include school reform through teacher education. Email address is Cramer.5@osu.edu.

Cynthia Dickens was an Assistant Professor at Mississippi State University from 1993 to January 1997. This chapter is published posthumously. Cindy's research interests were in collaborative research among women especially women in university faculty positions.

Rhonda Dailey-Dickinson has been teaching 23 years. She got her M.A. degree in 1989 at OSU in the School of Policy and Leadership. Rhonda co-wrote the proposal for the EPIC PDS and was a clinical educator for four years. Her inquiry interests include using cooperative learning and literacy development.

Tim Dove is a doctoral student in social studies and global education at OSU. He is currently a secondary social studies teacher in Worthington, Ohio. His research interests include teacher education, instructional technologies, curriculum development, and global education. His doctoral research specifically includes the use of listservs and online courses in teacher education. Email address is TMDove@aol.com.

Francee Eldredge teaches kindergarten at Avalon Elementary School. She has been a Clinical Educator since 1993. She has a master's degree in early and middle childhood. She is currently studying literacy at OSU and is the Literacy Coordinator for Avalon Elementary School. Email address is eldredge.1@osu.edu.

Patricia Enciso is an Assistant Professor and co-coordinator of LEADS program at OSU. In addition to teaching in the MEd program, she also teaches masters and doctoral level courses related to multicultural education and literacy and sociocultural theory. She was the 1996 recipient of the postdoctoral fellowship on research related to reading and sociocultural theory.

Diana Erchick is an Assistant Professor at OSU at Newark. She teaches in the Integrated Teaching and Learning Section of the School of Teaching and Learning, working with pre- and inservice teachers at the elementary and middle school levels. Her education and research interests include feminist perspectives in all of qualitative research, mathematics education, and constructivist pedagogy. Email address is erchick.1@osu.edu.

William Gathergood is a secondary English and drama teacher at Reynoldsburg High School with a background of conducting numerous international email projects, incorporating computer communications into the study of literature. His previous and ongoing projects including literary personification, interdisciplinary cultural studies, and the use of text discs to replace textbooks are documented at http://www.coe.ohio-state.edu/wgathergood. Email address is gathergood.1@osu.edu.

Ralph Gardner, III is an Associate Professor in Special Education at OSU, in the School of Physical Activity and Educational Services. He earned his Ph.D. from OSU in 1989. His current research interests include researching academic strategies for students with mild disabilities and students at risk for academic failure.

Keith Hall is a Professor in the School of Educational Policy and Leadership with research and teaching interests in the integration of technology in learning and professional development of educators. The current version of his TIENET-team created course for preparing educators can be previewed at: URL http://www.hercules.coe.ohio-state.edu/tienet/Demo; Username: tienet-test; Password: 4college; email address is hall.25@osu.edu.

Timothy E. Heron is a Professor in the School of Physical Activity and Educational Services at OSU. Dr. Heron also served for 17 years as an Educational Consultant to Children's Hospital Learning Disability Clinic in Columbus, Ohio. He has published several books and articles, has presented numerous papers, and has served as a consultant to teachers, parents, and administrators on issues related to disabilities, inclusion, instructional programming, consultation, and applied behavior analysis.

Bill L. Heward is a Professor of Education at OSU, in the School of Physical Activity and Educational Services. He coordinates the doctoral program in special education. Bill's current research focuses on improving the effectiveness of group instruction by developing and evaluating "low-technology" methods classroom teachers can use to increase the frequency of active participation by each student in the class. He has published many books and articles on education and applied behavior analysis. Email address is heward.1@osu.edu.

Dan Hoffman has been in public education for 28 years. He was principal for 10 years at Reynoldsburg High School, where he lead educational reforms in the building and at the state level. He is currently a doctoral student in educational administration at OSU. He is also Co-director of the Ohio Principals' Academy and Executive Director of the Ohio Essential Schools Center in New Albany. His interests are educational reform particularly the connection between leadership and learning. Email address hoffman.7@albany.oh.us.

Steven E. Hoffman, for the last several years, has been involved in preparing teachers for the urban setting as a Peer Assistance & Review

(PAR) mentor for the Columbus Public Schools, as a clinical educator with the OSU Professional Introduction program, and as a cooperating teacher for the English Education MEd program. Currently he is a Critical Friends Group coach at Independence High School, where he is in his 30th year as an English teacher, and a sometimes doctoral student at OSU. Email address is hoffman.95@osu.edu.

Richard D. Howell teaches in Special Education in the School of Physical Activity and Educational Services at OSU. His research interests include assistive technology and distance learning for students with disabilities and their teachers. Email address is howell.4@osu.edu.

Kathleen Ibom teaches third grade at Avalon Elementary in the Columbus Public Schools. She has been teaching for 15 years and is interested in teacher change and professional development. Her present inquiry focus is how to create ownership in students while building community in her classroom. Email address is ibom.1@osu.edu.

Marilyn Johnston is a Professor of Social Studies Education and Social Foundations at OSU, in the School of Teaching and Learning and was an elementary teacher for 15 years. She has been the co-coordinator for the ECC/PDS since 1991. Her current research interests are collaborative research, professional development, and teacher education reform. Email address is johnston.8@osu.edu.

Lizbeth Kelley is a science teacher at Heritage Middle School in Westerville, Ohio. As an on-site field professor, she coordinates Project Learn activities and placements in her school. Lizbeth teaches integrated science, earth, life, and physical science. Her team has minicourses to meet the needs of adolescent learners. She also has a class of special needs students in science who are collaborating with Project Learn to work in their learning strength to process new and difficult information in science.

Todd Kenreich is a doctoral student in Social Studies and Global Education. As a graduate from the MEd program at OSU, he taught history in Bethesda, Maryland for three years. He has recently returned to OSU as a doctoral student to study instructional technologies, curriculum development, and geography education. Email address is kenreich.5@osu.edu.

Becky Wendling Kirschner is an Assistant Professor in the School of Teaching and Learning, Language, Literacy, and Culture. Her current educational/research interests include teacher research, school/university partnerships, sociocultural studies of literacy, and educational anthropology. Email address is kirschner.3@osu.edu.

Barbara Levak has been in public education for 28 years including teaching English at the Reynoldsburg High School. In the Reynoldsburg PDS, she played many roles, which included a clinical educator, a cooperating teacher, and co-author of book chapters and journal articles. She is currently curriculum coordinator for the Reynoldsburg school district and program coordinator for the Ohio Coalition of Essential Schools in New Albany.

Lisa Maloney has been teaching third grade for 15 years. She was a half-time clinical educator and co-coordinator of the ECC/PDS for five years. Her interests include community building and democratic classrooms, mentoring new teachers, and classroom inclusion. Email address is westhoven.4@osu.edu.

Eugenie Maxwell teaches science at Hilliard Darby High School, Hilliard, Ohio, which is one of the fastest growing districts in the United States. As a PDS clinical educator with Project Learn, she meets her high school science classes every morning and performs her clinical educator position at OSU during the afternoons. Chemistry in the community and geology are several of her teaching responsibilities.

Merry Merryfield, Associate Professor in Social Studies and Global Education in the School of Teaching and Learning at OSU, writes about teacher decision-making and teacher education in global education, cross-cultural experiential learning, and African Studies. Email address is merryfield.1@osu.edu.

Steven Miller is an Associate Professor of Social Studies and Global Education in the School of Teaching and Learning at OSU. His primary research and teaching interest is in economic education, and in recent years has been particularly involved in economic education in Central and Eastern Europe. Email address is miller.74@osu.edu

Rachel Moots was an MEd student in English Education and after her internship in the School-to-Work program at Independence High School she was offered a job in that school. She is in her third year of teaching at Independence.

George Newell is an Associate Professor of English Education in the School of Teaching and Learning at OSU. He teaches graduate seminars and serves as an advisor to the preservice English education students in the MEd program. His current research interests include the study of how the English education program contributes to the growth and development of prospective English teachers. Email address is newell.2@osu.edu.

Mary O'Sullivan is a Professor in Sport and Exercise Education in the School of Physical Activity and Educational Services at OSU. Her major teaching responsibilities at the graduate level include: MEd courses on secondary teaching methods and internship, professional seminar, and an Introduction to Teaching course. Her research interest are in the issues surrounding physical education curriculum and physical activity for urban youth. Other interests include professional development issues for preservice and inservice teachers. Email address is osullivan.1@osu.edu.

Michael Parsons is a Professor in the Department of Art Education at OSU. He is interested in art education, school reform, children's thinking. Email address is parsons.4@osu.edu.

Stanley Ray is a teacher in South Western City Schools at Franklin Heights. He currently teaches Advanced Placement European History, U.S. Government, and Sociology. His interests in research include thematic integrated teaching, and what makes successful learning environments. Email address is ray.50@osu.edu.

Deborah Wilburn Robinson is an Assistant Professor of Foreign and Second Language Education in the School of Teaching and Learning at OSU. Her educational/research interests include teacher education and early language learning. Email address is robinson.468@osu.edu.

Theresa Rogers is an Associate Professor of Language, Literacy and Culture in the School of Teaching and Learning at OSU, where she is actively involved in teacher education. She is co-editor of *Reading Across Cultures: Teaching literature in a diverse society* (Teachers College Press) and has published numerous book chapters and articles in journals such as *Journal of Literacy Research, English Education*, and *Urban Review*. Email address is rogers.2@osu.edu.

Diane M. Sainato is an Associate Professor who joined the Special Education faculty at OSU in 1989. She currently is involved in research with young children with disabilities in the areas of independent performance, language, and social behavior. Diane directs the personnel preparation program for teachers of young children with disabilities. Email address is sainato.1@osu.edu.

Barbara Seidl is an Assistant Professor at OSU in the School of Teaching and Learning. Her interests include preparing teachers for urban schools, partnerships between community organizations and teacher preparation, and urban school reform. Email address is seidl.5@osu.edu.

Anna Soter is Associate Professor at OSU in the School of Teaching and Learning. Her research and teaching interests have centered around the teaching and learning of language, writing, and literature in the contexts of both preservice and inservice education of English/Language Arts teachers. She can be contacted through either email at Soter.1@osu.edu or by phone at 614–292–8049.

Sandra Stroot is a Professor in Teacher Education and Physical Education at OSU, in the School of Physical Activity and Educational Services. Her research interests focus on the socialization of teachers into the teaching profession. Email address is stroot.1@osu.edu.

Deborah Tannehill is a Professor in Sport and Exercise Education at OSU, in the School of Physical Activity and Educational Services. She teaches in the undergraduate Sport and Leisure Studies program, the MEd in Sport and Exercise Education, and the MA/PhD in Sport and Exercise Education. Her research is on teaching and teacher education as it relates to physical education and sport, secondary curriculum and instruction, supervision, mentoring, skill analysis, and technology applications in education. Email address is tannehill.2@osu.edu.

Mike Thomas taught middle and high school for 12 years. He has worked as a full-time clinical educator and co-coordinator of the ECC/PDS for five years. He has a BA in physics from Otterbein College, an MS in future studies from the University of Houston, and a PhD in Educational Administration from OSU. His interests include connections between adult personal and professional development and organizational development.

Barbara Thomson is an Associate Professor at OSU, in the School of Teaching and Learning in the section of Mathematics, Science, and Technology Education. She is currently Co-director of the Regional Center of Learning and Teaching Styles at OSU (COLTS-OSU). She partners with field professors and clinical educators from 10 different K–12 schools in the LEARN PDS.

Holly Thornton is involved with middle grades education as a sixth-grade teacher and at Augusta State University. She was part of the OSU/PDS Middle School Network site, a PDS building coordinator, and a policy board co-chair. Her current research interests include school/teacher education reform, educative research, implementation of middle school philosophy and best practices in middle grades classrooms, and teacher preparation. Email is hthornto@aug.edu.

Nancy Zimpher is currently the Chancellor at University of Wisconsin at Milwaukee and was formerly the Dean of the College of Education at OSU. Dr. Zimpher lead the reforms associated with the Holmes agenda at OSU and currently is the President of the Holmes Partnership Board.

INDEX